MW01097707

PATENT PORTFOLIOS

Quality, Creation, and Cost

LARRY M. GOLDSTEIN

Published by True Value Press
ISBN-10: 0-9895541-2-0
ISBN-13: 978-0-9895541-2-1

Layout: Marzel A.S. — Jerusalem
Cover Design: Studio Paz

Books by Larry M. Goldstein

THE PATENT QUALITY SERIES:

PATENT PORTFOLIOS: Quality, Creation, and Cost (published January, 2015)

LITIGATION-PROOF PATENTS: Avoiding the Most Common Patent Mistakes (published October, 2014)

TRUE PATENT VALUE: Defining Quality in Patents and Patent Portfolios (published July, 2013)

TECHNOLOGY PATENT LICENSING: An International Reference on 21ˢᵗ Century Patent Licensing, Patent Pools and Patent Platforms (co-authored with Brian N. Kearsey) (published July, 2004)

Dedication

The Jewish Talmud tells the story of an old man who was planting a carob tree. A passerby asked him:

"Tell me, old man, how long will it be before this tree bears fruit?"
"Seventy years," the man replied.
"Are you certain you will live another seventy years?"
Said the old man, "When I was born into this world, I found many carob trees planted by the elders. Just as they planted trees for me, so I plant trees for my children."[1]

The story expresses the way I feel as I complete this book. When I came into the world, I was naked, but the world was not. Just as I found the world clothed, so do I add my own cloak for those who come later. I thank the Lord I have had this opportunity to make a small contribution to people in the patent business.

This book is dedicated to those who clothe the world for the generations to come.

---

[1] Babylonian Talmud, *Tractate Ta'anit*, page 23a.

Summary Table of Contents

DEDICATION 4

ACKNOWLEDGEMENTS 10

PREFACE 11

Chapter 1 — "Quality": What is an Excellent Patent Portfolio? . .19

Chapter 2 — "Creation": How to Create an Excellent Patent
Portfolio? 73

Chapter 3 — "Cost": What is the Cost to Create an Excellent
Patent Portfolio? 133

Chapter 4 — Summary 209

AFTERWORD 239

APPENDIX: List of Principles for Excellent Patent Portfolios . . 241

GLOSSARY (Including Acronyms) 244

BIBLIOGRAPHY .265

INDEX OF TABLES 276

INDEX OF NAMES AND SUBJECTS 279

ABOUT THE AUTHOR 299

Detailed Table of Contents

DEDICATION 4

ACKNOWLEDGEMENTS 10

PREFACE 11

Purpose of this Book 11

Excellent Patent Portfolios 12

The Patent Quality Series .13

Chapter Summaries 14

Chapter 1 — "Quality": What is an Excellent Patent Portfolio? . .19

Introduction to Chapter 1 .19

1. Definition of a Patent Portfolio 19

2. Ten Principles of Excellent Patent Portfolios 25

   a. Corporate and Patent Strategies 26

   Principle 1: *A technology company must determine its strategy with regard to patents*. 26

   Principle 2: *A good patent portfolio matches the strategic focus of its owner* 27

   Principle 3: *Invest the "right amount" in patents* 28

   b. Characteristics of an Excellent Patent Portfolio 30

   Principle 4: *Balance of quality and quantity* 30

   Principle 5: *Geographic balance* 33

   Principle 6: *Time balance* 37

   c. Managing the Patent Portfolio 39

   Principle 7: *Identify and fill holes in coverage* 39

   Principle 8: *Time management, including divestment* 40

   Principle 9: *Establish criteria for measurement* 41

   Principle 10: *Place the patenting function within the organization* 43

3. Four Examples of Patent Portfolios 45
    Example 1 — Check Point Software Technologies. 45
    Example 2 — Silanis Technology 51
    Example 3 — Fuji Photo Film 56
    Example 4 — Qualcomm. 61

Conclusion to Chapter 1 70

Chapter 2 — "Creation": How to Create an Excellent Patent
Portfolio? 73

Introduction to Chapter 2 73

1. Key Concepts for Creating Patent Portfolios. 73

2. Cultivating Patent Portfolios Through Technology Inflection
    Points 84
    a. Introduction 84
    b. Basing a Portfolio on Breakthrough Patents 86
    c. "Good concepts" are the basis of patent value 87
    d. What is a Technology Inflection Point?. 89
    e. Examples of Technology Inflection Points 90
    f. Mega Trends as the Basis of Technology Inflection Points 93
    g. Summary of Technology Inflection Points and the Models
        of Patenting 93

3. Two Classic Questions 94
    a. Build or Buy 94
        (i)   Example 1 of Buying — Broadcom. 95
        (ii)   Example 2 of Buying — Silanis Technology 97
        (iii) Building by Operating Companies 97
        (iv)   Build versus Buy. 102
        (v)   The Processes of Building and Buying 104
        (vi)   Conclusion About Building or Buying 106
    b. Quality or Quantity. 107
        (i)   Strategy 1 — Quality Before Quantity. 108
        (ii)   Strategy 2 — Quantity Before Quality 111
        (iii) Strategy 3 — Quality and Quantity Together 114
        (iv)   Summary of Strategies 118

4. Portfolio Development Within a Company 120
    a. Introduction 120
    b. Elements of a Successful Patenting Program Within a
        Company. 120
        (i)   Commitment. 120
        (ii)   Criteria for Success 123
        (iii) Patent Decision-makers. 125
        (iv)   The Driver 127
        (v)   Problems 129
        (vi)   Time Frame 129

Conclusion to Chapter 2 130

Chapter 3 — "Cost": What is the Cost to Create an Excellent
Patent Portfolio? 133

Introduction to Chapter 3 133

1. Top Down Budgeting: Targeting a Cost 135
    a. First Analysis 136
    b. Second Analysis 141
    c. Third Analysis 142
    d. Fourth Analysis 144
    e. Factors Impacting the Ratio for Specific Companies 145
    f. Summary of Top Down Budgeting 148

2. Bottom Up Budgeting: Targeting a Result 149
    a. Examples of Bottom Up Budgeting 150
        Example 1 — Check Point Software Technologies. 150
        Example 2 — Qualcomm. 155
    b. Summary of Bottom Up Budgeting. 157

3. Competitive Budgeting: Targeting Costs and Results Based
    on Competitors 157
    a. Examples of Competitive Budgeting 161
        Example 1 — The Firewall Industry. 161
        Example 2 — The Electronic Signature Industry 179
    b. Summary of Competitive Budgeting 205

  4. Hybrid Budgeting: Balancing Costs, Results, and Competitors . . 205

  Conclusion to Chapter 3 206

Chapter 4 — Summary 209

  Topic 1: Basic Characteristics of an Excellent Patent Portfolio
    (Questions 1–10) 209

  Topic 2: Managing the Patent Portfolio (Questions 11–14) 221

  Topic 3: Budgeting for Patents (Questions 15–19) 228

  Topic 4: Special Topics (Questions 20–30) 233
    (a) Technology Inflection Points (Questions 20–22) 233
    (b) Patent Aggregation (Questions 23–27) 234
    (c) Patent Evaluation (Questions 28–30) 236

AFTERWORD 239

APPENDIX: List of Principles for Excellent Patent Portfolios . . 241

GLOSSARY (Including Acronyms) 244

BIBLIOGRAPHY 265

INDEX OF TABLES 276

INDEX OF NAMES AND SUBJECTS 279

ABOUT THE AUTHOR 299

Acknowledgments

Thank you to the following people who read all or portions of the book: Jeffery L. Carter (President and CEO of HighTech-Solutions, Colorado Springs), Natalya Dvorson (Partner at Sughrue Mion, PLLC, Washington, D.C.), and Eli Jacobi (Patent Consultant, Ra'anana, Israel).

Thank you as always to Paz Corcos for her excellent cover graphics, and to A.S. Marzel for his outstanding layout work.

Preface

PURPOSE OF THIS BOOK

Abraham Lincoln, the only American president to hold a patent,[2] said in 1858, "The patent system…added the fuel of interest to the fire of genius in the discovery and production of new and useful things."[3]

Surely President Lincoln was speaking only of excellence in the patent system. I believe very strongly in the importance of quality in patents and patent portfolios. Like Mr. Lincoln, I believe that high-quality patents are of great value both to the holders of the patents and to society as a whole. I believe also that poor-quality patents are, at best, a waste of time and money, and at worst, a burden on society.

This book is about quality in the aggregation of patents known as a "portfolio". The book tries to answer three basic questions:

---

[2] The patent held by President Lincoln is US 6,469, "Buoying Vessels Over Shoals", filed March 10, 1849, issued May 22, 1849. The President claimed a system with expandable chambers to float vessels over physical obstacles. The idea was almost certainly derived from the President's travels on the Mississippi River.

[3] "Lecture on Discoveries and Inventions", Abraham Lincoln, April 6, 1858, Bloomington, Illinois, available at *http://www.abrahamlincolnonline.org/lincoln/speeches/discoveries.htm* (last viewed on November 15, 2014). The quoted portion is the conclusion at the very end of the lecture.

1. What is an excellent patent portfolio?
2. How is it possible to obtain an excellent patent portfolio?
3. What would be the cost to obtain an excellent patent portfolio?

The purpose of this book is to help increase the quality and value of patent portfolios. The book achieves its purpose by identifying the characteristics of a patent portfolio that make it excellent (Chapter 1), discussing various ways to obtain an excellent portfolio (Chapter 2), and reviewing the main methods by which companies budget the investments to obtain such a portfolio (Chapter 3). The book concludes with a summary of the main ideas discussed in the book, presented in a Question & Answer format (Chapter 4).

EXCELLENT PATENT PORTFOLIOS

Why do patent portfolios matter? Or to be more precise, what is so important about patent portfolios as opposed to individual patents?

The truth is that no individual patent can begin to match the power of an excellent patent portfolio. Every individual patent, regardless of its quality or its value, is subject to the vagaries of continuing review at the patent office, and litigation in various judicial and administrative forums. No matter how good the individual patent is, it may be invalidated entirely, or individual claims may be cancelled, modified, or rendered unenforceable. There is no absolute protection for the individual patent.

Similarly, there is no absolute protection for the patent portfolio, but an excellent patent portfolio has vastly greater strength than an individual patent. The chance is infinitesimal that all of the claims in an excellent portfolio will be invalidated. Further, the various patents and claims in an integrated portfolio create maximum coverage of innovative concepts. Such concepts are called in this book "Points of Novelty". Both in terms of "breadth of coverage", that is, the variety of embodiments and implementations of a Point of Novelty, and "depth of coverage", that is, the extent to which dependent claims back up independent claims, a patent portfolio is a completely different entity than an individual patent.

THE PATENT QUALITY SERIES

The current book, **PATENT PORTFOLIOS: Quality, Creation, and Cost,** completes a trilogy of books which together comprise "The Patent Quality Series", the compilation of my thoughts on patent quality and patent value.

The first book in the trilogy, **TRUE PATENT VALUE: Defining Quality in Patents and Patent Portfolios**, published July, 2013, contains detailed discussions of quality and value in individual patents. Some of the concepts in that first book are cited here, and the earlier book is referenced as "*TPV*". The second book in the series, **LITIGATION-PROOF PATENTS: Avoiding the Most Common Patent Mistakes,** published October, 2014, identifies ten of the most common mistakes found in patents, and explains how to avoid these mistakes in order to boost patent quality and patent value. The current book, **PATENT PORTFOLIOS**, is the third book in The Patent Quality Series, and focuses exclusively on portfolios of patents, although by the nature of things individual patents may be discussed for their contributions to portfolios.

As with all of my other books, the patents here relate to industries in the "ICT" space, which is an acronym for "information & communication technologies". ICT includes essentially all industries in the fields of physics, communication, electronics, and mechanics, but does not include technologies known as "BCP", an acronym for "biological, chemical, and pharmaceutical" industries. Some of the principles discussed here in regard to ICT do indeed apply to BCP patents, but there are also various differences between BCP patents and ICT patents which are not discussed here. This book discusses specifically portfolios based on the ICT technologies.

CHAPTER SUMMARIES

Chapter 1 presents basic concepts of patent portfolios, and particularly the concept of "quality" in the sub-title of the book, "Quality, Creation, and Cost". Chapter 1 does three things.

First, it defines the concept of "patent portfolio", and explains the key ways in which a portfolio is different from an individual patent.

Second, it presents and explains ten principles related to high-quality patent portfolios. These principles are allocated among, respectively, Corporate and Patent Strategies, Characteristics of an Excellent Patent Portfolio, and Managing the Patent Portfolio.

Third, it presents four examples of patent portfolios that illustrate many of the principles discussed. These examples are taken from a variety of companies and industries, including Check Point Software Technologies (firewalls), Silanis Technology (software for electronic signatures), Fuji Photo

Film (single-use handheld cameras), and Qualcomm (cellular technology). All of these examples appeared first in my earlier book *TPV*, but the focus here is entirely on portfolios and the principles of excellence in portfolios.

Chapter 2 discusses various ways of generating an excellent portfolio, and focuses specifically on the concept of "creation" in the sub-title of this book, "Quality, Creation, and Cost". Chapter 2 does four things.

First, it explains key concepts in generating an excellent portfolio of patents.

Second, it discusses a particularly important concept called "Technology Inflection Points".

Third, it presents two of the classic questions frequently arising in patent portfolios. The first question, "build or buy", asks whether a company should develop its portfolio entirely from in-house innovations, or rather buy patents from outside parties. The second question, "quality or quantity", asks whether the company should focus its initial patent efforts on obtaining a small number of high-quality patents or rather on obtaining a large number of moderate-quality patents.

Fourth, it presents a model by which a company may set up and manage an in-house patenting program. In this sense, "in-house" means that the patenting process is managed within the company, as it must be. The patents may be written either by corporate employees or by outside patent professionals.

Chapter 3 discusses various ways of budgeting for an excellent portfolio, and focuses specifically on the concept of "cost" in the sub-title of this book, "Quality, Creation, and Cost".[4] Chapter 3 does four things.

First, it presents the first of four commonly used approaches for patent budgeting. This is a top-down approach, in which the amount of investment is allocated according to a general investment benchmark, and the patent portfolio is then planned in accordance with the budgeted investment. This approach, that is, first setting aside some specific amount and later planning the results, is very common, particularly in larger companies.

Second, it presents the second of four commonly used approaches for patent budgeting. This is a bottom-up approach, in which certain results (that is, numbers and locations of patents and patent applications) are targeted, and then funds are allocated to obtain these results. This, also, is a commonly used approach, particularly in smaller and startup companies.

Third, it presents the third of four commonly used approaches for patent budgeting. This is a competitive approach, in which the company first identifies its competitors, and second identifies the relative investments of these competitors both by amounts of monies invested and by patent results obtained. The company then uses this information as a

4 The terms patent "cost" and patent "investment" are heard interchangeably, and are used interchangeably here. From an accounting point of view, "costs" are typically expenses deducted in the year incurred, whereas "investment" creates an asset that may only be amortized over time. In fact, the outlays for patents built in-house are considered "costs" that may be expensed immediately, whereas patents purchased create an asset that may only be amortized over time. None of these accounting differences are discussed or intended in this book — the two terms "patent cost" and "patent investment" are used interchangeably without reference to accounting treatment or taxation.

benchmark to decide where it wishes to place itself in relation to its competitors. For industries with large public companies, the logical approach is to create benchmarks relating revenues, R&D investments, and patents — this approach is explained, and an example is given of the firewall industry. For industries dominated by private companies, where financial information is not readily available, the logical approach is to create benchmarks solely from patent information — this approach is explained, and an example is given of the electronic signature industry.

Fourth, it presents the fourth of four commonly used approaches for patent budgeting. In practice, most budgeting systems are not pure top-down (investments and costs), bottom-up (results), or competitive. Rather, they are one of a variety of possible combinations of investments, results, and competitive position. Chapter 3 ends with a discussion of Hybrid Budgeting, and the resolution of conflicts between targeted results, targeted costs, and targeted competitive position. Conflict will arise, and will be resolved, regardless of the type of approach ultimately chosen.

Chapter 4 is a SUMMARY of the main ideas in the book, presented in Question & Answer format. The following main topics are covered:

Topic 1: Basic Characteristics of an Excellent Patent Portfolio
Topic 2: Managing the Patent Portfolio
Topic 3: Budgeting for Patents
Topic 4: Special Topics
    a. Technology Inflection Points
    b. Patent Aggregation
    c. Patent Evaluation

Chapter 1

What is an Excellent Patent Portfolio?

Introduction to Chapter 1

In Chapter 1, the concept of a "patent portfolio" is defined, and differences are explained between an individual patent and a portfolio. Also, ten key principles of strong patent portfolios are listed and explained. Four examples of portfolios are then presented. Not all of these examples demonstrate good portfolios, but they all provide insight into the meaning of "an excellent patent portfolio". Finally, in the section "Conclusion to Chapter 1", the specific characteristics of an excellent patent portfolio are listed.

1. Definition of a Patent Portfolio

What is a patent portfolio? The broadest possible definition is "a collection of related and unrelated patents and patent applications owned by a single entity such as a corporation or individual."[5] This definition is broad because it includes every patent owned by a company or an individual. The definition

---

5 This a paraphrase of the definition of the term "patent portfolio" found at Wikipedia on November 15, 2014.

is also useless, because patents that are "unrelated" function as completely separate entities — they do not act together and they do not reinforce one another. A group of ten unrelated patents represents, in essence, ten separate portfolios, where each patent becomes its own portfolio.[6]

A more useful definition of patent portfolio is "a group of patent items[7] *on a related subject* that are owned or controlled by one entity". The patent items, both patents and applications, must be "related" in that they address a single technical subject or problem, which could be, for example, a single technology, or different methods of achieving the same result, or one technical standard, or one system, or different Points of Novelty in a single product.

For most companies, there is no fundamental difference between these two definitions, because all of the patents owned by the company address a related technical subject or problem. That is not true, however, for corporate conglomerates. For example, it would simply not be sensible to link or to judge as a group the patents of the various divisions of General Electric. Each of these divisions — GE Capital, GE Power & Water, GE Oil & Gas, GE Aviation, GE Healthcare, GE Transportation, and GE Home & Business Solutions — has its own problems, its own management, and its own patents.

---

6 This particular definition of "patent portfolio", that is, a group of "unrelated" patents and patent applications, is useful primarily to evaluate the entire company for sale or merger, or to sell all items in the portfolio. This definition is useful for these limited purposes, but it is not useful for defining excellence in patent portfolios, or for discussing how an excellent portfolio may be obtained, or for budgeting to create an excellent portfolio. The definition of interest in this book is a group of patents and patent applications that are "related" by technical subject, Point of Novelty, patent family, or some another aspect that allows the patents to be managed as a separate group.

7 By "patent items", I mean both patents and patent applications.

Similarly, there are different kinds of "patent aggregators", and their patents need to be considered differently. For example, an aggregator such as the administrator of the MPEG-2 patent pool will control patents directed at only one technology. In contrast, an aggressive aggregator, such as Intellectual Ventures (commonly referenced as "IV"), or a defensive aggregator, such as RPX, will have patents in a variety of businesses, some of which are totally unrelated to one another, and in such case, each business should be reviewed separately, and the concept of the "portfolio" should apply to the patents for each business separately.

Nature of a patent portfolio: Are patent portfolios primarily an extension of individual patents? In other words, would be it be correct to say that portfolios are like individual patents, but with more claims? This is an important question, and a person could argue either side of it.

A portfolio as a single super-patent: On the one hand, a portfolio is indeed like a single large patent, with more claims than an individual strength. The strength of every patent is evaluated according to three specific factors, which I link in the acronym VSD. This acronym stands for **V**alidity of claims, **S**cope of claim coverage, and **D**iscoverability of infringement. A patent is worthless if its claims are not valid and enforceable, so **V**alidity of claim is a basic question. Similarly, infringement is meaningless if it cannot be reasonably ascertained by a patent holder, so **D**iscoverability of infringement is also a basic question. Validity of claims and discoverability of infringement are often viewed as gateway questions — that is, they themselves do not create the value, but if they are absent, then the patent may be valueless.

Once an evaluator is satisfied as to validity and

discoverability, infringement of the patent becomes critically important. The questions are, "How broad is the Scope of coverage for the claims? What markets are covered? What specific companies? What products? Is the scope of coverage sufficient so a potential infringer could not avoid infringement by designing around the patents?" In other words, is there infringement of the patent claims either right now or in the near future? If so, the patent has value. If not, value will not be apparent.[8]

These factors, V, S, and D, apply to every patent and also to every patent portfolio, and in that sense a patent portfolio is an aggregation of the claims of all the patents in the portfolio. The value of the portfolio, like the value of an individual patent, is based on the Validity, Scope, and Discoverability of all its claims. In this sense, it might be correct to say that a patent portfolio is primarily an extension of an individual patent.

A portfolio as a creation different from any single patent: On the other hand, a portfolio is also fundamentally different than an individual patent, and again the reason derives from the VSD model of evaluating patents. Each one of the three factors — **V**alidity of claims, **S**cope of coverage, and **D**iscoverability of infringement — is strengthened significantly, in some cases dramatically, by the aggregation of multiple patents and claims. Consider Validity of claims, for

---

[8] Infringement happening now, or expected in the near future, is clearly the dominant criterion on which scope of claim coverage is judged. If there is infringement, the patent can be monetized by licensing or litigation. If there is infringement, infringing parties may be unwilling to initiate lawsuit on their own patents — the infringing parties are too vulnerable to countersuit. In that sense, infringement can enable freedom of operation, without fear of lawsuits, for the patent owner.

example. There are very many reasons why a claim issued by the patent office might later be limited, invalidated, or rendered unenforceable by the patent office, an administrative body such as the ITC, or a court. These reasons could be (1) internal to the patent (such as a poorly defined term in the claims), (2) part of the patent process (such as the failure to find relevant prior art that may be used later against the claim), or (3) entirely external to the patent process (such as a failure to guard the confidentiality of the invention prior to filing an application, or misuse of a patent after its issuance). These reasons are discussed at length in my prior books, and will not be reviewed here.[9] For all these reasons, individual claims, or full claim sets, or even entire patents, are invalidated all the time, on a frequent basis. An individual patent involved in litigation or contentious negotiations is always exposed to these dangers. In contrast, a portfolio, with dozens or even hundreds of patents, cannot realistically be invalidated. Some of the claims or patents may fall, but others will survive. A portfolio is much tougher, much more resilient, than an individual patent.

Similarly for Discoverability of infringement. It might be difficult to discover infringement of individual claims in a single patent, particularly if the claims relate to hidden aspects such as a method of manufacture or the nano-scale structure of a semiconductor. But a portfolio, with claims for methods of use, methods of implementation, components, products,

---

[9] Quality and defects in quality is the main theme of *TPV*. Another of my books, **LITIGATION-PROOF PATENTS** (2014), lists and discusses the ten most common mistakes appearing in ICT patents. Patent quality, patent defects, and mistakes in patents, are vital topics related to both patents and portfolios, but they will not be repeated here other than the specific examples noted in the text.

systems, and other aspects, will almost never face a serious problem related to Discoverability of infringement.[10]

However, the major advantage of a portfolio over an individual patent is neither Validity nor Discoverability, but rather Scope of claim coverage. This is true for two distinct, albeit related, reasons. First, a single inventive concept, which I call a "Point of Novelty" or "PON", can be covered in multiple types of claims, certainly in a single patent, but even more so in a multiplicity of patents covering every nuance and every possible implementation of the Point of Novelty.

Second, multiple inventive concepts that are related realistically cannot be covered in a single patent — there are just too many concepts, and too many ways of expressing each concept, to cover everything in a single patent. To cover multiple Points of Novelty on the same technical issue or problem is most realistically approach by a portfolio rather than an individual patent. If such a portfolio is properly crafted, the result is what is called a "patent thicket", an example of which is discussed below in the case of Fuji Photo Film. In both respects, that is, Scope of coverage for either a single Point of Novelty or for multiple PONs, a portfolio is much stronger than an individual patent.[11]

---

[10] As a practical matter, lack of discoverability is very rarely a problem. It happens, but not frequently. For this reason, although again a portfolio is superior to an individual patent, the relative degree of difference is less pronounced for Discoverability than for Validity.

[11] This general theme, that is, the relative advantage of a portfolio over a patent due primarily to enhanced Scope of coverage, was expressed in the article "Patent Portfolios", by Gideon Parchomovsky and R. Polk Wagner, *University of Pennsylvania Law Review*, Vol. 154, No. 1, pp.1–77 (2005), available at *http://papers.ssrn.com/sol3/papers.cfm?abstract_id=582201*. Wagner and Parchomovsky review two advantages. One advantage they call "scale", which is the action of a portfolio as a kind of "super-patent" covering a single

In all respects — Validity of claims, Discoverability of infringement, and especially Scope of claim coverage — a patent portfolio is superior to a sole patent, to the extent that one could argue that these are two different entities, and a portfolio is much more than a mere extension of an individual patent.

2. Ten Principles of Excellent Patent Portfolios

There are a number of key principles that should be understood and observed to create and obtain excellent patent portfolios. These principles are based upon experience in managing portfolios, as well as benchmark reviews of various portfolios in the ICT space.[12] Here are the principles that will be discussed in this section:

Corporate and Patent Strategies
Principle 1: *A technology company must determine its strategy with regard to patents.*

PON or a few closely related PONs, what they call "coterminous subject matter", at pp.31–38. This first advantage is analogous to the first advantage mentioned in the text — coverage of a single PON. The second advantage they call "diversity", which is the coverage of "related-but-distinct" concepts, such as, for example, different technical implementations related to the same technical problem, pp.31–33 and 38–41. This second advantage is analogous to the second advantage mentioned in the text — coverage of multiple distinct yet related Points of Novelty.

[12] Some of the principles discussed here were first presented in Chapter 7 of *TPV*. Where that is the case, I will make a footnote reference to the earlier book. The form of each reference shall be *"TPV"* for the earlier book. For example, *"TPV* 7-2-3 (Portfolio)" indicates that this principle is discussed and illustrated in Chapter 7 of *TPV*, in the second case presented in Chapter 7, and as the third portfolio principle explained. The sole purpose of these footnote references is to allow the reader to access additional material, if that is the reader's desire.

Principle 2: ***A good patent portfolio matches the strategic focus of its owner.***
Principle 3: ***Invest the "right amount" in patents.***

Characteristics of an Excellent Patent Portfolio
Principle 4: ***Balance of quality and quantity.***
Principle 5: ***Geographic balance.***
Principle 6: ***Time balance.***

Managing the Patent Portfolio
Principle 7: ***Identify and fill holes in coverage.***
Principle 8: ***Time management, including divestment.***
Principle 9: ***Establish criteria for measurement.***
Principle 10: ***Place the patenting function within the organization.***

a. Corporate and Patent Strategies: As a general matter, patent strategy must be coordinated with the overall strategy of the company. This implies three principles.

Principle 1: ***A technology company must determine its strategy with regard to patents.***[13] This principle may seem so obvious that it is not worth stating, but unfortunately, the principle is often not observed. To be clear, a company must make a conscious decision that it wants a strategy for its patents, it must decide what that strategy will be, and it must then implement the strategy. The strategy will include, at a minimum, the target results in terms of patent items generated, and a target budget. The strategy may include, at a maximum, other targets such as licensing income, a specific financial return on R&D, disincentives for competitors to

---

[13] *TPV* 7-3-1 (Portfolio).

initiate patent lawsuits (for fear of being counter-sued), or inhibiting competitors from freely developing their own R&D (for fear they may infringe the company's patents).

Many high-tech companies, particularly as they start out, will not make any explicit decision about patent strategy, but will instead file one or two patents for what are considered to be key technologies. That is simply an error. There should be a plan and a strategic focus from the very beginning, although of course the plan must be flexible in response to changing needs.

Principle 2: *A good patent portfolio matches the strategic focus of its owner.*[14] This is another principle that might seem too obvious for words, but unfortunately, one that is often not observed. A good patent strategy is not made separately from the corporate strategy, but rather as a result of the corporate strategy, and in support of the corporate strategy. This implies that the top executives must be involved in setting both the corporate strategy and the supporting patent strategy. Although these executives do not make typically make decisions about specific patent filings, they should at least give some general directions for certain aspects, such as: (1) the technologies, markets, and products to be protected by patents; (2) the absolute size of the portfolio; (3) the geographic balance; (4) the balance over time; and (5) the company's competitive position with respect to both relative quantity and relative quality of the portfolio. All of these aspects may be part of a patent strategy derived from the corporate strategy.

Investment: The two critical elements that must be

---

[14] *TPV* 7-3-3 (Portfolio).

included in every patent strategy are targeted results and targeted investment/cost. As to the latter, what is the correct amount to invest? All of Chapter 3 is devoted to this question, but we can summarize some basic ideas here.

Principle 3: ***Invest the "right amount" in patents.*** How can a company, or an evaluator of a company, know if the company is investing "the right amount" in patents?[15] This question is at the heart of Chapter 3, which presents and review specific companies and specific industries that have invested estimated sums in patent portfolios. Here, in contrast, we will simply list some of the major principles in determining what the "right amount" should be. Unfortunately, there is no magic formula, but at least we can approximate some possibilities, or let's say a possible range of investment, with various benchmarks.

3a. ***For a standard technology company, one possible rule is that the investment in patents should be about 1% of the amount invested in R&D.*** There is a great amount of material that supports 1% as a benchmark. This evidence will be presented in Chapter 3, below. However 1% is only a benchmark, and must be modified to support the specific needs of each company. Factors supporting more than a standard 1% are very rapid technology change, groundbreaking discoveries, new companies and new industries, system integration, consumer sales, patent attacks by competitors, and an aggressive patent strategy by the company. Conversely, a slow rate of technology change, incremental technology, mature companies, mature industries, component sales only, and a relatively

---

15   *TPV* 7-1-2 (Portfolio).

complacent industry with regard to patents, would all suggest a possible investment less than 1% of the R&D investment.

Why is R&D investment relevant at all? Because the patents are intended to support the results of the R&D effort. Despite this reason, are there measures other than R&D that could be used as a base to estimate a desired level of investment in patents? Yes, it would be possible to use revenue as a base. Of course, the investment in patents would be much less than 1% of revenues for the great majority of companies, but revenues could be used as a base. Some companies take a standard ratio for R&D to revenue, for example 7%, in which case the investment in patents might be 7% (for R&D/revenue) × 1% (for patent investment/R&D) = .07% investment in patents as a percentage of revenues. Again, this is a benchmark only.

3b. *Set your patent investment with regard to the perceived patent investments of your key competitors.* To be discussed in Chapter 3 in the section "Competitive Budgeting".

3c. *Compare patent costs to the likelihood of being sued, the possibility of losing the litigation, and costs either in financial damages or in being enjoined from selling products.* Costs to litigate patents are very high in the United States, easily in the millions of dollars for a single lawsuit that goes to trial. The costs in other countries are more moderate, but still significant. However, litigation costs are merely a leaf on the tree in comparison to the business costs of losing a patent litigation. One possibility is liability for tens of millions to hundreds of millions or even billions of dollars of damage. Perhaps worse, the company may be barred from an entire line of business. If litigation is a serious possibility, this threat should incentivize the company to increase significantly the company's investment in patents. Further, it is ironic perhaps that the biggest companies in each field are the companies most at risk. These large and successful product companies have higher market shares, larger unit sales, larger dollar sales, and more profits, than other product companies, which means the large companies have more to lose *and means also that these are exactly the companies that are targeted by patent plaintiffs.* This is the ju-jitsu of corporate patenting — the more successful the company in its products and services, the more the company is exposed to patent litigation, and the more it must invest in its own patents.

b. Characteristics of an Excellent Patent Portfolio: As with many other investments, we begin at the end. That is, we need to know what the end result should be before we invest time, money, and effort.

Principle 4: *Balance of quality and quantity.* A patent portfolio should be judged according to both the quality and quantity of its patents.[16] The quantity of patent items (patents and pending applications) in a portfolio is fairly obvious. The quality of patent items should also be obvious, but in fact people make two very common mistakes related to patent quality in a portfolio.

First, they ignore entirely the quality of a portfolio, and focus solely on the quantity of items in the portfolio. This mistake is very common, even among the largest companies. Both in direct experience, and from what I have heard in many seminars on patents, companies like to focus on quantity but not quality. In response to the question, "What does

---

16   *TPV* 7-1-1 (Portfolio.)

the company do to insure the quality of its patents as opposed to quantity?", typical answers are, "We review our applications carefully", or "We use outstanding patent attorneys", or "We periodically trim the portfolio to retain only the high-quality items". These answers are honest, but they are not responsive to the question.

The main problem is that "quality" is commonly perceived to be difficult to judge and hard to measure. Therefore, quantity is used as a proxy for quality. While it is true that quality is not as obvious as a countable number, nevertheless the common perception is at least seriously exaggerated. Correct responses to the question about quality might be, "We identify the Key Claim Terms in every application and specifically explain each such term in the way most favorable to us", or "We review every application for the most common quality mistakes, those mistakes that infect more than 99% of ICT patents, and we make sure to wipe them out of the applications", or "We consciously use claim parallelism to insurance the most powerful protection possible for our key Points of Novelty". All of these statements relate to individual patents rather than portfolios, but in the end, every portfolio is comprised of individual patents.

There are indeed ways to judge the quality of a patent. At a minimum, a high-quality patent has good claims that are well-supported in the written description, and the patent does well in a VSD evaluation. All of these concepts, "good claim", "well-supported", and "VSD evaluation", are defined and discussed in great detail in my earlier book, *TRUE PATENT VALUE*. At a minimum, a high-quality patent avoids the most common patent mistakes that destroy both quality and value. The ten most common patent mistakes — how to identify them and how to avoid them — are the main theme of my earlier book, *LITIGATION-PROOF PATENTS*. Contrary to popular belief, there *are indeed* ways to judge the quality of the patents in a portfolio, and these ways should be used.

A company should always understand the relative quality of its patent portfolio, and should know whether the general trend of the portfolio is towards increasing or decreasing quality.

Second, people sometimes say, in error, "All our patents must be and are of the highest quality". This simply is not true, and realistically cannot be true. To make every patent as good as it can possibly be would require far too much investment of money, effort, and engineering time, with no justification. The truth is that the strength of every patent portfolio is judged on *both quality and quantity*. This means that the best portfolios will have at least several outstanding patents, whereas the rest of the patents do contribute, but primarily to quantity and to backup for the outstanding patents. The company can and should identify what it considers to be its outstanding inventions, and try to obtain very strong patents for relevant Points of Novelty, but the rest of the inventions, while they surely do contribute, should not require over-investment to the point of illogic.

In fact, in planning their patenting activities, companies often employ ranking systems in which various inventions are rated by both type of invention and potential impact. Inventions that are considered to be particularly important strategically receive special attention — their applications are drafted and prosecuted with great care. Breakthrough inventions, innovations that may be considered "Technology

Inflection Points" (as discussed in Chapter 2), and inventions that cover critical features of technical standards,[17] are all inventions that should be patented with great care.[18]

For other inventions that are considered less important strategically, the attitude and approach are to "get something down on paper", or "file quickly", or "obtain some kind of allowance on the application as soon as possible".

In general, the approach that says, "All patents must be treated equally" is wrong, and ranking systems are one counter to this erroneous approach.

Principle 5: **Geographic balance.** A good patent portfolio is balanced geographically.[19] The owner of a portfolio must consider at least three geographic markets.

5a. **Protection in the U.S. is critical**: The U.S. is the main market for much ICT technology and products. Further, it is a market where patent damages can run into the many millions or even billions of dollars. If the owner of a portfolio is or aspires to be a worldwide player, patent protection in the U.S. is critical.

5b. **Protection in a home market is often appropriate**: Many companies want patent protection in the country they call home. This is often appropriate, since it deters

---

[17] *TPV* 7-3-4 (Portfolio.)

[18] Standard-essential patents (or "SEPs") are a matter of controversy today. Some people feel such patents are used to extract unjustified rents from the users of the technical standard. Other people feel that the value generated by such patents is the justified return for early investment in important new technologies. The debate is simply beyond the scope of the current book, but for a detailed review of such patents, see my prior book, *TECHNOLOGY PATENT LICENSING*, especially Chapter 3, pp.88–141, entitled "The Determination of Essentiality".

[19] *TPV* 7-2-1 (Portfolio)

disruption in a main location of activity. Conversely, some countries are not known for strong patent enforcement, and in such countries, the need for local protection may be less pronounced.

5c. *Other markets for geographic protection.* In addition to the U.S. and the home market, it often makes sense to file in the company's most serious revenue locations. This not only protects local efforts of the company, but also provides downstream patent protection for the company's customers in these markets.[20]

Also, some companies like to have patents in the countries in which major competitors are based. The attitude is that such patents deter threats of patent litigation from such competitors. However, the costs for such protection can be quite high and possibly unjustified, unless there is a realistic chance that the company will engage in patent litigation against such competitors.

How does a company determine which geographic markets to emphasize in its patenting activity? Focusing efforts is critically important, particularly for ICT patents. Owners of BCP patents, particular patents for new drugs, often pursue worldwide patent protection at a cost of several million dollars per patent. In contrast, for ICT patents it is doubtful that worldwide protection is ever justified. The cost of worldwide protections is simply too great to bear for ICT patents. Considerations that ICT companies use to achieve geographic balance include:

---

[20] In some case, a company may provide an intellectual property indemnity with the product, but even without such an indemnity, local patents may be comforting to local customers.

Market Importance: Importance of the geographic market to the company, as discussed above.

Cost: Cost in terms of time, effort, and money, to obtain effective patent protection in the country. Some people consider the cost of obtaining patents in the U.S. to be high, but the costs in a country like Japan, including both translations and specific procedures required by the Japanese Patent Office, are higher still. The costs of obtaining protection throughout Europe are very high — it is possible to reduce these costs by obtaining a European-wide patent at the European Patent Office, and then "validating" this patent in specific countries, but the costs of validation (for translation and for country-specific fees) are also high. There are other methods for reducing international patent costs, such as the program known as the "Patent Prosecution Highway", but even with these programs, international protection is very expensive and must be planned in advance.

Enforceability: People sometimes assume that patents are equally enforceable in all countries, but that is simply untrue. For example, patents that are called "software patents" or "business method patents" are enforceable in the United States,[21] but will be much harder to enforce in Europe and are unlikely to be unrecognized at all in most Asian countries. It is questionable whether any such patents should be pursued in any country other than the United States. As a second example, the People's Republic of China has the unfortunate

---

[21] After the U.S. Supreme Court decision in *Alice Corporation v. CLS Bank*, slip opinion 13-298, 573 US _____ (decided June 19, 2014), software and business method patents are also in doubt in the United States, but as of this writing, at least some "software patents" and some "business method patents" are still valid and enforceable in the United States.

reputation of being highly resistant to enforcing patents held by non-Chinese nationals. In these circumstances, should patents be pursed at all in the PRC?[22]

Timing: If a chain of priority is preserved, later filings in multiple countries may all rely for their priority date on an original filing in one country.[23] Nevertheless, despite maintenance of early priority date in multiple countries, the specific order in which applications are filed in various countries is of great importance, for two reasons. First, applications that are filed earlier will very likely be granted earlier than applications that are filed later. Second, the "tone" or character of the application is very often set by the original filing. For example, the special form of patent claim known in the United States as the "Jepson claim" (known in Europe as the "two-part claim") almost never appears in patents derived from an original U.S. filing, but appears frequently in patents derived from an original European filing.

Extensive international filing quickly becomes extremely

---

22 I have heard it said that the situation in the PRC is changing in favor of enforcement, and that the situation is likely to change even more in the future as the country comes to rely more on developing its own technology rather than applying the technology developed by other countries in years past. I cannot evaluate these statements, and perhaps filing in the PRC is warranted for what may happen in future years, but the current reputation of the PRC is that its courts will be extremely reluctant to enforce patents held by non-Chinese nationals.

23 Relying on foreign priority depends on the membership of the involved countries in the Paris Convention for the Protection of Industrial Property of 1883 (still in force in 2014). Countries that are members of the Paris Convention may also be members of the Patent Cooperation Treaty of 1970, in which case priority dates may be preserved in some cases up to thirty months from the date of the original filing. Specific provisions of the Paris Convention and the Patent Cooperation Treaty are not within the scope of this book.

expensive. To control cost and achieve geographic balance, a company needs both a clear understanding of the costs and benefits from filing applications in various countries, and a plan to achieve maximum result at reasonable cost.

Principle 6: *Time balance.* A good patent portfolio is balanced over time.[24] A company goes through several stages in its life. This is true of every company, and particularly of a company that is heavily based on technology. The initial stage is very R&D intensive with major technical advances, followed by a middle stage with R&D that is typically less intensive and more gradual in its improvements, followed by a decline phase in which R&D tends to be reduced significantly. Patent activity needs to match the stage, as demonstrated in the table below.

Table 1-1: R&D and Patent Investments by Stage of Company

Stage of Company	R&D	Patents
Early stage — startup	Very intensive. Oriented to major advances.	Must be intensive. Oriented to small number of high-quality patents.
Middle stage — growth	Moderate. Important improvements, but not breakthroughs.	May be intensive or moderate. Often oriented to produce quantity.
End stage — decline	Reduced or eliminated.	Minimal.

There is likely to be a resource confrontation in the early stage. Just at the time the company is investing heavily in

---

24   *TPV* 7-2-2 (Portfolio).

R&D — to develop and prove the concept — the company must also invest heavily in patents. Here, the "investment" is not only money, but also the time of senior R&D people. This conflict cannot be avoided. The company's most significant technical contributions are likely to be at the beginning, and they must be patented. Failure to patent early technology is a mistake that cannot be recovered 5 years down the road. The investments can be moderated through various techniques, by focusing on only the highest technical contributions, by producing a small number of outstanding patents, by intelligent use of patent continuations to put off much of the cost in the U.S., by use of the international application known as the PCT to put off international investment, and by area applications (such as in the European Patent Office rather than in multiple European countries) to further delay international investment. In the end, however, no matter what specific techniques are used to reduce or delay costs, significant investments of time and money must be made in patents at the earliest stage of the company's life.[25]

That which is true for an entire company is true also for a new product line or a new technology within a company. The

---

[25] Startup companies often file very few patent applications, but include multiple inventions in each application. An application that has many inventions is called a "jumbo application". The strategy is to reduce filing and preparation costs by including many inventions in the written description. Individual inventions described in the original application may then be claimed and prosecuted in subsequent continuation applications. In that sense, the jumbo application becomes a "daddy" and "granddaddy" application, spawning many offspring with the same early priority date. Needless to say, this strategy can work only if the written description in the original application is very high-quality. The multiple inventions need not be claimed in the original application, but they must be well described. See "Jumbo Application" in the Glossary.

concept of corporate renewal requires companies to perpetually reinvent themselves with new technologies and products, each of which will go through life cycle stages, and each of which must receive patent investment appropriate to the specific stage of the technology or product.

c. Managing the Patent Portfolio: Even if an excellent portfolio has been matched to the corporate strategy, the portfolio must be managed over time.

Principle 7: *Identify and fill holes in coverage.* Management of a portfolio requires that holes in the portfolio be sought out, identified, and closed. This must be an active process. There must be an ongoing process to identify holes in the portfolio. These holes may be caused by expiration of patents over time, or by changing needs, or by decisions to allocate significantly more resources to patents, or by prior errors, but whatever the reason, there must be an active and ongoing effort to identify and close holes.

There are only two ways to fill holes in a portfolio — prepare and prosecute your own application, or buy existing patents. Each way has an advantage and a disadvantage. Creation of one's own application gives much greater control, but even the fastest patent will take at least one year from application to grant, and a more realistic estimate is 3–5 years for each patent. The only guaranteed way to quickly close a hole in patent portfolio is to identify existing patents owned by others, and buy them.[26] In purchasing patents, one can select exactly what is desired, and the purchasing process can be fast. On the other hand, buying patents tends to cost more

---

[26] *TPV* 7-2-3 (Portfolio).

money, sometimes vastly more money, than internal building. The decision to build or buy is discussed further in Chapter 2.

Principle 8: *Time management, including divestment.* To maintain portfolio value, patenting activities must continue over time.[27] Patents expire over time. Untended, a portfolio will gradually decline in both quantity (as patents expire) and quality (as the best patents expire). If a company intends to continue its existence, it must invest in patents over time, to insure continuity of coverage. The nature and size of the investments may change, but until a company reaches the terminal stage in its life, some investment must continue to be made to insure continuity of coverage. This principle may appear obvious, but many companies engage in bursts of patenting activity in a concentrated period of time, then stop their efforts. That may be true, for example, of Silanis Technology, which is discussed in the examples below. An opposite example is Qualcomm, which has not only maintained its portfolio, but rather intensified its patenting activity, as discussed in the examples below.

There should be no doubt about this. In every portfolio, a very few patents create the great majority of value — that is, they create most of the portfolio value either for aggression (that is, to generate licensing revenue for the company or to inhibit the R&D efforts of competitors) or for defense (that is, to deter patent lawsuits by competitors and obtain for the company freedom to operate).[28] When the main drivers of value in a patent portfolio expire, the company has reached

---

[27] *TPV* 7-3-3 (Portfolio).

[28] The relative value of patents in a portfolio is discussed in Chapter 2, below. See also "Types of Patents by Value Contribution", in the Glossary.

CHAPTER 1: WHAT IS AN EXCELLENT PATENT PORTFOLIO?   **41**

a decision point.[29] An example of this appears in the case of Check Point, discussed in the examples below.

In addition to the few great patents, there are likely to be many patents in the portfolio that for one reason or another are simply not useful. Perhaps there were expectations of value that were not realized? Perhaps the patent suffered defeat in litigation? Perhaps a change in the law renders questionable, or even valueless, claims that were formerly valuable? Perhaps the patent was formerly valuable, but its technology has been supplanted by a new approach? Perhaps there is nothing inherently wrong with the patent, but the company wishes to concentrate is resources on new and more promising innovations? Maintaining issued patents costs money, primarily in maintenance fees payable to the patent office.[30] A company cannot achieve success in its patenting efforts unless it focuses its efforts on current, not past, activities. The patenting strategy must include a plan to divest, by sale to outside parties or by simple abandonment, patents that are currently of little or no use to the company.

Principle 9: ***Establish criteria for measurement.*** Corporate strategy comes first, then patent strategy as a support to corporate strategy, and then measurement criteria for determining whether the patenting efforts are achieving their intended

---

[29] *TPV* 7-1-3 (Portfolio).

[30] In the United States, for example, as of now the maintenance fees after issuance are $1,600 at 3.5 years, $3,600 at 7.5 years and $7,400 at 11.5 years. Fees for so-called "small entities" are half these sums, and fees for so-called "micro entities" are one-quarter of these sums. At any of these levels, however, maintenance fees quickly add up, particularly for large portfolios. Many countries levy maintenance fees for issued patents. For pending, unissued applications, the United States does not require maintenance fees, but many countries do require such fees.

goals. The specific criteria depend on the specific goal, and if the company is pursuing multiple goals in its patenting efforts, the portfolio will be judged by suitable criteria for each goal.

For example, is the goal to generate income by licensing or litigation? Then revenue generation will be measured over time. Or more likely, there will be a comparison of revenue generation versus total cost to generate the revenue. These measurements may be of particular relevance to the financial officers of the company.

For example, how effective is R&D in creating value? One measure, of course, is the number of new products and services developed over time. Another measure is the number of patent applications and patents generated over time. Another measure is the amount of licensing revenue as a percentage of R&D over time. This last measure is reviewed in the specific case below for Qualcomm. These measurements may be of particular relevance to top R&D officers of the company.

For example, how effective is the patent portfolio in inhibiting competitors and generating value by a predominant position for a particular innovation? This is more difficult to judge. In one specific case discussed below, Fuji Photo Film excluded competitors from its marketplace and thereby created tremendous value for the company in exchange for a relatively modest investment in a patent portfolio. These measurements may be of particular relevance to the general managers of specific businesses, sometimes called "Strategic Business Units" (or "SBUs") within the company.

No strategy is complete unless it includes also criteria by which implementation will be measured.

Principle 10: **Place the patenting function within the organization.** Where should the patenting function fit within the organization? Who should have control of it, and hence also responsibility for it? This is far from a trivial decision, because the attitude of the various departments in the company towards patents is likely to vary greatly. There are four options, and each option is in fact used by various companies.

First, to place patents within the Legal Department. This makes a good deal of sense, since patents are, after all, a legal concept, and they are created primarily by legally oriented professionals working with the inventors. Further, the Legal Department is the group in the company most likely to be aware of, and understand, new court decisions and other legal changes affecting patents.

Second, to place patents with the office of the Chief Technology Officer. The CTO is very interested in the success of the R&D efforts, and success with patent creation is one measure of R&D success. Further, the office of the CTO is most likely to understand the technical implications of each invention, and to be the group best placed within the company to set priorities of technical importance on the various inventions.

Third, to place patents with the VP of Business Development. This might not seem sensible, since the Business Development Department is not likely to understand legal implications as well as the Legal Department, or technical implications as well as the CTO. But patents are not written to create plaques on a wall. They must be of specific use to the company, else why invest so much in creating them? The Business Development Department may be in charge of licensing intellectual property, creating joint venture and joint R&D efforts, and managing merger & acquisition activity in which patent value can play a critical role. Placement here may make less sense on the front end (that is, patent generation) but more sense on the back end (that is, revenue and business generation).

Fourth, to place patents and patent responsibility within the Strategic Business Units responsible for creating technology, developing products, and generating revenue from the products. There are strong advantages, and also strong disadvantages, for such a placement. On the plus side, the SBU managers are likely to have the best understanding of the technology protected by the patent, the best understanding of the specific business implications of the patent, and the most incentive to use patents in every way possible to meet the financial goals of the SBU. On the negative side, the SBU managers will likely have no legal expertise, will probably be less interested in the long-term technical implications of the patent (since the managers want short-term results), and will likely be unable to prevent duplication of technical and patenting efforts with other SBUs within the company.

It is of course possible to include various combinations of the four placements listed above. As one example, the Legal Department might be responsible for generating patents, whereas the Business Development Department might be responsible for monetizing or otherwise generating value from the company's patents. Split placement of the patenting function helps maximize the natural expertise of different groups within the company, but also creates problems of coordination. In some way, however, patenting must be placed within the company to help achieve the goals of the patent function, and hence the goals of the corporate strategy.

3. Four Examples of Patent Portfolios.

Each of the following examples of high-tech patent portfolios could justify its own book, but we will focus solely on
the principles discussed above. Not all of these portfolios
are "good", let alone "excellent", but they are all illustrative of
principles of excellence. In order to shorten the discussion,
each portfolio will be represented by a figure showing either
the development of the portfolio over time, or the state of the
portfolio on a specific date.[31]

Example 1 — Check Point Software Technologies

Check Point is one of the pioneers in electronic firewall
protection, both Internet and intranet. The company has been
active since the early 1990's. Here is a summary of its sales and
R&D activities over the past few years.

---

[31] These four examples were presented first in *TPV* — Check Point, Silanis
Technology, and Qualcomm in Chapter 7 of *TPV*, and Fuji Photo Film in
Chapter 4 of *TPV*.

Table 1-2: Revenue and R&D Summary
for Check Point Software[32]

	2007	2008	2009	2010	2011	2012	2013	Totals	CAGR
Annual Revenue ($M)	731	808	924	1,098	1,247	1,343	1,394	7,545	11.4%
Annual R&D ($M)	81	92	90	106	110	112	122	713	7.1%
R&D/ Revenue	11.1%	11.3%	9.7%	9.6%	8.8%	8.3%	8.7%	9.4%	

Here is a view of the company's patent portfolio from its beginning through June, 2014.

Table 1-3: Check Point Software's Patent Portfolio[33]

	US pats	US apps	EU pats	EU apps	DE pats	JP pats	Int'l apps	Totals
1994	0	0	0	0	0	0	0	0
1995	0	0	0	0	0	0	0	0
1996	0	0	0	0	0	1	0	1
1997	1	0	0	0	0	0	1	2
1998	1	0	0	0	0	0	0	1

[32] Information in this table comes from Check Point's annual reports, and is available at *http://www.checkpoint.com/corporate/investor-relations/earnings-history/index.html*.

[33] Throughout this book, US patents and US applications are derived from the web site of the U.S. patent office, *www.uspto.gov*, and from the commercial web site, *www.freepatentsonline.com*. Throughout this book, European patents, European patent applications, German patent items, Japanese patent items, and PCT International applications, are from *www.freepatentsonline.com*.

	US pats	US apps	EU pats	EU apps	DE pats	JP pats	Int'l apps	Totals
1999	0	0	0	0	0	0	0	**0**
2000	0	0	1	0	1	0	0	**2**
2001	0	0	0	0	0	0	1	**1**
2002	1	0	0	0	0	0	0	**1**
2003	0	1	0	0	0	0	0	**1**
2004	0	0	0	0	0	0	0	**0**
2005	2	2	1	0	0	0	3	**8**
2006	0	2	1	1	2	0	0	**6**
2007	2	3	0	0	0	0	0	**5**
2008	2	1	0	0	0	0	0	**3**
2009	4	1	0	1	0	0	1	**7**
2010	5	7	1	1	1	0	0	**15**
2011	5	1	0	0	0	0	0	**6**
2012	10	5	0	0	0	0	0	**15**
2013	9	6	0	2	0	0	0	**17**
2014	8	6	0	0	0	0	0	**14**
Other	6	14	N/R	N/R	N/R	N/R	N/R	**20**
Totals	**56**	**49**	**4**	**5**	**4**	**1**	**6**	**129***

[*: Total number as a sum of the various categories is 125 rather than 129. However, Check Point has also one additional patent in each of Canada, Republic of China — Taiwan, Republic of Korea, and Singapore. When these are added, the total is 129, as shown.]

What could we conclude from these views of Check Point's sales, R&D, and patenting activities over time? Let's start with two preliminary observations.

First, no conclusion whatever can be made about reasons

for the changing level of R&D investment. Yes, R&D investment is increasing gradually over time, and yes, it is decreasing as a percentage of sales, but these trends may be entirely appropriate.

Second, evidence suggests that Check Point has, over its entire life, either built or bought about 129 patent items. As explained in Chapter 3 below, this kind of portfolio probably cost about $3M to assemble and maintain.

On the characteristics of excellent portfolios, how could we review this portfolio?

1. Fit with corporate strategy: I have no independent knowledge of Check Point's corporate strategy, apart from the patent portfolio itself. I cannot draw a conclusion.
2. Coverage of key technologies and markets: The general topics of the patents are directly within Check Point's business. Key technologies are covered. I cannot draw conclusions about specific products.
3. Mix of quality and quantity:
    a. Check Point's two earliest patents are US 5,606,668, "System for Securing Inbound and Outbound Data Packet Flows in a Computer Network", and US 5,835,726, "System Securing the Flow of and Selectively Modifying Packets in a Computer Network". These patents were reviewed at great length in *TPV*, and they are very good patents covering breakthrough inventions. The quality of the portfolio was very high with these two patents.[34]
    b. Approximately 129 patent items for a company of

---

[34] These two patents were filed in 1993 and 1996, respectively, and were

this size and in this area of technology is insanely low. That is true by any measure. (1) On an R&D budget of $713M over the past six years alone, $3M does not approach 1%. There are factors that call for investing more or less than the 1% benchmark, but for a company like Check Point, the factors (high-technology, rapidly changing technology, strong market position, integrated products rather than components) would seem to suggest *more than 1%*, and certainly not less. (2) In comparison to the costs of a single patent litigation, $3M is a very low investment. (3) Check Point is a market leader, with almost $1.5B in annual sales and an operating profit rate that is over 50% of total revenues. A loss in patent litigation could be very expensive for a large and profitable market leader such as Check Point. (4) Check Point's investment in patents in comparison to the investments of Check Point's main competitors is very poor. This is discussed further in Chapter 3, in the section "Competitive Budgeting".

4. Geographic coverage: Coverage in the U.S. is good. Coverage in European and Asian countries is weak, because that there simply are not enough patents in these locations.

5. Continuity over time: Everything said above is dwarfed by this portfolio's great weakness of continuity. Check Point's two earliest and probably its best patents, refer-enced above, expired in February, 2014. By law, Check

---

issued in 1997 and 1998, respectively. They both expired, solely due to the passage of time, in early 2014.

Point could still sue for damages of patent infringement occurring in the past, but no damages will accrue for any current or future activities, and Check Point cannot obtain an injunction on these patents. Nothing appears to have replaced these two outstanding patents. If we look at the patent table above, we see that there was almost no patenting activity within the period 1998–2004. Although it does appear that Check Point has boosted its patent activity in the period 2012–2014, no amount of patenting activity within the company can redress the deficit from the late 1990's to the mid-2000's.

6. Special considerations for this portfolio: The firewall market continues to grow strongly, and Check Point as a major player might be exposed to significant patent liability. Both these factors indicate that patent investment might be higher than an overall industry average.

If Check Point wanted, how might it address the gaps in its portfolio, particularly the loss of its best patents and the break in continuity of time? It could, for example:

(1) Buy early patents in this field, but patents with more years of life left. This would likely cost millions of dollars, but it is possible. At this point of time, there is no build option that can repair the almost absence of patent activity in period 1998–2004, so the only way to fill the holes is to buy patents.

(2) Join commercial defensive patent aggregators, such as RPX, to access additional patents, that is, to increase its access to pooled patents.

(3) Identify players who hold key patents in the industry, and license-in those patents, or acquire the companies.

(4) Create production and marketing alliances with other companies that can bear part, most, or even all of the risk and cost of patent litigation.

(5) Create an ownership alliance with another company that has a stronger patent position. This could be achieved by Check Point and the other company taking equity positions in one another, or more simply by Check Point selling a significant portion of its equity to the other company.

Example 2 — Silanis Technology

Silanis Technology, a Canadian company based in Montreal and founded in 1992, provides electronic signature and electronic approval software for commercial and governmental customers. Its technology allows the addition of electronic signatures to MS-Word and Excel, MS-Outlook, Adobe Acrobat, and other kinds of application programs.

Silanis is a private company, with limited public disclosure. Its R&D figures are not published. Revenues are also confidential, although they appear to be in the range of $5M — $10M/year. Here is a review of the Silanis patent portfolio since the company's founding through June, 2014.

52   PATENT PORTFOLIOS

Table 1-4: Silanis Technology's Patent Portfolio[35]

	US pats	US apps	CA pats	CA apps	EPO pats	EPO apps	DE grant	Int'l apps	Totals
1992	0	0	0	0	0	0	0	0	0
1993	0	0	0	0	0	0	0	0	0
1994	0	0	0	0	0	0	0	0	0
1995	0	0	0	0	0	0	0	0	0
1996	0	0	0	0	0	0	0	0	0
1997	1	0	0	0	0	0	0	0	1
1998	0	0	0	0	0	0	0	0	0
1999	0	0	0	0	0	0	0	0	0
2000	0	0	0	3	0	0	0	6	9
2001	0	0	0	4	0	3	0	1	8
2002	0	3	0	2	0	1	0	3	9
2003	0	0	0	3	2	2	0	0	7
2004	1	0	0	0	0	0	2	0	3
2005	2	0	0	0	0	0	0	0	2
2006	0	0	1	0	0	0	0	0	1
2007	0	0	0	0	0	0	0	0	0
2008	1	0	0	0	1	0	2	0	4
2009	0	0	0	0	2	0	1	0	3
2010	0	0	2	0	0	0	0	0	2
2011	0	0	0	0	0	0	0	0	0
2012	1	0	0	0	0	0	0	0	1
2013	0	0	0	0	0	0	0	0	0
2014	0	0	0	0	0	0	0	0	0
Totals	6	3	3	12	5	6	5	10	50

[35] Canadian patents are from the web site of the Canadian Intellectual Property Office, *http://www.cipo.ic.gc.ca/eic/site/cipointernet-internetopic.nsf/eng/Home.*

Let us make some preliminary remarks. First, for a portfolio like this, with 19 patents and 31 applications, a reasonable estimate of total investment would be about be about $1.0M-$1.5M. This is a small number in absolute terms, but for a company with perhaps $5M-$10M in sales per year, and perhaps $100M in sales over its lifetime, this is a significant investment.

Second, the portfolio appears to be entirely self-generated, that is, filed and prosecuted by Silanis, with the exception of US 5,606,609, acquired for an unknown sum in the year 2000. This was an outstanding patent, discussed at length in *TPV*. However, this patent expired in September, 2014.[36]

Third, although the absolute size of the portfolio may be reasonable for a company of this size, about 66% of the portfolio was built or acquired in the period 2000–2003. There has been almost no patent activity in the past five years.

On the characteristics of excellent portfolios, how could we review this portfolio?

1. Fit with corporate strategy: I have no independent knowledge of Silanis' corporate strategy, apart from the patent portfolio itself. The Silanis portfolio has provided protection against hostile lawsuits, and that perhaps was Silanis' objective, both in obtaining US 5,606,609, and in developing relatively strong protection in Canada. Silanis' corporate strategy is discussed further in Chapter 3.

2. Coverage of key technologies and markets: The general topics of the patents are directly within Silanis'

---

36 This patent was filed in 1994, issued in 1997, acquired by Silanis in 2000, and expired in 2014.

business. Key technologies are covered. I cannot draw conclusions about specific products.

3. Mix of quality and quantity:

    a. For reasons discussed in my earlier book, US 5,606,609 is a very good patent, and has provided significant protection to Silanis during the patent's life. However, the patent expired in September, 2014.

    b. 50 patent items for a company of Silanis' size is a very substantial number. Silanis has been a leader in its industry, but the industry dynamics are changing. Silanis is now being challenged by a company called DocuSign that is investing heavily in patents. Other patent changes are also occurring, and in general, the next few years will likely see significant changes in the electronic signature industry. These changes are discussed in Chapter 3.

4. Geographic coverage: The U.S. is almost certainly the #1 market for electronic signature products and services. Silanis' coverage in the U.S. has been good, but that changed with the expiration of the main U.S. patent. Silanis, a Canadian company, has invested relatively heavily in home-country patents. This kind of investment would probably not be seen in a non-Canadian company, but it may be reasonable here to give Silanis peace of mind. Over 50% of patent investments have been in European and international markets (not Canada or the U.S.), which is extremely high for a non-European company. In sum, the main challenge of geographic coverage is the recent loss of U.S. protection, and a secondary challenge is a possible

over-investment in European and international patent items.

5. Continuity over time: This is the serious concern. In its early years, the company did not invest in patents. Then, in 2000–2003, the company invested heavily and generated about two-thirds of its present portfolio, including the acquisition of US 5,606,609 in 2000. However, the company has invested almost nothing in patents over the past five years, its portfolio is aging, and it is now facing new patent threats, as will be discussed further in Chapter 3. Overall, lack of continuity over time is a great weakness of the portfolio.

6. Special considerations for this portfolio: There are weaknesses in this portfolio, but these are not special considerations, and there are no such considerations on the face of the portfolio. However, there are indeed special considerations that are derived from the nature of the electronic signature industry. The character of the players in this industry, and the great variety of investments by the players in patents, may have an impact on Silanis' patent strategy. These considerations will be discussed further in Chapter 3

Silanis has holes its portfolio due to low investment in recent years and the expiration of its key U.S. patent. What might Silanis do at this point to fill the holes in its portfolio? Although it does appear that Silanis is a leader in electronic signatures, given the nature of this industry most of the possible strategies listed above for Check Point are probably not relevant for Silanis. It is unlikely the company can join defensive aggregators, or cross-license patents from companies in its industry, or create production or marketing alliances (given the nature of the electronic signature business). Silanis' potential problem with patents can probably be addressed by either of two strategies:

(1) To buy another U.S. patent to replace the expiring US 5,606,609, at a significant price;

(2) To create an ownership alliance, or possibly even to sell itself to larger company. One of its major competitors, EchoSign, did in fact sell itself to Adobe in 2011.

Patent changes in the electronic signature industry, and challenges to Silanis, are discussed further in Chapter 3.

Example 3 — Fuji Photo Film

This example is different from the first two examples. Whereas the prior examples show development of a portfolio over time, this example shows the impact of a portfolio at a single point in time. This example is intended to demonstrate the tremendous power of a properly constructed portfolio — a portfolio that covers the right products, in the right geographic market, at the critical moment in time. In sum, this is an example of a "Patent Thicket".

Fuji Photo Film, founded in Tokyo in 1934, has been one of the leaders of consumer photography products. In 1986, the company invented the QuickSnap line of handheld disposable ("one-use") cameras. It has been a leader in this market from the late 1980's through the 1990's and 2000's.

In the 1990's, various companies in the United States were acquiring disposable cameras, repairing or refurbishing them with new batteries and film, and selling them to consumers. In 1998, Fuji filed an action with the International Trade

Commission ("ITC") to prevent the importation into the U.S. of such refurbished cameras. In 1999, the ITC granted this petition, and forbid the importation of such products into the U.S. After various litigation, the U.S. Court of Appeals for the Federal Circuit, which is the highest court entitled to decide patent actions in the U.S. (apart from the Supreme Court), reversed the ITC, finding that if cameras were first sold in the U.S., such sale exhausts the right to sue for patent infringement. In other words, Fuji's opponents won this round of litigation. However, the litigation continued, and the lower court determined that most of the cameras, almost 40 million units, were not first sold in the U.S., and therefore did infringe at least 33 independent patent claims in 15 patents. This decision went to the Court of Appeals a second time, which affirmed the decision against the defendants Jazz Photo Corporation and others. Ultimately, about 20 companies were found to infringe, the main defendant Jazz Photo was driven to bankruptcy, and Fuji continued to enjoy a dominant market position based on its patent portfolio. All of this despite the fact that Fuji lost on the main issue, which was Fuji's claim of patent infringement for cameras first sold in the U.S. and later refurbished. The ITC decision is Case No. 337-TA-406, entitled, "In the Matter of Certain Lens-Fitted Film Packages", *Fuji Photo Film Co., Ltd., of Japan v. Achiever Industries of Hong Kong* and twenty-six other defendants from various countries in Asia, Europe, and North America (order of June 2, 1999). The decision of the Court of Appeals for the Federal Circuit is reported at 394 F.3d 1368 (Fed. Cir. 2005).

Why was this portfolio so valuable? Because it did exactly what a portfolio is supposed to do. It covered a single core invention, which was disposable cameras, but covered multiple Points of Novelty related to this invention, with multiple types of claims (structure of a system, a component structure for packaging, method, and product design). Note that the specific product, one-use then throw-away cameras (and NOT simply "cameras"), must be a low-tier offering within the general market for cameras, because consumers will not simply throw away higher tier cameras. As a low-tier offering, the product relies upon Japan's key traditional strengths — design, engineering, and production to cut cost, and mass distribution. This product line was ideally suited to Japanese strengths, and the patent portfolio was ideally suited to protect the product line.

Here is the portfolio considered by the ITC, with the aspect noted, the patents related to that aspect, and the number of claims in that aspect that the ITC found were infringed by the defendants.

Table 1-5: Fuji Photo Film's U.S. Patent Portfolio in 1999

Aspect of the Point of Novelty that was Patented	Patents Focused on this Aspect of the Subject	Number of Patents Focused on this Aspect	Number of Independent Claims Infringed by Defendants
Film units = handheld cameras	US 5,361,111 US 5,381,200 US 5,408,288 US 5,436,685	4	9
Film packaging	US 4,833,495 US 4,855,774 US 4,884,087 US 4,954,857 US 5,063,400 US 5,235,364 RE. 34,168	7	19
Methods for assembling film packaging	US 4,972,649	1	2
Ornamental design of handheld cameras	Des. 345,750 Des. 356,101 Des. 372,722	3 (all design patents)	3
TOTALS		15	33

The ITC found that the defendants had infringed thirty-three independent claims covering the cameras, the packaging, assembly, and design of the cameras.

Some of the independent claims in this portfolio were strong, while others were not. The key point, however, is that the patents worked together at a particular point in time to cover multiple aspects of the same inventive concept. This is an example of what is sometimes called a "Patent Thicket", which is a particular kind of patent portfolio with reinforcing patents covering multiple aspects of a single concept. A patent thicket provides vastly stronger protection than a single patent, even if, as here, not all of the patents in the portfolio are strong.

On the characteristics of excellent patent portfolios, how could we review this portfolio?

1. Fit with corporate strategy: Fuji's obvious strategy was to achieve dominance in the U.S. market with its disposable cameras. Fuji achieved this through patent litigation. There was a perfect fit between the corporate and patent strategies.

2. Coverage of key technologies and markets: Even a cursory glance at the table above demonstrates how well Fuji achieved this coverage. All of the key aspects of design and structure appear to be covered by the portfolio.

3. Mix of quality and quantity:
    a. As noted, some of the patents were stronger than others, and some of the claims were stronger than others, but at least 33 claims were considered of sufficiently high quality to catch 20 infringers.
    b. In this case, 15 patents were sufficient for the patent owner to dominate an industry.

4. Geographic coverage: The U.S. was the only market of relevance here, and it was covered by these patents.

5. Continuity over time: These patents were all in force during the critical time period, which was the late 1990's and early 2000's. Disposable cameras are still used today, in 2014, but their heyday has passed with the rise of the cell phone camera.

6. Special consideration for this portfolio: The product, one-use cameras, had a particular problem in that it created its own after-market that could seriously

undermine new sales in the main market. Fuji's challenge was to extend its market legitimately by temporarily reducing the after-market, thereby increasing market demand for its one-use cameras. There are several ways Fuji might have dealt with this challenge. The solution it chose, that is, to protect its market through intellectual property, was a very effective approach. Bear in mind, however, this solution was "temporary" only. As the patents in the portfolio expire over time, the strategy becomes untenable. Here the patents were of vital, but temporary, importance to the company.

Example 4 — Qualcomm

Qualcomm was founded in 1985, and has been, from its very beginning, one of the pioneers in the development of CDMA technology for cellular technology. The following table makes clear the extent of Qualcomm's commitment to R&D.

Table 1-6: Revenue and R&D Summary for Qualcomm[37]

	2007	2008	2009	2010	2011	2012	2013	Totals	CAGR
Annual Revenue ($B)	8.9	11.1	10.,4	10.9	15.0	19.1	24.9	100.3	18.7%
Annual R&D ($B)	1.8	2.3	2.4	2.5	3.0	3.9	5.0	20.9	18.6%
R&D/ Revenue	20.6%	20.5%	22.6%	22.3%	20.0%	20.5%	20.1%	20.8%	

---

[37] Information in this table comes from Qualcomm's annual reports, and is available at *http://investor.qualcomm.com/sec.cfm?DocType=annual.*

Let us compare Check Point and Qualcomm.

Check Point is very technology-oriented. It has invested heavily in R&D to achieve its market position, its average investment in R&D as percentage of revenue in the period 2007–2013 was 9.4%, and its annual high was 11.3% in 2008. More typical for a technology company would be about 7%-8%, which Check Point exceeded in every year within the period 2007–2013.

Qualcomm is in a different category altogether, not only in comparison to the technology-heavy Check Point, but also in comparison to technology companies generally. An average R&D/revenue ratio of 20.8% in the period 2007–2013, and a range of 20.1%-22.6%, are astounding numbers, way above average. This percentage, R&D/revenue, is generally called in the technology industry "R&D intensity" or "the R&D intensity ratio". In Qualcomm's case, this ratio shows an extremely strong commitment to R&D. In short, Qualcomm's corporate strategy clearly relies very heavily on R&D investments that far exceed industry norms.

Also, Qualcomm's reliance on patents far exceeds industry norms, in two respects, that is, investment in patents, and financial return from patent licensing. Consider the following table summarizing Qualcomm's patent holdings on May 22, 2013, and on May 22, 2014.

Table 1-7: Snapshots of Qualcomm's Patent Portfolio

Patent Item	5/22/2013	5/22/2014	Growth	% Increase
U.S. patents	6,878	9,277	2,399	34.9%
U.S. patent applications	8,752	11,354	2,602	29.7%
European patents and applications	12,347	14,058	1,711	13.9%
Japanese patents and applications	1,687	2,534	847	50.2%
German patents and applications	1,990	1,995	5	0.3%
PCT int'l applications	15,259	17,908	2,649	17.4%
TOTAL	**46,913**	**57,126**	**10,213**	**21.8%**

First, what has been the total cost to Qualcomm to generate its current portfolio (as of 2014)? As a rough estimate, assume $30,000 per patent item to prepare, file, and prosecution patent applications, then maintain and defend the granted patents. For issued patents held to the end of their legal life, the number will almost certainly be higher. For pending applications, and for patents that are issued but not maintained to the end of their lives, the number will be lower. This average estimate is not unreasonable. It yields a total of investment in patents by Qualcomm of about 57,126 items × $30,000/item = $1.714 Billion.

Second, it is very significant that despite Qualcomm's massive patent investments in prior years, the company is continuing to invest significant amounts in its patent portfolio. The company has been in existence 30 years, but last year alone its entire portfolio grew almost 22% (that is, 10,213 divided by 46,913).

Third, according to its published reports, since its

inception in 1985 through the end of April, 2014, Qualcomm has invested $30.0 billion in R&D. The patent investment of $1.714B represents 5.71% of the investment in R&D. I call this the "patent activity intensity".[38] This ratio, the "patent activity intensity", will be explained and discussed further in Chapter 3, but for now it is noteworthy that a general benchmark investment for technology companies, as explained later in Chapter 3, is about 1% investment in patents / R&D investment. Qualcomm's ratio, at 5.71%, is an off-the-chart outlier.[39]

In short, both Qualcomm's R&D intensity and its patent activity intensity are extremely high. Both are multiples of industry norms, in which Qualcomm's R&D intensity ratio of 20.8% is about three times the norm, and its patent activity intensity of 5.71% is almost six times the norm.

What is happening here? With one more piece, the puzzle will become clear.

Qualcomm relies very heavily on patent licensing to generate both revenues and particularly profits. This represents

---

[38] There is no accepted industry term for the ratio (Patent investment / R&D investment). I have created the term "patent activity intensity". This is not at all the same thing as "patent intensity", which some technology people use for the ratio (patents / 1,000 employees) and other technology people use for (patents / 1 million inhabitants).

[39] The 5.71% patent activity ratio is based on an assumption that Qualcomm has invested $30,000 one each patent items in its portfolio, for a total investment of $1.714 Billion. If we assumed, instead, $30,000 for every U.S. patent and $20,000 for every other item in the portfolio, total investment would be $1.235 Billion, and the patent activity ratio would be 4.11% instead of 5.71%. If we assumed, instead, $30,000 for every U.S. patent, $15,000 for every international application, and $20,000 for every other patent item, total investment in patents would be $1.146 Billion, and the patent activity ratio would be 3.82% rather than 5.71%. This comparative sensitivity to assumed patent costs demonstrates that in Qualcomm's case, different cost assumptions simply do not matter. Qualcomm's patent activity is massively higher than the norms of high-tech industry, and that is true both at 3.82% and at 5.71%.

the marriage of the corporate and patent strategies. Consider the following information about Qualcomm's various lines of business:

Table 1-8: Qualcomm Equipment, Service, and Licensing Revenues and Profits[40]

	2008	2009	2010	2011	2012	2013	Total	CGR
Total Revenue ($B)	11.1	10.4	11.0	15.0	19.1	24.9	91.5	17.5%
Equipment & Service Revenue ($B)	7.2	6.5	7.0	9.2	12.5	17.0	59.4	18.7%
% of Total	64.9%	62.5%	63.6%	61.3%	65.4%	68.3%	64.9%	
Licensing Revenue ($B)	3.9	3.9	4.0	5.8	6.6	7.9	32.1	15.2%
% of Total	35.1%	37.5%	36.4%	38.7%	34.6%	31.7%	35.1%	
Total EBT	4.9	4.5	4.7	6.9	7.9	9.8	38.7	14.9%
Equipment & Service EBT ($B)	1.8	1.4	1.7	2.1	2.3	3.2	12.5	12.2%
% of Total	36.7%	31.1%	36.2%	30.4%	29.1%	32.7%	32.3%	
Licensing EBT ($B)	3.1	3.1	3.0	4.8	5.6	6.6	26.2	16.3%
% of Total	63.3%	68.9%	63.8%	69.6%	70.9%	67.3%	67.3%	

---

[40] All information from Qualcomm's annual 10-K statements. Numbers for 2011–2013 were simply copied in the form given. Category numbers for 2008–2010 were estimated on the basis of published information — there may be some errors, but for present purposes they simply do not matter. The published information tells a consistent story.

This table clearly demonstrates that for at least the past six years, and probably for much longer, Qualcomm has relied on licensing revenue for the great majority of its profits. In fact, whereas only about one-third of its sales come from licensing, about two-thirds of its profits come from licensing. Licensing can include all kinds of intellectual property and know-how, but in Qualcomm's case, with almost 60,000 patent items, it is clear that patents have driven the great majority of these revenues. Further, it is inferable that Qualcomm's corporate strategy, even from its beginning in the mid-1980's, has been to invest strongly in technology, and to derive financial gain from the patents derived from this technology.

Qualcomm is an aggressive developer and licensor of technology. We can judge this by the magnitude of its perennial investment in R&D, its investment in patents, its patent portfolio, its revenues derived from technology licensing, and its profits derived from technology licensing. We can judge this also by benchmark ratios such as R&D investment/ revenue, Patent investment/R&D investment, Technology licensing revenue/Total revenue, and Licensing Profits/Total Profits. In all these benchmarks, Qualcomm's numbers are much higher than those of the average technology company. All of this information is consistent with the company's strategic focus on aggressively developing and licensing technology.

To summarize for Qualcomm: (1) Its R&D intensity of 20.8% is way above the average, about three times what one would expect in an average technology company, and even higher in comparison to relatively established companies such as the 30-year old Qualcomm; (2) Its patent activity intensity of about 5.71% is close to 500% greater than a benchmark for technology companies, discussed further in Chapter 3; (3) Although it derives only one-third of its revenue from patent licensing, the profit margin on this revenue is extremely high, generating about two-thirds of Qualcomm's profits. Indeed, Qualcomm's total profit solely from licensing in the six-year period 2008–2013 ($26 Billion) almost equals the total R&D investment since the company was founded thirty years ago ($30 Billion).

On the characteristics of excellent portfolios, how could we review the Qualcomm patent portfolio?

1. Fit with corporate strategy: Qualcomm wanted to develop technology, and profit on its technology investment. That is what it has done, and what it continues to do. This is an outstanding patent portfolio in support of Qualcomm's aggressive licensing strategy.

2. Coverage of key technologies and markets: Its coverage of CDMA technology, including fundamental concepts, aspects appearing in the various CDMA technical standards, and specific problems, is excellent.

3. Mix of quality and quantity:
   a. As explained in my earlier book, Qualcomm has many patents that are heavily cited and relied upon in the industry.[41] Not all of Qualcomm's patents are outstanding, and indeed some of the claims in some of the patents are very weak, but Qualcomm certainly has many high-quality patents.
   b. Almost 60,000 patent items, of which more than one-sixth have been generated in the last year alone. On any kind of comparison, the quantity

---

[41] *TPV*, Table 7-8.

is outstanding. In particular: (1) The patent activity intensity is well above 1%. (2) Costs of single litigations are small in comparison to Qualcomm's total investment in patents of perhaps $1.5B — $2.0B. (3) Qualcomm has been engaged actively in patent litigation, as both plaintiff and defendant, and although it has lost some sizable amounts in some cases, its overall litigation activities have been strongly on the plus side. (4) I do not here compare Qualcomm's investment in patents to the investments of any particular competitors, except to say again that Qualcomm is an extreme outlier on a continuum of patent investment.

4. Geographic coverage: All major markets in Asia, Europe, and North American, are covered by various Qualcomm patents.

5. Continuity over time: The surprising thing about Qualcomm is that it has not only continued but indeed intensified its patent activity over time. Excellent continuity.

6. Special considerations for this portfolio: The cellular industry is unique among high-tech industries, for two reasons.

First, unlike many high-tech industries, cellular companies typically do not supply entire systems, but rather the various products of different companies *must work together* to produce a service useful to the customer. There are at least three separate segments of the cellular business, including the customer's handset, base stations that communicate with the handsets, and control centers that communicate with the base stations. (Such control centers may be called network controllers, or mobile switching centers, or by some other name, but essentially they all control base station traffic and communicate with the public switched telephone network.) Different companies supply handsets, as opposed to base stations and control centers, and indeed different companies may supply the base stations as opposed to the control centers. A system can operate successfully only if all products function in accordance with a specific technical standard, and that is a key feature of cellular technology — there are very many technical standards. Some of Qualcomm's most heavily cited patents predate the first CDMA standards, and are in fact essential to the implementation of CDMA standards.

Second, there are very many patents in the cellular business. By one count, 250,000 patents cover various functions of smart phones.[42] In these circumstances, where quantity is such that no one can license-in all relevant patents, the quality of the patents is vitally important. Qualcomm's most heavily cited patents pre-date the technical standards for CDMA, many of its patents are essential to implementation of the technical standards, and these patents have been the basis for Qualcomm's multi-billion dollar licensing program. This also, is a special consideration of the Qualcomm patent portfolio.

---

[42] Estimate by defensive patent aggregator RPX Corporation, Registration Statement (Form S-1), at 59 (Sept. 2, 2011), available at *http://www.sec.gov/ Archives/edgar/data/1509432/000119312511240287/ds1.htm*.

Conclusion to Chapter 1

There are similarities between a single patent and a patent portfolio, but a patent portfolio is typically much stronger than a single patent in all of the VSD factors, particularly in Validity of claims and Scope of claim coverage. The difference in strength is so great that an individual patent and a patent portfolio should be considered different entities.

In Chapter 1 we looked at ten principles of excellent patent portfolios. We also considered four examples of portfolios — some good, some less good, but illustrating together the key factors that determine the quality of a portfolio. These key factors are (1) the portfolio's fit with the corporate strategy; (2) its coverage of key technologies and markets; (3) its mix of quality and quantity of patents; (4) its geographic suitability for the company; (5) its continuity over time; and (6) special considerations in this industry or for this portfolio.

Each of the four companies discussed here is a leader in its product or technology market. How did these companies perform in the building and management of their patent portfolios? Table 1-9 provides a summary:

Table 1-9: The Portfolios of Check Point, Silanis, Fuji Photo, and Qualcomm

Characteristic	Check Point	Silanis Technology	Fuji Photo Film	Qualcomm
1. Fit with corporate strategy	Not clear — the patent strategy is unknown	Portfolio good for defensive purposes	Portfolio outstanding to exclude competitors from the market	Perfect coordination of corporate and patent strategies
2. Coverage of key technologies and markets	Good	Good	Excellent: covers multiple Points of Novelty	Excellent: Focus on cellular technology
3. Mix of quality and quantity	Good	Good	Outstanding	Outstanding
4. Geographic coverage	Over 80% U.S. May be unbalanced	Unique, but may not be suited to needs	U.S. coverage was needed and achieved	Excellent: All geographic markets
5. Continuity over time	Poor	Poor	Excellent	Excellent: Strong and increasing
6. Special considerations	Strong market growth	Changing industry	Excellent	Excellent
OVERALL	**Vulnerable over time**	**Vulnerable over time**	**Perfectly suited for market dominance**	**One of the best**

Chapter 2

How to Create an Excellent Patent Portfolio?

Introduction to Chapter 2

In Chapter 2, key concepts related to creating patent portfolios are presented and discussed, including three alternative ways that companies look for patentable ideas. Also presented is the concept of "Technology Inflection Points" for generating inventive concepts as a basis for an excellent patent portfolio. Next, two classic questions are reviewed, "Build versus Buy" to fill needs in a patent portfolio, and whether to emphasize "Quality or Quantity" in the building of the portfolio. Finally, a process is described by which a company may set up an internal patenting program for identifying patentable inventions, selecting certain inventions to be patented, and managing the patenting activity within the company.

1. Key Concepts for Creating a Patent Portfolio

A patent portfolio is not born fully formed. Rather, it develops gradually over time. How do companies manage the development of a portfolio? In the most general sense, every portfolio is managed in the same way, with three generic steps.

(1) Corporate strategy => (2) Patent strategy => (3) Implementation of patent strategy.

In every case, some kind of direction is set for the company, either a formal "corporate strategy", or perhaps a general intent of what the company is doing and where it wants to go. Whether there is a formal document called "Corporate Strategy", and whether the process is entirely formal or informal, this step occurs within every company in some way.

On the basis of the corporate strategy, the patent strategy is then set. Again, the strategy for the patents may be the result of a formal process, discussed below, or may be completely ad hoc and informal. To say, "We don't want to bother with patents right now", is also a patent strategy. The only criterion for judging the patent strategy is whether the acts of implementation and the resulting patents fit what the company wants to do.

Assume, however, that the patent strategy is not, "We don't want to be involved in patents", and rather that the company wants to engage in some kind of patenting in pursuit of corporate goals. In real life, what do companies do? They basically use one of three approaches, which I will call "Models". These three Models are presented in the table below.

Table 2-1: Three Models of Patenting Activity in a Company

	Description	Kinds of Patent	Who?	Build or Buy?	Novelty
Model I Gathering	Patent whatever comes up.	Serendipi-tous patents.	Often individual inventors and non-technical companies.	Build only. Buy not relevant.	Most tradi-tional method
Model II Matching	Patents support R&D for products and processes.	Portfolio shaping = a few lead patents and many supporting patents.	Mainly corpora-tions, both technical & non-technical.	Mainly build, buy to supple-ment.	Well estab-lished in 20th century
Model III Cultivating	Patents lead the business.	Search for break-through patents.	High-tech startups, technical visionaries, licensing-driven companies (Apple, Google, Qualcomm).	Both build and buy. The mix varies greatly by the type of company.	Much newer — late 20th century and 21st century

I call Model I "Gathering", because its essence is to pick up the patent ideas that happen to be lying about the company. Of course there is a selection, so that not every idea is patented, but the emphasis is on finding individual inventors who happen to have patentable ideas. There is no serious possibility of buying patents, because no one at the company is looking for them. Model I is entirely legitimate and is suitable for many companies, such as those in non-technical fields, or those that are covered by the patents of another entity (either by ownership or by an indemnity agreement), or those that are gradually exiting a business and do not wish to make major efforts in patenting. Model I is not suitable for technology-oriented companies in their initial or early maturity stages. Model I is the most traditional of the three methods, and has been in existence essentially since the very beginning of patents.[43]

Model II is named "Matching", because the essence is to match patent protection to technologies and products that the company wants to protect. In Model II, the company is attempting to create a typical kind of high-quality portfolio, that is, a portfolio with a few lead patents that are very good, and with many other patents that make incremental improvements and that support the lead patents. There is a conscious decision to shape the portfolio to protect the intellectual knowledge of the company. This Model II may be suitable for any company in an area with moderate to heavy innovation, meaning it may be suitable for the great majority of technological and non-technological companies. The emphasis of activity is still likely to be on developing inventions inside the company, but the company may also identify holes in the portfolio and try to fill them by purchasing patents. In every case, patenting follows research — protection of developed technology and products is the essence of Model II. In my experience, Model II is the model most typically used by companies to protect innovation. Model II has been a dominant mode for corporations from at least the 20th century, although

---

[43] Patents might be considered to have started with the Venetian Statute of 1474, or in the UK with the 1624 Statute of Monopolies, or in the U.S. in the late 18th century with the United States Constitution in 1787 and the Patent Act of 1790.

patent pools, which are a form of Model II, date back to at least the mid-19th century.

Model III is called "Cultivating". Here there is a deliberate decision to create and patent breakthrough innovations. Contrary to public perception, actually very few companies engage in this kind of activity. By their nature, technical startups try to do this — they are often looking for the "wow factor" that will allow them to create a new market. Certainly the earliest patents of Check Point Software are an example of a startup company that in its early years was pioneering a concept, and that patented breakthrough innovation. There are also a few established companies, typically those that are strongly oriented toward generating license fees, who try to find and patent this kind of innovation. Qualcomm jumps to mind immediately as the holder of the strongest patent portfolio in the communications business.[44]

---

[44] Qualcomm is certainly a strong candidate for this honor. The magazine of the Institute of Electrical and Electronics Engineers, called the *IEEE Spectrum*, each year ranks the strengths of patent portfolios for various segments of the information & communication technologies business. The magazine rates the patent portfolios of 20 companies in each of 17 segments. In its most recent rating, for 2013, the *IEEE Spectrum* ranked Qualcomm's patent portfolio #1 in the segment "Communication/Internet Equipment", but #6 overall, according to the following company ratings in their respective industry segments:

1. Google: #1 in the segment "Communication/Internet Services", score of 8,890.39.
2. Apple: #1 in the segment "Electronics", score of 7,893.51.
3. DigitalOptics: #1 in the segment "Semiconductor Manufacturing", score of 4,993.34.
4. IBM: #1 in the segment "Computer Systems", score of 3,974.49.
5. Microsoft: #1 in the segment "Computer Software", score of 3,909.67.
6. Qualcomm: #1 in the segment "Communication/Internet Equipment", score of 3,766.31.

For all of the ratings in 2013, see *http://spectrum.ieee.org/static/interactive-patent-power-2013* (last viewed on November 15, 2014). The *IEEE Spectrum*

In Model III, "Cultivating", patents play a very important
role in the business. Here, patenting activity either precedes
R&D and is the basis of the business, or is coterminous with
R&D and acts as an essential part of the business. For this
reason alone, that is, the relatively high importance of patents
in Model III, many companies favor the filing and prosecution of their own applications rather than the purchasing of
patents created by other parties. That is not a fixed rule, however. In some cases, critical patents are purchased in order to
fill holes in a portfolio. The objective may be aggressive, that
is, to secure revenue and market share, or defensive, that is, to
deter lawsuits by others. Model III is relatively new. Although
it certainly existed in the mid-20th century, it has become
much more prevalent in the late 20th and now 21st centuries.
It is the preferred mode for patent assertion entities without
significant products,[45] for some mixed companies with both

---

constructs these ratings with five factors, which are explained at *http://
spectrum.ieee.org/at-work/innovation/patent-power-2013/constructing-the-
patent-power-scorecard* (last viewed on November 15, 2014).

[45] Patent assertion entities, or "PAEs", are sometimes called by the pejorative term "patent trolls". Such entities acquire patents, very often although
not exclusively by purchase, and then assert them in licensing & litigation
programs against many companies. I do not have a moral position about
PAEs, but I do state that (1) the parameters of patents are determined by
law, (2) assertion activities have occurred and will continue to occur in
accordance with law, (3) changes in law may decrease or increase the extent
of such activity, and (4) whatever changes in law may occur in the future,
it is almost certain that significant assertion activity will always exist in a
modern, innovation-driven economy.

products and patents,[46] for aggressive patent aggregators,[47] and for defensive patent aggregators.[48]

By "portfolio" under Model II, I mean a few lead patents, and many supporting patents. By "portfolio" under Model III, I mean a few *breakthrough patents*, possibly some other very valuable patents, and many supporting patents. The line between these types of portfolio is not always clear, although the relative emphasis is quite different — Model II emphasizes products whereas Model III emphasizes either patents or patents & products jointly.

How might a "portfolio" look under either Model II or Model III? There was published very recently a study of patents in the renewable energy business, particularly in wind and solar power.[49] Part of that study included a comparison of

---

[46] The chief example of a mixed company using patents to generate a return on R&D efforts is Qualcomm. That is true also of IBM, and of Apple to a lesser degree. Other companies, such as Microsoft, Nokia, Samsung, and others, are mixed product & patent companies that use their portfolios primarily, although not exclusively, to deter litigation by other companies. Qualcomm started, from its inception, with a joint focus on products and patents. The other companies mentioned may have started primarily with a product focus, but have evolved, as least somewhat, to a joint product & patent focus.

[47] The prime example of an aggressive patent aggregator is Intellectual Ventures. Patent pools that are formed to generate revenues are also aggressive aggregators. Such pools often are not considered to be aggregators, but they engage in licensing & litigation programs as the very purpose of their existence. The chief example of a successful pool is the MPEG-2 patent pool, but there are many others, as discussed in my earlier book, *TECHNOLOGY PATENT LICENSING*.

[48] Prime examples of a defensive aggregator are Allied Security Trust and RPX Corporation. Some people consider open source licensing, which requires non-compensated contributions of intellectual property and waiver of rights to sue, to also be a form of defensive aggregation.

[49] The study is "Clean Tech Trends — Intellectual Property & Transactions", by Ron Epperson of Intellectual Energy LLC, and Myron Kassaraba of

patent ownership by leading companies in the wind industry. Here is a summary of some of that comparison.

Table 2-2: Comparison of Patent Portfolios in the Wind Energy Industry[50]

Patent Relevance	GE Num.	GE %	Vestas Num.	Vestas %	Siemens Num.	Siemens %	Mitsubishi Num.	Mitsubishi %	Industry Num.	Industry %
High	22	1.9%	9	1.2%	5	0.8%	4	0.9%	60	0.9%
Medium High	124	10.7%	88	12.0%	66	10.9%	46	10.1%	496	7.3%
Medium	742	63.9%	471	64.2%	420	69.5%	243	53.4%	3,664	54.2%
Low	247	23.6%	166	22.6%	113	18.7%	162	35.6%	2,535	37.5%
TOTAL	1,162	100%	734	100%	604	100%	495	100%	6,755	100%

Pluritas, LLC, published in *les Nouvelles: Journal of the Licensing Executives Society International*, June, 2014, at pp.84–95.

50   Table 2-2 is a modification of "Figure 14: Leading Companies' Portfolios Ranked by Industry Relevance", which appeared in the previously cited article by Epperson and Kassaraba from *les Nouvelles*.

Figure 14 as it appears in the Epperson and Kassaraba article is taken from page 5 of a 2013 report by Totaro & Associates, a Houston-based IP & innovation consulting firm with a particular expertise in the wind energy industry. That report from 2013, entitled "Reduction of Cost of Energy Through Innovation", is summarized at *http://www.totaro-associates.com/#!ip-landscape/c1k7h*, and is posted in full at *http://media.wix.com/ugd/ba1f58_3e4296160be0621aae30878bdc11c066.pdf*.

An update to the 2013 report, entitled "Global Wind Innovation Trends Report: Q3, 2014", includes results for 2013 and 2014, and may be viewed in part at *http://media.wix.com/ugd/ba1f58_53696aacea22418b8621e386f9963c03.pdf*. The entire report may be purchased at *http://www.totaro-associates.com/#!landscape/c1qms*.

The Totaro & Associates web site, *www.totaro-associates.com*, presents an interesting example of a company that has chosen to specialize in the intellectual property of a specific industry. All of the pages of that web site that are noted above, were last viewed by me on November 15, 2014.

Table 2-2 is a comparison of the worldwide patent port-folios of the four largest patent holders and of the industry as a whole, including patent items from the beginning of the wind industry, in 1990, through 2012 (including both issued patents and pending applications, aggregated and reported by numbers of patent families).

The other relevant piece of information is the definitions of the various categories. "High" relevance to the industry means, "Critical filings which have been asserted, licensed or enforced, or are otherwise highly likely to be in the future due to claim breadths". "Medium High" means, "Important filings that the industry needs to be cognizant of, but these can likely be avoided/mitigated". "Medium" means, "May have been relevant in the past or simply not broadly applicable. Multiple methods of design around exist". "Low" means, "Patent/Application is not relevant to the pervasive set of technologies and products in the industry".

The exact parameters of these definitions are not vital. Rather, we need to understand that the great value lies in the "High" items, perhaps with some support in "Medium High" and "Medium", whereas "Low" patents do not contribute significantly to the portfolio's value.[51]

---

[51] The authors of the 2013 Totaro report, "Reduction of Cost of Energy Through Innovation", had a different interpretation of the four categories. They said, at p.4,

> "The industry relevance results indicate that only about ~1% of issued patents are a high impact on the industry as a whole, with another ~7% which may become relevant in the future. The remaining ~92% of filings are merely providing companies with basic defensive IP protection".

It is important to understand the authors' view, but ultimately the interpretation is subjective. For example, it is very difficult for me to see how the "Low" patents could contribute to "basic defensive IP protection", when such patents have been defined as "not relevant...to the industry". Perhaps Low

The percentages presented in Table 2-2 are more or less what we may expect to find in any industry, including technology-oriented businesses.

(1) A very few patents, called "High" in Table 2-2, create most of the value. These typically represent only 1–2% of all the patents in the portfolio. Patents called "High" value in Table 2-2 may be sub-divided into various categories, such as "breakthrough patents", "seminal patents", and "very valuable" patents.[52] In Table 2-2, the volume of these patents among the leaders ranges from 0.8% of Siemens wind energy patents to 1.9% of GE wind energy patents, with a total industry average of 0.9%.

(2) A much larger percentage, called "Medium High" in Table 2-2, create most of the remaining value. These typically represent about 10% of all the patents in the portfolio. In

---

patents contribute in the sense that an owner can point to a specific number of patents, but these patents are so weak as to be almost without value. On the other end, I doubt that "Medium High" patents, which are defined as "important filings that the industry needs to be cognizant of...[although they] can likely be avoided/mitigated", contribute merely to "basic defensive IP protection". Patents that must be designed around are patents that have value, in my opinion. In any case, I agree with the authors that only 1% of the patents, the "High" items, contribute much of the value in the portfolio.

[52] Specific definitions of "Breakthrough Patent", "Seminal Patent", "Very Valuable Patent", "Valuable Patent", and "Supporting Patent", appear in the Glossary under the general category, "Types of Patents by Contribution to Value". In general, "breakthrough patents" cover unique and vitally important inventions, "seminal patents" are high-value patents that meet certain criteria (early filing date, many forward non-self citations, technical problem, and scope of patent), ""very valuable patents" have a high-score on a VSD evaluation but do not fall into either of the two prior categories, "valuable patents" have or will soon have some infringement but do not fit into the prior categories, and "supporting patents" have little value in themselves but either cover minor improvements or contribute solely to the bulk of the portfolio.

Table 2-2, the volume of these patents among industry leaders ranges from 10.1% of Mitsubishi wind patents to 12.0% of Vestas wind patents, with an industry average of 7.3%. The dramatic difference between the numbers for leading companies and the average for the entire industry suggests that non-leaders have many fewer "valuable" patents as a percentage of the portfolio, which of course implies mathematically that much of the portfolios of non-leaders are lower-value "Medium" and "Low" patents.

(3) The bulk of the patents in a typical portfolio, close to 90%, may be supporting patents either in that they cover relatively minor improvements, or they contribute solely as part of the bulk of the portfolio. In Table 2-2, these are called "Medium High" and "Low" patents, and they range among the leaders from 86.8% of Vestas wind energy patents to 89.0% of Mitsubishi wind patents, with an industry average of 91.8%.

This is what we mean when we say an "excellent patent portfolio". A very small number of the patents, say 1% — 2%, are outstanding, a larger number, about 8% — 12%, also create value, and the very large number, about 90%, are supporting either in the sense of representing minor improvements or in adding to the bulk of the portfolio. These kinds of numbers are not surprising or unusual. Therefore, when we speak of an "excellent portfolio", we understand that the great bulk of value (and hence of the revenue-generating ability of the portfolio) is provided primarily by about 10%-12% of the patents, while the rest of the patents contribute primarily to quantity.[53]

---

[53] The study of the wind energy business by Ron Epperson and Myron Kassaraba, cited in footnote 49, and in particular Table 2-2 based on the work of Totaro & Associates cited in footnote 50, is the clearest breakout of patent portfolios I have seen. This of course is not the only evidence

2. Cultivating Patents Through Technology Inflection Points

a. Introduction

Let's be clear about the differences among R&D, science, technology, patents, and business innovation. R&D is generally categorized as either "fundamental", meaning that it contributes to science without directly leading to results, or "applied", meaning that it contributes to technology, which in turn is used to create new goods and services. By law, concepts of science are not patentable, and so the results of fundamental R&D cannot be patented.[54] Patents relate only

---

supporting the common understanding that very few excellent patents create most of the value of a portfolio. In the $1.056 Billion purchase by Microsoft of the AOL portfolio in 2012, one article pointed out 12 particularly interesting patents out of a portfolio of 800, that is, about 1.5% of the portfolio. Jay Green and Stephen Shankland, "Why Microsoft spent $1 billion on AOL's patents", April 9, 2012, available at *http://www.cnet.com/news/why-microsoft-spent-1-billion-on-aols-patents/(last* viewed on November 15, 2014.). Similarly, in 2011, a consortium comprised of Apple, EMC, Ericsson Microsoft, Research in Motion, and Sony, purchased the Nortel portfolio of 6,000 patents for $4.5 Billion. The price was therefore $750,000 per patent on average, but this number is almost useless since in reality a small number of patents create most of the value. "There are likely about 60 patents in the portfolio that are the 'real diamonds', according to Joff Wild of IAM Magazine", quoted in, "The Nortel Six — $4.5 Billion Peace of Mind?", by Jim Hallenbeck, July 18, 2011, available at *http://www.patents4software.com/2011/07/the-nortel-six-%E2%80%93-4-5-billion-peace-of-mind/* (last viewed on November 15, 2014). Sixty (60) "high-value patents" out of 6,000 comes to, not surprisingly, 1% of the portfolio. No one can say for certain that 1% is the exact percentage of high-value patents, and of course the actual percentage will vary somewhat from portfolio to portfolio, but there seems to be an industry consensus that a very small number of patents drives most of the value in the typical portfolio.

54 35 United States Code sec. 101 states that only "new and useful" concepts may be patented. Since fundamental R&D is, by its definition, not immediately "useful", it cannot be patented. All this in theory. The reality is

to applied R&D. The applied R&D may be directed at creating a new industry — some people call this R&D "disruptive". Alternatively, the applied R&D may be directed at creating a specific product or improving an existing product. These relationships may be summarized in a table.

Table 2-3: Research, Science, Technology, Products, and Patents

Type of Research	Result	Is it Patentable?	If so, What Kind of Patent?
Fundamental R&D	Science	NO	— — — — —
Applied R&D — Disruptive	Technology	YES	High-value*
Applied R&D — Gradual	Products	YES	Improvement**

[*: "High-value" means the combination of "breakthrough", "seminal", and "very valuable" patents.]
[**: Patents for minor improvements to specific products will be, in many cases, "supporting patents" rather than "high-value". It is possible, however, that a patent will cover a major improvement to an important product, in which the case the patent may be a "valuable patent" or, in a small number of cases, a "very valuable patent".]

Only a very small percentage of applied R&D is disruptive, just as a very small percentage of patents, certainly no more than 2% (and probably less), could be called "breakthrough" or "seminal" or even "very valuable". The rest of this section of Chapter 2, Technology Inflection Points, explains one method by which disruptive technology and high-value patents may be identified and developed.

---

always messy, however, and the line between patentable "applied R&D" and non-patentable "fundamental R&D" is not always clear.

b. Basing a Portfolio on Breakthrough Patents

What does it take to create a "good portfolio", meaning a portfolio that is based on (1) a few breakthrough or other "lead" patents (that is, seminal or very valuable patents); (2) some "valuable patents"; and (3) very many supporting patents?

(1) A "good concept". This is an idea, or inventive concept, that can create a new industry or that is truly disruptive in a current industry.
(2) "High-value patents", which include breakthrough patents, seminal patents, and other very valuable patents that do not meet the criteria of the first two categories. All high-value patents both embody the good concept, and are in themselves "good" or "high-quality" patents.
(3) Valuable patents that do not meet the criteria of high-value patents, but that are probably infringed now and that add significant value to the overall value of the portfolio.
(4) Supporting patents that cover a relatively minor or less important feature of the technology, or patents that might be easily designed around by potential infringers to avoid liability. By themselves, these patents are almost without any value. As part of a portfolio, their main value is to provide bulk in cases in which parties compare the relative sizes of portfolios to estimate the relative values of the portfolios.

This point is vital to understand. An opportunity for breakthrough or other high-value patents exists only if the

*underlying Point of Novelty is disruptive. However, the
opportunity for breakthrough patents and other high-value
patents is realized only if these patents are themselves "high-
quality" patents.*

The remainder of this discussion will focus on "the good
concept", which is the basis for both high-value patents and
good portfolios.

c. "Good concepts" are the basis of patent value

AT&T's Bell Labs was probably the most productive and
innovative R&D center in the history of humankind, producing 14 Nobel Prize winners and fundamental breakthroughs
in semiconductors, lasers, computer programming, and many
other innovations. What was the secret to this success? How
did Bell Labs discover the transistor or the C programming
language? In fact, the researchers were *not* looking for technical breakthroughs, or fundamental change of any kind. They
were looking instead for "good problems", which they defined
by "discovering the weak points [of a system] that could be
improved upon".[55] The "good problems" led to "good concepts", which became technical breakthroughs and the foun-
dations of new businesses.

Is the AT&T Bell Labs model relevant today? How can
people today find "good concepts"? A recent article suggests
at least one approach. Entitled, "IBM Reveals Its Top Five
Innovation Predictions for the Next Five Years", this article
lists "five big innovations that will change our lives in the next

---

[55] Jon Gertner, *The Idea Factory: Bell Labs and the Great Age of American
Innovation* (Penguin Press, New York, 2012), pp.15, 33.

five years".[56] Although the specific innovations are interesting in themselves, perhaps more important is what this article says about innovation and patents:

- First, innovations that are "good concepts" for cultivating patents occur within the short to medium term, here up to 5 years. Predictions beyond 5 years are extremely difficult, and require a large degree of luck.
- Second, a good concept starts with an important innovation, or perhaps what may be called a "wave" or a "market movement". The good concept is not created by the patent cultivators, but rather the patent cultivators will ride this market movement.
- Third, the innovation creates its own technical problems which must be solved in order to realize the benefits of the innovation. Patents that address and solve these problems are the kind of "good patents" required by Models II and III.

What are examples of "good problems"? The answer involves a concept I call "Technology Inflection Points".

56 The article, by Dean Takahasi, is available at *http://venturebeat.com/2013/12/16/ibm-reveals-its-top-five-predictions-for-the-next-five-years/* (last viewed on November 15, 2014). The five big innovations are (1) educational classes customized for each student; (2) improving the local shopping experience with POS service; (3) using DNA to create customized medicine; (4) customized digital guardians based on a person's behavior; and (5) learning cities that keep residents informed of relevant events and that improve urban management.

d. What is a Technology Inflection Point?[57]

A Technology Inflection Point, or "TIP" for short, is a point in an existing technology that is important, perhaps vital, for the advancement of that technology. It is an important criterion, or a factor, in technical development. Some people view a TIP as a "problem to be solved", but that view is useful only if the solution to the "problem" will boost the technology forward.

How is it possible to find a TIP? There are at least two ways to find a Technology Inflection Point:

(1) Find a major weakness or bottleneck in an existing method or system, and ask: Would resolution of this weakness or bottleneck create a major technical advance? If so, that is a Technology Inflection Point. If you have, or if you can cultivate, an innovation that turns this weakness into a TIP, then you might be able to create patent value.

(2) If the technology is undergoing, or is about to undergo, a paradigm shift, then that shift is almost certainly a TIP. One serious difficulty is that this kind of shift is often well-understood and expected long before it occurs, so finding innovative concepts based on the TIP may be hard to do — competitive approaches may already exist.

---

[57] This part of the discussion of Technology Inflection Points is based on my earlier book, *TPV*, at pp.78–81.

e. Examples of TIPs[58]

1. **The engine in motorized vehicles**: The standard internal combustion engine, based on the four phases of fuel intake, compression, combustion, and exhaust, has been extremely valuable to humankind, but unfortunately creates serious problems which are begging for a technical inflection. Such engines are extremely inefficient, wasting about 70% of the energy burned in heat and vibration, and they create pollution on a global scale. A solution that will provide private transportation at a reasonable price, without the massive waste of internal combustion engines or without massive pollution, would almost certainly create a Technology Inflection Point.

2. **Battery power in mobile devices**: The world has gone mobile. It was foreseeable, and foreseen by some, that battery power would become an increasingly important issue in the provision of services to mobile devices. This is probably not the "paradigm shift" suggested by a new type of motor engine, but it is certainly a bottleneck in existing systems, and its removal could create major technical and business opportunities. Massive investments are being made in battery technology, but no one yet knows which path will succeed.

3. **Video on the Internet**: With current technology, sooner or later the explosion of video on the web will cause the Internet to crash. Although a crash appears inevitable, no one believes a crash will happen, even though everyone believes that the demand for video will continue to explode. How can this be? Because technologies will be developed that insure that no crash will happen. Which technologies? Maybe

---

58   This part of the discussion is based on *TPV* at pp.81–86.

storage, maybe compression, maybe data throughput, maybe modulation, maybe encryption, maybe some of these or all of them, and probably others as well. Innovations that solve this problem can create breakthrough patents.

4. **Low-power chips for data servers**: Steve Mollenkopf, the CEO of Qualcomm, stated at the Consumer Electronics Show in Las Vegas on January 6, 2014, that Qualcomm will develop low-power chips for Internet cloud servers.[59] This statement is not a solution, however, but rather the identification of a problem. Internet cloud servers currently consume tremendous amounts of power, and create massive pollution from the power they consume. This problem in Internet servers was foreseeable ten years ago, and any patents addressing this problem might have very great value indeed. The pressing need to reduce power consumption suggests that the cloud server industry has reached a Technology Inflection Point.[60]

5. **3D Printing**: This is an area of innovation that is very new and has enormous potential. The general idea is that concepts are translated almost immediately from design to a

---

[59] "Qualcomm CEO sees opportunity in data center server market", by Noel Randewich, January 6, 2014, at the CES show in Las Vegas, *http://www.reuters.com/article/2014/01/06/us-ces-qualcomm-idUSBREA0510U20140106* (last viewed on November 15, 2014).

[60] Thus from the CEO of Qualcomm, on January 6, 2014. Two days later, on January 8th, there is a report of what appears to be a tremendous breakthrough in the storage of energy, "Cheap battery stores energy for a rainy day," by Mark Peplow, Nature.com, January 8, 2014, available at *http://www.nature.com/news/cheap-battery-stores-energy-for-a-rainy-day-1.14486* (last viewed on November 15, 2014). The new technology, which will apparently allow cheap storage of energy from intermittent sources such as wind or the sun, would seem to have great potential to reduce energy consumption of data server centers. Any existing patents on this technology, or similar technologies, could potentially be very valuable.

product created by the printing of thin layers of material. This idea is basically a marriage of CAD (computer aided design) and CAM (computer aided manufacturing), but with two particular advantages.

- First, much lower cost than traditional manufacturing, in some cases by orders of magnitude.[61]
- Second, the potential for new kinds of manufacturing, such as products that will in essence manufacture themselves.[62]

There are clearly many problems involved before the potential of 3D printing can be realized, but these are exactly the kind of problems that can give rise to outstanding patents followed by, or together with, new businesses based on these patents. This marriage of patents and business is what I have called Model III of patenting.

---

[61] "Man Compares His $42,000 Prosthetic Hand to a $50 3D Printed Cyborg Beast", by Eddie Krassenstein, 3DPrint.com, April 20, 2014, *http://3dprint. com/2438/* (last viewed on November 15, 2014). Although the printed hand is three orders of magnitude less expensive than the traditionally manufactured prosthetic hand, no one would say that these two products are equal. They certainly are not, but they point the way to the future. See also, "3-D printing creates customer knee replacements", by Jean Tarbett Hardiman, The Washington Times, August 23, 2014, *http://www.washingtontimes.com/ news/2014/aug/23/3-d-printing-creates-custom-knee-replacements/?page=all* (last viewed on November 15, 2014), which implies very strongly that knee replacements created by 3D will dominate the market for knee replacements, despite a price that is at the moment "slightly higher" than prior methods of creating knee replacements.

[62] "3D-Printed Robot Self-Assembles When Heated, So the Robot Apocalypse Just Became Inevitable", by Seth Millstein, Bustle.com, May 26, 2014, *www.digitaltrends.com/cool-tech/mit-researchers-developed-3d-robots-self-assemble-heated/* (last viewed on November 15, 2014).

f. Mega Trends as the Basis of TIPs

What about the five trends listed by IBM in its article? The time frame, that is, within five years, is definitely right. The five trends — customized education, improved local buying, customized healthcare, customized digital guardians, and improved cities — are certainly big enough and important enough to be TIPs, although the trends may also be a bit vague to identify "inventive concepts" that might be patentable. IBM says that the common element among all five of these trends is "that everything will learn". That is an interesting characterization, but perhaps more useful would be say, "All of these trends will enable services that are customized for individuals". Where we formerly had to say, "In this specific technology, one size needs to fit all", we can now say, "With the new technology, each person can receive his or her own service, with maximum value to that person".

What technical innovations will allow these inflections to be made in education, health, and urban living? IBM highlights (1) cloud computing; (2) big data analytics; and (3) adaptive learning techniques. Innovations that enable one of these three are candidates to create Technology Inflection Points.

g. Summary of Technology Inflection Points and the Models of Patenting

Creation of an excellent patent portfolio after development of technology or products, called Model II, and creation of an excellent patent portfolio prior to or coterminous with a new business, called Model III, both require (1) good concepts; (2) breakthrough, seminal or other "high-value patents" embodying these good concepts; and (3) a portfolio with the right mix of high-value patents, valuable patents, and supporting patents.

The identification of Technology Inflection Points is one method for generating good concepts. The creation of good patents is not the subject of this book,[63] but is rather the culmination of the process that begins when a company consciously begins to pursue an outstanding patent program to develop an excellent patent portfolio.

3. Two Classic Questions

The development and management of a patent program within a company is the subject of the Section 4 of Chapter 2. However, before we consider patent programs, let's consider here, in Section 3, two issues that come up repeatedly in the planning and management of patent portfolios.

a. Build or Buy

It makes no difference whatever how ownership of a patent item occurred. Nevertheless, some companies have a "Not Invented Here" syndrome, and they will be reluctant to purchase patents built elsewhere. Although one may under-stand and sympathize with the psychological motivation of

---

[63] The creation of good patents is the subject of two of my other books. *TPV* explains the concept of "good patents", and provides examples of such patents. ***LITIGATION-PROOF PATENTS*** discusses the most common mis-takes that prevent patents them from becoming "good patents", and provides examples of such mistakes.

these companies, this reluctance is misplaced. Economically, it makes no difference if a patent has been built or bought. Consider two examples where companies purchased patents to fill holes in their portfolios. Both examples were touched on in Chapter 1.

(i) Example 1 of Buying — Broadcom

Broadcom and Qualcomm were engaged in litigation in the period 2005–2009. Broadcom sued at the International Trade Commission and in Federal court. Although Broadcom owned at that time about 1,000 U.S. patents, it asserted a total of eight patents, of which five were asserted at the ITC and three were asserted in court.[64] There was no overlap at all between the patents in the two lawsuits. Here are the results of these lawsuits:

---

[64] The selection of specific patents from a large portfolio is the norm in litigation. Courts will not allow a plaintiff to assert hundreds of patents — the resulting litigation would be simply unmanageable.

Table 2-4: Patents in the Litigation Broadcom v. Qualcomm
(winning patents in boldface)

Litigation	Dates of Litigation	Patents Sued On	The Winning Patents
ITC 337-TA-543	June, 2005–October 14, 2008	Filed & Prosecuted by Broadcom: US 6,583,675; US 6,359,872 ——————— Application purchased by Broadcom & prosecuted to issuance: Application Number 08/513,658 which became **US 6,714,983** Patents Purchased by Broadcom: US 6,374,311; US 5,682,379 ———————	**US 6,714,983, purchased by Broadcom as an application**, and then prosecuted by Broadcom to issuance as a patent. The other patents dropped out of the case.
District Court for the Central District of California, and the Federal Circuit Court	May, 2005–September 24, 2008	Filed & Prosecuted by Broadcom: US 6,847,686 ——————— Patents Purchased by Broadcom: **US 6,389,010; US 5,657,317**	**US 6,389,010** and **US 5,657,317, purchased by Broadcom**, win. The other patent falls.

Broadcom acquired all three of the winning patent items in a single transaction from one company on December 24, 2002.[65] Of these three patent items, Broadcom acquired

65 In fact, Broadcom paid about $24M to buy from Intermec 150 U.S. and non-U.S. patent items, both patents and applications, related to areas such as IEEE 802.11 networking, power supplies, and digital video recorders. See, for example, "Broadcom Picks a Peck of Patents", by Craig Matsumoto, LightReading, December 26, 2002, available at *http://www.lightreading.com/ethernet-ip/broadcom-picks-a-peck-of-patents/d/d-id/587217* (last viewed on November 15, 2014).

US 6,389,010 and US 5,657,317 as issued patents, whereas Broadcom obtained US 6,714,983 as a pending application 08/513,983 and completed the prosecution to issuance.

This is a clear example of an established company, with hundreds of patents filed and prosecuted by itself, which nevertheless supplemented its portfolio by acquiring issued patents and also a pending application that it prosecuted to completion. The purchased patents were then used for aggressive litigation.

(ii) Example 2 of Buying — Silanis Technology

As a second example of a company that bolstered its portfolio by purchase, in the case of Silanis Technology, discussed in Chapter 1, all items in the patent portfolio were filed and prosecuted solely by Silanis, except US 5,606,609, an outstanding patent that was acquired by Silanis on January 26, 2000. Here is an example of a small and relatively young company, acquiring a patent as part of its earliest efforts to establish a defensive patent portfolio.

(iii) Building by Operating Companies:

The examples given above are all based on "buy", but purchasing patents from outside parties is contrary to the common expectation. Among operating companies (that is, to say, the companies whose chief occupation is supplying goods or services rather than aggregating patents), the chief mode is to build patents internally rather than to buy them, although buying may be used to supplement a portfolio.

In the book *TPV*, the clearly predominant mode by which companies acquired great patents was to file and prosecute them, rather than to buy them.[66] That sample includes out-standing patents, but the sample number is very small.

On June 10, 2014, the Intellectual Property Owners Association (hereinafter "IPO") published its annual list of the top 300 recipients of U.S. patents for the prior year.[67] The vast majority of these companies are operating companies — in fact, of these 300 top recipients of U.S. patents, only two might seem to be involved primarily in the patent business.[68] Here is the list of just the top twenty companies, all of

---

[66] In *TPV*, fifty-five patents are reviewed, of which sixteen patents are analyzed in great detail. Of the patents analyzed in detail, ten, or 62.5%, were built entirely in-house, including patents of AT&T, Check Point Software Technologies, i4i, Philips, Qualcomm, Siemens, TiVo, Trend Micro, Uniloc. Of the patents that were intensively analyzed, six, or 37.5%, were purchased from another entity, including patents purchased by Broadcom, Comcast, Microsoft, Sharp, and Silanis Technology. Each one of the companies that has purchased excellent patents has also engaged actively in filing & prosecuting applications in-house.

[67] The list of 300 recipients is at *http://www.ipo.org/wp-content/uploads/2014/06/2013-Top-300-Patent-Owners_5.9.14.pdf* (last viewed on November 15, 2014). One could review also a competing list by IFI Claims Patent Services, division of Fairview Research, which is extremely similar to the IPO list, albeit with a few differences in both numbers of issued patents per company and in overall rankings. The IFI Claims list is at *http://www.ificlaims.com/index.php?page=misc_top_50_2013&keep_session=1800844745* (last viewed on November 15, 2014).

[68] The two that apparently specialize in the patent business are Invention Science Fund I, LLC, a division of Intellectual Ventures ("IV"), and InterDigital Technology Corp. Based solely on quantity, and without review of quality, both of these companies are relatively minor players in the acquisition of U.S. patents. The Invention Science Fund is rated as #133, with 252 U.S. patents received in 2013, a decline of 15.4% from 2012. InterDigital is rated at #163, with 284 patents received in 2013, a decline of 12.0% from 2012. However, both of these entities, that is, IV and InterDigital, have been very significant players in the patent market — IV in generating licensing revenues, and InterDigital in both generating licensing revenues and selling patents. Most significantly for present purposes, despite its internal patent

which are active operating companies that rely primarily on revenues from products and services, and whose main patent-generating activity is through internal building rather than in purchasing patents from other parties:

Table 2-5: Top 20 Recipients of U.S. Patents in 2013
(according to the IPO Association)

Rank	Company	U.S. Patents Received in 2013	% Growth from 2012 to 2013
1	IBM	6,788	5.1%
2	Samsung Electronics	4,652	(7.8)%
3	Canon	3,918	18.5%
4	Sony	3,316	(8.1)%
5	LG Electronics	3,117	16.2%
6	Microsoft	2,814	4.1%
7	Toshiba	2,679	3.0%
8	Panasonic	2,649	(6.4)%
9	Hitachi	2,399	(11.9)%
10	Google	2,190	90.3%
11	Qualcomm	2,182	48.3%
12	General Electric	2,086	2.3%
13	Siemens	1,828	(8.6)%
14	Fujitsu	1,802	(6.3)%
15	Apple	1,775	56.3%
16	Intel	1,730	34.4%
17	AT&T	1,658	17.9%
18	General Motors	1,621	18.0%
19	Seiko Epson	1,488	2.3%
20	Ricoh	1,469	4.4%

---

efforts, IV's predominant mode of acquisition has been to purchase patents, whereas InterDigital mainly patents its own inventions.

The list in Table 2-5 is based on the recipients of the most U.S. patents issued in 2013. What might happen in the future? We can apply the percentage growth rates from 2012 to 2013, in the last column, to predict future rankings. Taking 2013 as the baseline, and applying the percentage growth rates from 2012 to 2013, the predicted top recipients of U.S. patents in the years 2014 — 2020 appear in Table 2-6:[69]

Table 2-6: Predicted Top Generators of U.S. Patents

(based on a continuation of the 2012–2013 growth rate)

Rank	2013	2014	2015	2016	2017	2018	2019	2020
1	IBM	IBM	Google	Google	Google	Google	Google	Google
2	Samsung	Canon	IBM	IBM	Apple	Apple	Apple	Apple
3	Canon	Samsung	Canon	Qualcomm	Qualcomm	Qualcomm	Qualcomm	Qualcomm
4	Sony	Google	Qualcomm	Apple	IBM	Canon	Canon	Intel
5	LG	LG	Apple	Canon	Canon	IBM	Intel	Micron

Some observations may be made about Tables 2-5 and 2-6:

1. Many of the top companies have not changed in recent years. IBM and Samsung have rated very highly for years. Many of the Japanese and Korean companies

---

[69] I have excluded from this list any ranking for Samsung Display, a company that focuses on "smart" digital signs. Samsung Display had 237 U.S. patents in 2012, and 1,259 U.S. patents in 2013, a growth rate of 431.2% per year. If this rate were to continue, Samsung Display would be #2 in patents in 2014, #1 in 2015 with more patents than the next five largest patent generators combined, almost half of all U.S. patents in 2016, and about 70% of all U.S. patents issued in the year 2017. Clearly this trend cannot continue. There must be a limit to this statistical madness, but I do not know where that limit is, so I state only that this company, Samsung Display, very clearly wants to dominate the market for digital signs, and beyond that I will not include them in this review.

listed in Table 2-5 have also been major generators of U.S. patents in recent years.

2. It is perhaps somewhat surprising that some of the well established U.S. companies, particularly Qualcomm, but also AT&T, General Motors, and Intel, continue to invest significantly in building their patent portfolios. Micron Technology is another well-established company, which has not previously been known for patents, but which is now investing significantly in patents.

3. Companies such as Apple and Google have been perceived as relatively hostile to patents. Not any more.[70] If current trends continue, Google and Apple will be #1 and #2, respectively, as soon as 2017.

4. If current trends continue, by the year 2020, the top-five list will be comprised solely of U.S. companies, the first time that will be true in many years.[71]

---

[70] Apple's interest in patents is obvious from this list, not to speak of its extremely active worldwide litigation against Samsung. Google's transformation from being almost completely indifferent to one of the top players is very striking. See "Google's evolution from IP refusenik to major patent owner continues", *Intellectual Asset Magazine blog,* June 10, 2014, available at *http://www.iam-magazine.com/blog/detail.aspx?g=963240a0-e700-4a99-a676-c34e00f00c79* (last viewed on November 15, 2014), which points out that Google first appeared on the list in 2008, ranked #290, with 58 patents. In 2013, Google is ranked #10, with 2,190 patents, a growth rate of 90.3% from 2012 to 2013, or a CAGR of 107% per year in the period 2008–2013. All this, in addition to Google's purchase in 2011 of 17,000 patents and 7,000 applications from Motorola. Microsoft also, was viewed originally as being relatively indifferent to patents, perhaps even hostile, but that appears no longer to be the case.

[71] "If current trends continue". Table 2-6 is based upon extrapolation of the results from year 2012 to year 2013. I am very aware of the limitations of extrapolation, especially for long-term predictions. The American humorist Mark Twain pointed out that in a period of 176 years, the Mississippi

What does all this mean? I have indicated that companies have a perennial decision whether to build or buy their portfolios. Operating companies overwhelming favor building portfolios from internal inventions, rather than buying external patents. Companies will indeed purchase patents, particularly what they perceive as outstanding individual patents or strong portfolios, but overall, operating companies will probably continue to rely on building, rather than buying, as their main mode of generating patent portfolios.

(iv) Build versus Buy

Although operating companies clearly favor building portfolios rather than buying them, this is not true for other segments. Consider this view of operating companies and patent aggregators.

River had shortened itself 242 miles, or a bit more than 1.33 miles per year. Therefore, extrapolating backward in time, it is clear that in the Silurian Period, about 1 million years ago, the Mississippi River must have stuck out over the Gulf of Mexico like a fishing rod, and extrapolating forward in time, in only 742 years Cairo, Illinois and New Orleans would be conjoined, with a single mayor and unified board of aldermen. Mark Twain, Life on the Mississippi (1883), viewed at *http://www.markwareconsulting.com/miscellaneous/mark-twain-on-the-perils-of-extrapolation/(last* viewed on November 15, 2014). In short, extrapolation has its limitations. Nevertheless, in some cases, and I do believe here, extrapolation points to directions that show general trends, even if there are will be some errors in the particulars. Relatively speaking, companies such as Google, Apple, and Qualcomm, seem to be placing an enormous emphasis on patents and competitive positioning in patenting activity.

Table 2-7: Preferred Modes of Patent Activity by Type of Company

Type of Company	Examples	Preferred Patent Activity
Most operating companies	Fuji Photo Film, General Electric, Google, Microsoft, NEC, Samsung, and many others	Building is the preferred mode, although purchase may be done in special cases.
Mixed operating/patenting, with aggressive licensing efforts	Broadcom, IBM, Qualcomm	Clear preference for building, but Broadcom has bought some top quality patents.
Aggressive aggregators	Acacia Research, Conversant IP Management (formerly called "Mosaid"), Innovatio IP, Intellectual Ventures (also referenced as "IV"), InterDigital, Rembrandt IP Management, Unwired Planet, and WiLAN	Predominantly buy or acquire right to license, although internal building is common as a secondary activity. (InterDigital and Unwired Planet mainly build.)
Defensive aggregators	Allied Security Trust (also referenced as "AST"), License on Transfer Network (also referenced as "LOT Network"), Open Invention Network (also referenced as "OIN"), RPX, and Unified Patents	Overwhelmingly buy rather than build.

Several observations may be made about the patent activities of various types of companies:

1. The preferred activity of most operating companies, as discussed above, is to build rather than buy.
2. Mixed companies with aggressive licensing efforts are active in operations, but also derive a significant portion of their profits from patents. For example,

Qualcomm's products and services generate about two-thirds of its revenues but only about one-third of its profits, whereas its licensing activities generate about one-third of total revenues and about two-thirds of profit.

3. Aggressive aggregators are willing to build portfolios, but their main mode is to buy the patents of outside parties. Intellectual Ventures had to bulk up its portfolio quickly, and in the early years from its founding in 2000, IV was almost totally dominated by buying. Today IV engages in both activities, although to the best of my knowledge its main mode is still buying. Acacia typically does not buy, but does not build either — rather, it acquires rights to sue from patent owners, and splits the proceeds. Innovatio IP engages mainly in buying, although it may also engage in contingency litigation, which is the Acacia approach. InterDigital is unique in this category — mainly it develops its own ideas and builds its own portfolios.

4. Defensive aggregators are overwhelmingly buyers rather than builders.

(v) The Processes of Building and Buying

There are significant similarities between creating a portfolio through building and creating it through buying. There are of course differences, but the processes are much more similar than might first appear.

Table 2-8: The Processes of Building and Buying Patents

Step	Building Portfolios	Buying Portfolios	Differences in the Process
1	Plan the Corporate Strategy.	Plan the Corporate Strategy.	Very little or none.
2	Plan the Patent Strategy.	Plan the Patent Strategy.	Very little or none.
3	Determine specific technologies and products to be protected.	Identify holes in the portfolio.	Again, very little. In both cases, the company must determine what it wants but doesn't yet have.
4	Identify relevant inventive concepts within the company.	Identify patents and applications available for purchase, possibly through brokers or other middlemen.	Internal versus external focus.
5	File applications and prosecute them to issuance.	Purchase and maintain patents; possibly purchase applications and prosecute them to issuance.	Dramatically different. Building costs some money, but is very intensive in terms of engineering & management time. Purchasing generally requires much less commitment of time, but generally at a much higher financial cost.

The two great advantages to building portfolios in-house are that the financial price is typically much lower than purchasing high-quality patents, and the degree of flexibility is much greater since the builder can write and prosecute its own patents.

The two great advantages of buying is that it is much faster than internal patent building, and it has superior control of the outcome in that the buyer knows what is being purchased (since both the patent and its prosecution history are known). To the extent that a buyer buys pending applications rather than issued patents, the degree of controlling the outcome will fall (since the future prosecution events cannot be known), but so will the price per patent item.

Let's summarize these observations visually.

Table 2-9: Advantages and Disadvantages of Building and Buying Patents

Factor	Building	Buying
Cost	+ Usually much less	– Usually much more
Flexibility	+ Ability to write the patent	– The patent is given
Certainty of a patent	– Can never know what will be allowed	+ An issued patent is a known product
Speed	– Typical 3 to 5 years per patent	+ Immediately upon acquisition

(vi) Conclusion About Building or Buying

Generally, operating companies tend to prefer building rather than buying, and aggregators of all kinds (with a few exceptions) tend to prefer buying rather than building. In all segments, there is a willingness to either build or buy as the occasion demands, although some specific companies have a very strong preference for one or the other. In short, most companies today, whether operating or patent oriented, and whether aggressive or defensive, recognize the need to develop their portfolios with whatever tools are available, and are willing, in specific cases, to either build or buy. The processes of building and buying are extremely similar on the front end (i.e., the development of strategies), but tend to be quite different at the back end where an internal application must be prosecuted to issuance as part of the building process, or a patent must be identified and acquired as part of the buying process.

b. Quality or Quantity

In addition to build or buy, the other decision very frequently confronted by companies is whether to focus initial patenting efforts on acquiring a relatively small number of high-quality patents, or rather on acquiring a significantly larger number of middle-quality patents. In other words, quality or quantity?

First, let's assume that the company's objective in the long-run is to create a balance in its patent portfolio between quality and quantity. The contrary assumption is simply insensible. That is, to have a portfolio with only a very few high-quality patents is not viable in the long-run. Patents expire, they are subject to attack at the PTO and in the ITC and in the courts, their claims are frequently limited or invalidated, and even some of the best claims may be designed around by competitors to avoid infringement. To rely entirely on a few high-quality patents is not sensible. Similarly, a large portfolio without any quality is like an elephant in a city apartment. What are you going to do with it? How will you pay for its maintenance? There may be legitimate reasons to have such a portfolio, but only in the short-run.[72] In the end, the only good portfolio will have a mix of quality and quantity.

---

72 I understand full well that there are entities, both companies and individuals, that acquire low-quality and low-value patents, threaten legal action, and then offer to drop the threat if the alleged infringer will pay a licensing

There are three strategies that may be employed over time.

Strategy 1: Obtain high-quality patents first, then bulk up on supporting quantity.

Strategy 2: Obtain a large quantity of patents, possibly through building but more likely through a mass purchase, then build or buy a small number of high-quality patents to complement the quantity.

Strategy 3: Develop together quality and quantity, if that is possible.

In fact, each of these three strategies is employed by various companies.

(i) Strategy 1 — Quality Before Quantity

Small companies in particular focus on quality over quantity in their patent efforts, and this for two reasons. First, small companies exist because they believe that have found some innovation of great value to the market. This could be a technology innovation, a new usage or application of known technology, or a unique method not previously known. There must be some kind of innovation, because innovation is the raison d'être of the small company. This innovation is the heart of the company, and it must be protected by the highest quality patent that can be achieved (or by a small number of high-quality patents).

Second, small companies are generally resource-hungry, often in money and almost always in the time of senior

---

fee significantly less than the cost of defending against a lawsuit. This form of legalized extortion happens in many areas of law and business, but it is not the subject of this book. I speak here only of serious companies who wish to build an excellent patent portfolio.

managers and engineers. If a patent program is launched, only a few patents may be affordable, but they should be the best ones the company can achieve. Startups and other small companies often stick multiple inventions into a single "jumbo application", then prosecute each invention separately in a continuation application. The likely results are: (1) the single early priority date is preserved for the entire portfolio; (2) massive filing costs for multiple inventions are delayed, and may arise only years down the road when divisional or continuation applications are filed; and (3) the overall cost may be reduced — prosecution costs are probably not reduced, nor are filing costs (which will eventually be the same for the same number of filings), but preparation costs of a single jumbo application are likely to be less than preparing three, four, or even more individual applications, one for each invention. To be sure, a jumbo application will certainly cost more than a single ordinary Non-Provisional Application, but probably much less than filing multiple NPAs for multiple inventions.

The desire to focus on quality rather than quantity was almost surely the motivation of Check Point Software Technologies, discussed in Chapter 1, which filed and prosecuted two outstanding patents on firewalls in the mid-1990's. It may have been the case with Silanis Technology, also discussed in Chapter 1, which bought an excellent patent in the year 2000. This seems to be a pattern with small companies. According to one study,[73] the patents of "small firms" (defined

---

[73] The study is "Small Serial Innovators: The Small Firm Contribution to Technical Change", by CHI Research, Inc. of Haddon Heights, New Jersey, prepared for the U.S. Small Business Administration, Office of Advocacy, released February 27, 2003, available at *http://archive.sba.gov/advo/research/rs225tot.pdf* (last viewed on November 15). The study by CHI Research was later published in an article, "Highly innovative small firms in the markets

as 500 or fewer employees) are heavily cited by later patents.[74] Even after all patents have been normalized for age and technical area, the patents of small companies are much more heavily cited than the patents of large companies.[75] According to this study, higher rates of citations "represent economically and technically important inventions".[76]

This study is not surprising, and simply confirms what

-----

for technology", by Diana Hicks and Deepak Hegde, Georgia Tech Research Corporation, 2005, available at *https://smartech.gatech.edu/bitstream/handle/1853/24060/wp4.pdf* (last viewed on November 15, 2014). This study is frequently referenced, including in very recent articles. See, for example, "Why 'Patent Reform' Harms Innovative Small Businesses", by Robert N. Schmidt, Heidi Jacobus, and Jere W. Glover, IPWatchdog®, April 25, 2014, available at *http://www.ipwatchdog.com/2014/04/25/why-patent-reform-harms-innovative-small-businesses/id=49260/* (last viewed on November 15, 2014), at notes [i] and [iii], and "Killing The Golden Goose: The Dangers Of Strengthening Domestic Trade Secret Rights In Response To Cyber-Misappropriation", by Zoe Argento, *16 Yale Law Journal* 172 (2014), at p.175, note 7. (All articles last reviewed on November 15, 2014.)

[74] Citations received by earlier patents from more recent patents are called "forward citations" for the earlier patents, since the citations are forward in time. See the category, "Citation of One Patent by Another Patent", in the Glossary.

[75] This conclusion appears throughout the CHI Research study. For example, small firms are said to have created 6% of the sample of U.S. patents studied in the period 1996–2000, but 14% of "the most heavily cited patents" (that is, the 1% of patents with the most forward citations). That is, small firm patents are 14%/6% = 2.3 times more likely to be in the most heavily cited group than the patents of large firms. According to the study, even after patents have been "normalized" to account for age and technical area, the patents of small firms patents still receive about 30% more forward citations than the patents of large firms.

[76] The use of forward citation analysis to identify high-quality patents is discussed at great length in *TPV*. In general, I think that what are called "forward non-self citations", meaning forward citations by another party, are indeed an indication of technical or economic importance, but "forward self citations" (that is, a company citing its own patents) are not such an indication. See *TPV* at pages 66–70 and 307–319.

may be surmised by both logic and experience. Small and innovative companies, both by the nature of what they do and by their resources limitations, frequently focus their early patenting efforts on quality rather than quantity. Although most such companies fail, if a small company beats the odds and succeeds, that company may then supplement its patent quality with greatly enhanced patent quantity, possibly relying on a jumbo application for an early priority date.

(ii) Strategy 2 — Quantity Before Quality

Large companies clearly dominate the world of large portfolios. Of the entities receiving the most U.S. patents in 2013, the top 100 are almost all major corporations (with the exception of one research institute, one university, and the U.S. Navy).[77] Also, the U.S. patent office, in its 2013 Annual Report, finds that about 21.07% of patents issued in 2012 were issued to what are defined in the patent regulations as "small entities". This means that 78.93% of patents were issued to large entities.[78]

Is there some reason for this difference between small firms and large firms in the quantity of filings? Is that reason connected to the quality of filings? In the article "Patent Portfolios", previously cited, Parchomovsky and Wagner confirm that "large firms patent more, [whereas] small firms patent more carefully" (at p.53). They also say (at p.55),

"Under the patent portfolio theory, this pattern is both

---

[77] The IPO list of 300 largest recipients of patents in 2013, *ibid.*, at pp.1–2.

[78] US PTO "Performance and Accountability Report for Fiscal Year 2013", Table 11, "Utility Patents Issued to Small Entities (FY 2009 — FY 2013)", p.198, available at *http://www.uspto.gov/about/stratplan/ar/USPTOFY2013PAR.pdf* (last viewed on November 15, 2014).

explainable and expected...For large firms, a major drive...is the need to create substantial portfolios — independent of the expected values of any particular patents... Small firms, however, are likely to be substantially more resource-constrained..."

What is the "patent portfolio theory" that explains this pattern? Or stated otherwise, why do large firms patent extensively, irrespective of the quality of the patents? Parchomovsky and Wagner say that there are two key advantages of portfolios, which they call "scale" (that is, deep coverage of one or a very small number of Points of Novelty) and "diversity" (that is, breadth of the concept, different implementations of the main concept, and/or related Points of Novelty). Further, Parchomovsky and Wagner say that *both* "scale" and "diversity" become greater at the same time as the portfolio size increases, almost without regard to the "expected values" of the individual patents in the portfolio — that is to say, irrespective of the relative quality of the individual patents in the portfolio, even if the quality of patents in the portfolio is low and declining (at pp.42–43).

Is this true? Is it really the case that large firms patent even in the face of low and declining value of additional patents? Is it true that large firms view the advantages of "scale" and "diversity" as primarily or even solely *quantitative*, so that they are not concerned with the *qualitative* aspects of the portfolio? Consider:

- Some patent practitioners in patent management agree that large firms do indeed put an enormous emphasis on quantity and very little on quality;
- Speakers at various forums sometimes say that in

negotiations for mergers of companies, or in the purchases of large patent portfolios, parties often focus on the numbers and geographic locations of the patents and applications, but very little on quality;

- In licensing negotiations, serious consideration is often given to the relative quantities of patents held by the parties, rather than the quality of the patents. In some cases, only the most cursory review of patents is performed, or even no review at all.

On the other hand, some patent colleagues and speakers say that in large-scale transactions, the identification of high-quality patents is critical. This accords with my own experience as a patent evaluator and manager, but I am not sure if this is indeed the predominant view among large companies.

The problem is that evaluating quality requires time, expertise, and money. It is therefore easier and faster, not to mention much cheaper, to rely solely on a patent count rather than reviewing the quality of the portfolio. Until there are clear criteria for judging patent "quality", it is likely that many firms will focus primarily or even solely on quantity, and very little on quality.[79]

---

[79] Two of my earlier books were intended to deal with exactly this question. That is, **TRUE PATENT VALUE** defines the characteristics of excellent patents, and analyzes patents in order to find what is excellent and what is lacking. **LITIGATION-PROOF PATENTS** identifies and explains the most common mistakes in patents, mistakes that prevent the patents from being "high-quality". "High-quality" patents are those which achieve the characteristics of excellent patents, and that avoid the most common mistakes in patents. It is therefore my own opinion that "quality" in patents can be ascertained, that "high-quality" patents can be identified, and that a portfolio can be judged on both a very few "high-quality" patents and a mass of supporting patents. However, my "characteristics of quality in patents" and my "most common mistakes in patents" are neither common knowledge nor

(iii) Strategy 3 — Quality and Quantity Together

The earlier strategies create conflicts. There is tension between an early focus on quality and an early focus on quantity. Some people, including me, believe that quantity must be complemented by quality, but other people, particularly Parchomovsky and Wagner, say that large companies are almost completely consumed by quantity and in reality, whatever such companies say, the theory of patent portfolio means that these companies will continue to focus almost entirely on quantity.

Would it be possible to solve the conflict between quality and quantity? That is to say, would it be possible to develop quality and quantity together? Has anyone achieved such a feat? The answers are yes, this mix has been achieved, and therefore yes, it is possible to develop both quality and quantity together.

Recall the annual portfolio ratings by IEEE Spectrum. There are 17 categories of companies, universities, and research institutions, a total of 336 entities. Of these, the ratings include a total of 160 companies within 8 categories that clearly belong to the general field of information & communication technologies ("ICT"), which is the focus of this book.[80] The strength of Google's patent portfolio is rated #1 among all 160 ICT companies, and also among all 336 entities in the

---

accepted standards, and I am therefore not certain if indeed large companies focus entirely on a clearly-defined "quantity" of patents instead of what the corporations may perceive as a rather vague "quality" of patents.

[80] The 8 categories are clearly part of ICT are (1) Communication & Internet Equipment, (2) Communication & Internet Service, (3) Computer Peripherals and Storage, (4) Computer Software, (5) Computer Systems, (6) Electronics, (7) Semiconductor Equipment Manufacturing, and (8) Semiconductor Manufacturing.

report. The strength of Apple's patent portfolio is rated #2, again among all 160 ICT companies and also among all 336 entities in the report. Perhaps even more important, Google and Apple are not just #1 and #2, respectively, but in addition they are *way above* the rest of the field, rated as 8,890 and 7,984, respectively, in comparison to the third company DigitalOptics at 4,993, followed by a group of companies around 4,000 (IBM, Microsoft, and Qualcomm).

I have not reviewed these portfolios independently, and I neither endorse nor reject IEEE Spectrum's review. I say only that the IEEE is a very reputable organization, that IEEE Spectrum is a very reputable magazine, and that this magazine rates Google and Apple #1 and #2, respectively, in patent portfolio strength, which we will take here as a proxy for quality.

On the quantity side, Google and Apple are clearly not the largest holders of U.S. patents. Of all companies receiving U.S. patents in 2013, Google received the 10th highest number at 2,190, and Apple received the 15th highest number at 1,775. Their annual growth rates for U.S. patents from 2012 to 2013 are 90.3% and 56.3%, respectively. If current growth rates continue, Google will be the largest recipient of U.S. patents by 2015, Apple will be the second largest recipient by 2017, and they will both hold these positions to the end of the decade.

Probably the strongest evidence for the proposition that it is possible to marry quality and quantity is that both Google and Apple ramped up patent quality *at the same time*, that is, during the same period, that they were ramping up patent quantity. Table 2-10 makes this clear. Quality rankings are taken directly from the IEEE Patent Power Scorecard for the relevant year, and quantity measures are taken from the U.S.

PTO patent database by intersecting the name of the patent assignee with the relevant time range.[81]

Table 2-10: The Portfolios of Google and Apple on Quality and Quantity

Company	Measure	2010	2011	2012	2013	01/01/2014– 6/30/2014
Google	QUALITY (Rank among ICT companies)	Not on the list	#15	#3	#1	— —
Google	Quantity (number of US patents at end)	560	987	2,156	4,029	5,173
Google	Quantity (% of entire portfolio at end of period)	10.83%	19.08%	41.67 %	77.88%	100.00%
Google	Quantity (increase in that one period)	372	427	1,169	1,873	1,144
Google	Quantity (% of entire portfolio obtained in that one period)	7.19%	8.25%	22.60%	36.21%	22.11%
Google	QUANTITY (Running accumulation as % of entire portfolio)	7.19%	15.44%	38.04%	74.25%	96.36%

81   For example, by giving to the PTO database the instruction, "AN/Google AND ISD/1/1/1990->12/31/2011", the result will be the total number of U.S. patents issued to Google as assignee between 1990 and 2011, inclusive. Since Google was founded in 1998, this instruction will list all patents issued in Google's name from the beginning of the company's existence through December 31, 2011.

Company	Measure	2010	2011	2012	2013	01/01/2014–6/30/2014
Apple	QUALITY (Rank among ICT companies)	#55	#8	#12	#2	— —
Apple	Quantity (number of US patents at end)	3,578	4,383	5,673	7,757	8,679
Apple	Quantity (% of entire portfolio at end of period)	41.23%	50.51%	65.37%	89.38%	100.00%
Apple	Quantity (increase in that one period)	724	805	1,290	2,084	922
Apple	Quantity (% of entire portfolio in that one period)	8.34%	9.28%	14.86%	24.01%	10.62%
Apple	QUANTITY (Running accumulation as % of entire portfolio)	8.34%	17.62%	32.48%	56.49%	67.05%

Table 2-10 suggests that both Google and Apple have boosted their patenting efforts in the period from the 2010 to mid-2014. During this period, each company received the great majority of all U.S. patents in its portfolio — for Apple, 67.05% of all its U.S. patents were issued in this period, and for Google, a surprising 96.36%. Even though Google has been in existence since 1998, and received its first patent in 2003, over 96% of its U.S. patents have been issued within the past five years.

During this same period, Google was rising in "patent

quality" from being not even on the list of about 160 ICT companies, to being #1 of both the ICT companies and of all other companies in the IEEE Spectrum review. Similarly for Apple, rising in "patent quality" from #55 of ICT companies to #2 of both ICT companies and of all companies. It would seem, therefore, that these companies succeeded in achieving growth in both patent quality and patent quantity during this same period, 2010 to mid-2014.

(iv) Summary of Strategies

All three strategies are viable, and are used by companies. For reasons of cost and business need, smaller and newer companies tend to focus first on quality, and later on quantity. At least some larger companies focus first on quantity rather than quality, but there are a few companies, notably Google and Apple, that manage to develop both quality and quantity over the same period.

How have Google and Apple achieved this balance, whereas others have not? What do they have that other companies might lack?

- Superior management?
- Superior engineers and other technical people?
- Superior focus?
- Superior opportunities for innovation, given their market areas?
- Superior position in the market?

The answer is not clear. We can say only that neither quality nor quantity may be ignored.

To patent many concepts and/or buy many patents without regard to quality is insensible for three reasons. First, the beginning of any company or any new line of business[82] is likely to be the time of the most fundamental innovations. If that is true, then at least some of the patents protecting these fundamental innovations must be high-quality patents. Second, the time to write patent claims with the broadest scope is at the very beginning of the innovation — certainly not later on, after other innovations and other patents have limited the scope of what may be claimed. Third, a portfolio with all quantity and almost no quality is a sham. If the sham is discovered, and the chances are that it will be discovered at some point, the overall value of the portfolio must drop precipitously.[83]

On the other hand, to focus solely on a few high-quality patents is naïve. Large quantities of patents are impressive to many people, and will make an impact in the market. Whether the reason for this impression is increased scale and increased diversity, as Parchomovsky and Wagner say, or rather something else, individual companies and the market do believe in quantity as one measure of a portfolio's worth.

Over time, however a portfolio is assembled, equilibrium

---

[82] That which is true for an entire company is true also for a new line of business within the company. When a company, even a mature company, starts a new business based on innovation, particularly based on technical innovation, the quality of patents is essential for building the business. This is true whether the company employs Model II (products before the patents) or Model III (patents before or at the same time as the products).

[83] There is a common phrase from the world of media and advertising — "Perception is reality". This phrase is used cynically, and I would prefer rather the well-known statement by President Lincoln, "You can fool some of the people all of the time, and all of the people some of the time, but you can't fool all of the people all of the time." Sooner or later, a portfolio with no underlying quality will be seen as what it is, and that will create a problem for the owner of the portfolio.

can be achieved only by a balance of quality and quantity within the portfolio.

4. Portfolio Development Within a Company

a. Introduction

What is required to develop a portfolio within a company? Here the word "develop" does not mean that all the patents must be built on in-house ideas, but rather that the portfolio must be developed either through in-house ideas or by buying the patents of others, or by both. Here the phrase "within a company" does not necessarily mean that the patents must be written by full-time employees — that is one approach, but the company may prefer outside patent professionals (that is, patent attorneys and patent agents), or a mix of both employees and outside patent professionals to write the patents. The question rather is, what kind of commitment, what resources, and what functions, are required to create and implement a portfolio development plan? This section of Chapter 2 is based primarily on my experience over the past 20 years managing patent portfolios for multiple companies large and small.

b. Elements of a Successful Patenting Program Within a Company[84]

(i) Commitment — Strategy and Incentives

The "clear and well-understood commitment" of top

---

[84] My thinking about the elements of a successful patenting program is based primarily on my experience over the past 20 years managing patent portfolios for multiple large and small companies in the communications

management is essential. Indeed, without such commitment, no program should be undertaken — any efforts undertaken without such commitment are likely to be a frustrating waste of time and money.

Strategy

By "clear commitment" I mean that the top management sets a corporate strategy, that part of the corporate strategy includes a patent strategy, and that a budget of resources and people is created to implement the patent strategy. (Budgeting is the subject of Chapter 3, below.) Management is not required to oversee daily activities — some top managements do this, but others do not, and it is probably a function of the nature, size, and age of the company. To be precise, specific ideas need not be reviewed by senior managers, but these managers must give an indication of the technologies and products that should be the subjects of patents at the company.

Incentives

By "well-understood commitment", I mean that every-one in the company understands first that patents are an integral part of the company's mission, and second, that the company recognizes and rewards activities in pursuit of this

---

industry. Also, I rely on the suggestions and advice of Eli Jacobi, one of the reviewers of this book, who has helped create or manage patent programs at Amdocs, Comverse Network Systems, IBM, and Siemens. Finally, I am indebted to H. Ward Classen for a presentation he made on June 24, 2014, entitled, "Creating an Intellectual Property Program: The Initial Steps". This presentation is offered as a Webinair by Innography, Inc., an intellectual property consulting firm and producer of software to analyze patent portfolios. The presentation may be accessed at *https://go.innography.com/ Webinar-Downloads-The-Practitioners-Guide-to-Creating-an-Intellectual-Property-Program.html* (last viewed on November 15, 2014).

mission. There are different ways to make the commitment well-understood.

- Some companies give talks on patents and intellectual property to product groups or to new employees. These talks raise awareness about patents in general, explain the importance of patents to the company specifically, and promise enhanced recognition or compensation for those developing inventions and presenting their inventions to be patented.
- Some companies give various non-financial awards, such as meetings with senior managers, and opportunities for independent research, to those submitting inventions to be patented.
- Some companies include patent participation as part of annual reviews of employee performance, with potentially positive or negative implications for both compensation and promotion within the company.
- Some companies give financial rewards to those who patent inventions at the company. These awards may be tied to specific events, such as (1) submission of a patentable invention for review; (2) acceptance of the invention to be patented; (3) filing of a patent application for the invention; and (4) issuance of the patent. Typically the rewards are in the few hundreds to few thousands of dollars per stage, although a minority of companies base additional compensation on the money eventually generated by the patent.
- Some companies create a kind of competition among product groups to see which groups can submit the most patentable ideas or the most fully formed inventions. In a corporate environment, groups are always

fighting for resources, and this may be another form of competition among the groups.

- In some companies, advancement for some of the technical people is accelerated or decelerated based on the activity of these people in regard to the company's patents.

In whatever way the company chooses to make known its commitment, engineers and technical managers must be judged on their contributions to the patenting program and rewarded for their participation. A patent program will succeed only if (1) specific attention is paid to patent activities, and (2) incentives are provided to those whose contribution is essential to the success of the program.[85]

(ii) Criteria for success

Criteria must be created to measure success. Criteria will include at least quality and quantity of patents and patent applications, over time, by geographic area, and by coverage of key products and technologies. Quantity measures are

---

[85] In the great majority of technology companies, patents are not the main business activity and do not dominate the corporate agenda. For these companies, patent success is contingent upon creation and implementation of a program along the lines suggested here. Conversely, there are some companies for whom patents are so critically important that a separate and special program is not required. That is true, for example, of patent aggregators (both aggressive and defensive aggregators), and patent pool administrators. For such companies, patents are the entire business, and therefore a "special" program is a contradiction in terms, since a patent program at such a company may not be "special". Nevertheless, for all companies the general rule is true — activity that is recognized and rewarded will be received, whereas activity that is ignored by the company will be ignored also by the employees.

relatively clear, and they must be set for specific products and technologies, geography, and time.

Quality measures may include one of two basic approaches. The first basic approach to measuring quality is to have patent experts read and rank applications or patents.[86] This review should include, at a minimum, review of every patent application for the most common mistakes in ICT patents.[87] To insure quality in pending applications, there is no substitute for review by a patent expert — it is an essential and indispensable step.

The second basic approach to measuring quality is to apply some standardized criteria and algorithms to create numeric scores for patents.[88] The resulting scores are sometimes called "patent metrics". A company wishing to rate its patents can either turn to commercial suppliers of rating services[89] or create its own rating system.[90] Automated review is probably

---

[86] In *TPV*, this approach — review by a patent expert — is called "Expert Fundamental Analysis", or "EFA". It is explained in great detail in Chapters 2, 7, and 8, of *TPV*.

[87] The most common mistakes in ICT patents are identified, and explained with examples, in my book, **LITIGATION-PROOF PATENTS**. Once these common mistakes are clearly understood, they can be identified in drafts of patent applications, and deleted or corrected, producing, as the title says, the closest thing attainable to "litigation-proof patents".

[88] This approach — automated scoring — is called "Proxy Fundamental Analysis", "PFA", and is explained in great detail in Chapters 2, 7, and 8 of *TPV*.

[89] A number of companies provide automated rating services for patents. These would include, for example, Innography, IPVision, OceanTomo, PatentRatings International, and Perception Partners. There are also specialized raters, who provide services for particular industries, such as the previously mentioned Totaro & Associates for the wind energy industry.

[90] How would a company construct its own rating system? It is possible to use a system created by others. For example, the algorithm employed by IEEE Spectrum to create its Patent Power Scorecard is published and

essential when many patent items — hundreds or even thousands — must be evaluated within a short period of time. Details of automated reviews are beyond the scope of this book.[91]

(iii) Patent Decision-makers

There must a group of decision-makes to review inventive ideas, and to select the ideas to be patented. This group might be called "the Patent Committee", or "the Patent Review Committee". The group should have at least three kinds of expertise, and perhaps more. There should be a senior technical person, possibly an R&D manager, perhaps the Vice President of engineering, perhaps an outside expert who is hired specifically for this task. There should be an expert in patents. This may be a lawyer, a patent agent, a patent manger,

---

available to everyone. It is possible for a company to select its own criteria, give each criterion a suitable weighting, and create scores on the basis of this system. Fifteen of the most important factors commonly used by companies to evaluate patents are listed and critiqued in *TPV* at Chapter 2, especially pages 66–70, and at Chapter 7, especially pages 307–319.

[91] Numerous criteria could be applied in an automated manner. For example, prior to filing, relevant factors could include length of application, number of claims, number of independent claims, number of backward citations, and others. For example, after filing but before issuance, relevant factors could include length of prosecution, number of office actions, specific objections or rejections by patent examiners, and others. For example, after issuance, relevant factors could include challenges by outside parties, revenue generated, litigations, numbers of forward citations, and others. My earlier book, *TPV*, reviewed 15 of the most important factors, but it is possible to identify 120 factors or even more that might be applied in an automated review. See, for example, "PATENT EVALUATION: Building the tools to extract and unveil intelligence and value from patent data", Renaud Garat of Questel IP Business Intelligence, presentation at LES Moscow, May, 2014, slide #19. Automated review of patent items is a very complicated and interesting topic that would merit its own book, but it is a topic that is beyond the scope of the current book.

or an outside advisor, but again, someone who has expertise in the critical functions of patenting and patent portfolio management. There should be a person from marketing or business development. This expertise is sometimes ignored, but that is a mistake, in my opinion. Patents are a union of technology, law, and business — all three functions should be represented in the group that reviews ideas and selects those to be patented.[92]

This group has three main functions. First, it creates the patenting program. This means it creates the forms required to document ideas, it creates the criteria for review of ideas, and it is involved from the beginning in working with a patent manager or with in-house counsel.

Second, it creates the plan to generate patentable ideas. The plan will include specific goals for numbers of applications to be submitted per time period, and will also include areas of emphasis (possibly specific technologies, or products, or ideas from particular product groups). This plan should include activities for publicizing the patent program within the company. In some cases, the members of this group may themselves help implement this publicity, perhaps through talks to product groups, perhaps through development of a "patent primer" explaining key aspects of the patent program

---

[92] Some companies have representatives from product groups serve in the decision-making group. This is optional, and depends on the company's preference. On the one hand, senior representatives from the main technical groups will likely increase the prestige of the patent function, and may encourage people to file ideas as part of the ongoing business of the company. On the other hand, the time of senior managers is quite limited, and their inclusion in a group of this sort can create political tensions. An alternative, that is, to have lower level representatives in the group, may be a flawed idea — it creates the bureaucracy and tension of a larger group, without the prestige associated with senior technical managers.

at the company. Publicizing is very important to the success of the program. In many companies, especially in companies in which the patent program is just starting, many engineers will not take initiative to submit ideas — the patent activities must be explained, usually multiple times, and the patent manager must be very active in soliciting ideas. The plan may also include reward incentives for submitting ideas, for filing applications, and for obtaining patents. Many companies give financial incentives. Some companies give non-financial incentives, such as opportunities to present inventions, discussion with senior managers, and others.[93]

Third, the group reviews the ideas submitted, and selects those for further work. Further work might include a prior art search, a feasibility study, or a go-ahead to prepare the application. In some cases, the group may interact with the inventors by requesting and receiving additional information as required.

(iv) The Driver

There must be someone who acts as the point person to drive the work. I would call this person an "evangelist for the patent program". The person's formal title might be "VP of Intellectual Property", or Assistant General Counsel" (or

---

[93] How much money should be offered? Some companies give $1,000, of which part may be at idea submission, part at filing, and part at issuance. A sum less than $500 is probably not meaningful. Non-monetary awards may also include attendance at award dinners, lunches with the VP of R&D, publications in the company newsletter, participation in innovation development groups, and in some special cases, opportunities to create business or product lines that are based on patentable inventions. Also, performance reviews and advancement may depend, at least in part, on participation of innovation within the company — this is a large and important topic, but one which is beyond the scope of this book.

perhaps General Counsel in a patent-oriented company), or "Patent Manager". This person might be a patent professional, such as a patent lawyer or patent agent. That is not required, although it is in most cases preferable if a significant amount of the actual patent drafting occurs in the company.

The patent driver has four main tasks. First, to work with the patent decision-makers in all of their activities.

Second, to meet with the heads of projects within the company, to keep abreast of developments in the projects, and to identify areas for potential patenting activity.

Third, to work with the inventors at the company. This is an ongoing and time-consuming task, the essence of the patent manager's job. The patent driver will probably be the one who gives talks on patents to various employee groups within the company. He or she will explain the patent forms to inventors, sit down with them, work through ideas, and explain the patent policy of the company. The patent driver can answer questions about the forms and even help fill them out, but it is the inventors' responsibility to document their inventions.

Fourth, to work with outside counsel, or an in-house attorney if that is the choice of the company, to write and file the applications. The actual drafting of applications is not the main task of the patent driver, although this task may be undertaken if the patent driver is also a patent professional and if this is the intent of the company. If the patent driver does not write the applications, which is the more common model, he or she must still be closely involved in the selection of patent counsel. The decision may be made by either the patent driver or the Patent Committee, but the patent driver must at least be consulted, because the selection of the person or people to draft and prosecute applications is a vitally important part of the program's success.

(v) Problems

Many different problems arise in the execution of the patent program. There are problems with inventors — ideas that are not documented, tensions within an inventor group, disagreements regarding who is an "inventor" for a specific patent, premature disclosure of inventive concepts, etc. There are frequently problems with the group of decision-makers. Recruitment of members to the Patent Committee may be difficult, the members may not devote enough time to the task, they may have particular agendas that do not coincide perfectly with the patenting program, etc. Often the submission of ideas requires the agreement of product group leaders, which may or may not be forthcoming. In short, this is a complicated process, but it will succeed if given appropriate attention, resources, and time.

(vi) Time Frame

Starting from scratch, how long does it take to create a successful patent program? This depends to a large degree on the size and age of the company, the importance of the technology, and the level of resources commited. The commitment of senior management and creation of the patent strategy are part of the corporate planning process, and in reality predate the beginning of the patent program. To create a Patent Committee and find a patent driver may take a few weeks or a few months, depending on the criteria employed and the intensity of the efforts. The efforts to set up the program — criteria for success after a mandate has been received, creation of forms, and creation of publication material — should also require a few weeks. The educational effort is a major variable. In a small company, this can be very quick. In a larger company, this may require weeks to months. If the company is relatively large, relatively mature, and not patent-oriented, then the cultural mindset must be changed, and this may require a sustained effort over several years. The work of collecting ideas, sifting and selecting, then writing and prosecuting patent applications, will continue over several years, and will probably overlap the educational effort.

Based on my personal experience, in a relatively small company, with a substantial R&D effort, the commitment of top management, and the allocation of sufficient resources, significant progress can be made within a period of 6–12 months. In a large company starting from scratch, progress can be made within a year, but full development may require 3–5 years. If the cultural mindset must be changed, a realistic estimate is at least 5 years, perhaps longer.

Conclusion to Chapter 2

Chapter 2 is about the creation of an excellent patent portfolio. Companies typically pursue one of three basic models — patenting ideas as they arise (Model I), developing a portfolio to support R&D or products (Model II), and patenting very actively either prior to or coterminous with R&D efforts in order to create a business based on both the technology and the patents (Model III).

The development of an excellent portfolio requires good inventive concepts, good patents, and appropriate balances of various kinds of patents and various kinds of claims. One source of good concepts is Technology Inflection Points, several examples of which are noted.

Two classic questions arising in almost every portfolio are whether to build patents in-house or buy them, and whether to put the initial emphasis on either high-quality for a small number of patents or lesser quality for a larger number of patents. Some companies have managed to create a balance between quality and quantity, but this is not a trivial task.

Finally, Chapter 2 ended with a discussion of the structure and functions of a patent program within a company. In Chapter 3, we will look at budgeting to develop an excellent portfolio.

Chapter 3

What is the Cost to Create an Excellent Patent Portfolio?

Introduction to Chapter 3

Budgeting to create an excellent patent portfolio requires a company to ask and answer two questions — "How much money should the company invest in patent activities?", and, "What results does the company need to obtain from its patenting activities?" Chapter 3 presents four methods for answering these questions.

By the first method, the company allocates a certain budget to its patent activities, typically based on what the company perceives are the resources available for this activity. In some cases, the budget is determined as a percentage of annual R&D investments or as a percentage of annual revenues. This method, which I call "Top Down", is probably the most common method used for budgeting patent activities.

The second method, which I call "Bottom Up", determines numbers of required patent items (both patents and applications) in particular countries, and then budgets monies required to attain these numbers of patent items. This method is based on the perceived need for patent protection, which is determined, either consciously or unconsciously, by the company's perceptions of its area of technology, the state of the technology, and the nature of the company (that is, relative degree of R&D orientation). The nature of the patent strategy chosen by the company — relatively defensive or relatively aggressive — will have a major impact on this method. The second method is also commonly used.

The third method of budgeting for patents looks first at what the company's main competitors are doing. This method, which I call "Competitive Budgeting", may budget first cost (that is, the amount of money to be invested in patents in comparison to what competitors are doing) or budget first patent items (that is, the number of patents required by the company in comparison to the patent activities of competitors). Analyses of two industries, the firewall industry and the electronic signature industry, are presented in Chapter 3 as illustrations of Competitive Budgeting for patent activity.

The fourth method of budgeting for patents is a combination or any two, or all three, of the foregoing methods. I call this fourth method, "Hybrid Budgeting". In reality, very few companies (if any at all) will apply any of the first three methods in their pure forms. Two of the pure forms — exclusive focus on cost without regard to results or competitive position (pure Top Down), and exclusive focus on results without regard to cost or competitive position (pure Bottom Up) — are possible in theory, but are basically not employed, since even a strong emphasis on cost (Top Down) is likely to include at least some review of possible results, and even a strong emphasis on results (Bottom Up) is almost certain to include some review of cost. Pure Competitive Budgeting is a logical impossibility, since there must be a comparison to competitors' patent costs, or to competitors' patent results, or to both their costs and results. Therefore, Hybrid Budgeting, in one of its various forms, is the method of choice for almost all companies, although specific companies will continue to give relatively more emphasis to cost (Top Down with hybrid aspects), or to results (Bottom Up with hybrid aspects) or to competitive position (Competitive Budgeting with hybrid aspects).

In short, whichever method of budgeting is chosen, in the end the company will almost certainly try to balance costs, results, and possibly competitive position. Achieving balance is an iterative process which is explained in Chapter 3.

Finally, the last section, "Conclusion to Chapter 3", presents a table summarizing the four methods by which a company may budget to create an excellent patent portfolio.

1. Top Down Budgeting: Target Cost

The first method, "Top Down budgeting", is to determine first an amount of resources the company will invest in patents. For a company that is very constrained financially, the budget for patents may be simply what the company feels it can afford. In many cases, however, the company will compare itself to some kind of general benchmark, and allocate that level of resource. Of the first three common methods of budgeting for patents (that is, Top Down, Bottom Up, and Competitive), the Top Down method might be considered the least scientific, but in fact it is a method that is very frequently used, particularly among cost-conscious companies.

Is there any guidance or benchmark for the level of investment by an average technology company? To the best of my knowledge, there is no commonly accepted standard, but there is strong evidence that the economy as a whole invests in patents about 1% of the sum invested in R&D, and therefore 1% of R&D investment is a general benchmark that might be used.[94]

What evidence supports this ratio — 1% of R&D to be invested in patents? No measure will be exactly 1% and nothing else, but four analyses give strong support to this ratio.

a. First Analysis

It is possible to make a direct comparison between total annual R&D investment in the U.S. to total annual costs of U.S. origin patents and patent applications.[95]

Battelle Memorial Institute is a private, non-profit, applied science and technology development company. In recent years, it has published an annual report, entitled, "Global R&D Funding Forecast". Its forecast for 2014 includes historical information for the prior two years. In 2013, total R&D

---

[94] For these purposes, "invests in patents" means the cost of preparing, filing, and prosecuting applications to issuance as patents, plus the cost of maintaining issued patents. This sum does not include the costs of any patent litigation, or damages paid for patent infringement, or royalties paid for licensing patent rights, or sums paid to purchase patents. As orders of magnitude for the entire economy, costs of litigation plus damages might be twice the amount of investments in patents, and patent commerce — licensing or sale of patent rights — may equal the investment in patents. Therefore, it is possible that the investment every year in obtaining and maintaining patents is no more than 25% of the total cost of patent activity in a year. Investment in the patent portfolio is the only patent activity addressed in this book. Neither litigation costs nor the costs of patent commerce are discussed here.

[95] It would make no sense to compare R&D in the United States with patents generated from outside the United States. For that reason, the correct comparison is to patent items *only of U.S. origin.*

spending in the United States was $450 Billion, and in 2012, total U.S. R&D spending was $447 Billion.[96]

What were the total investments in U.S. origin patents? The elements of cost are:

1. Fees for attorneys and professional draftsmen to prepare the application.
2. Filing fees paid to the PTO.
3. Attorney's fees to respond to office actions.
4. Issuance fee for granted patents, paid to the PTO.
5. Maintenance fees payable at years 3.5, 7.5, and 11.5, from issuance.

1. Attorney's fees vary by type and complexity of application, but one account that is, in my opinion, very reasonable, estimates attorney's fees as $9,000 — $15,000 per application, depending very much on the technical area of the patent and the complexity of the invention.[97] I will assume an average cost of $12,000 solely for attorney's fees to prepare the application. Draftsmen fees are estimated at about $80-$100 per page of drawings, for a total of about $400-$500 on average, and I will assume $500.[98] Total professional fees to prepare

96 Battelle's "2014 Global R&D Funding Forecast" is available at *http://www.rdmag.com/sites/rdmag.com/files/gff-2014–5_7%20875×10_0.pdf* (last viewed on November 15, 2014). The specific R&D figures are on page 7.

97 "The Cost of Obtaining a Patent in the US", Gene Quinn, in IPWatchdog® Blog, January 28, 2011, available at *http://www.ipwatchdog.com/2011/01/28/the-cost-of-obtaining-patent/id=14668/* (last viewed on November 15, 2014). 27 types of patents are listed as examples, with a range from $5,000 for the most simple inventions such as a coat hanger, ranging to more than $15,000 for the most complex inventions such as telecommunication networks. For ICT patents, which are the focus of this book, a reasonable range would be, in my opinion, $9,000 — $15,000.

98 "The Cost of Obtaining a Patent in the US", suggesting $400 for

an application, including both attorney's fees and draftsmen's fees, would therefore be about $12,500.

The PTO breaks out applications and patents by U.S. and non-U.S. origin, and statistics exist for the years 1963–2012. In 2012, there were 268,782 U.S. origin patent applications. At an average cost of $12,500, this implies total investment to file these U.S. origin applications of about 268,782 applications × $12,500 per application equals $3.361 Billion, solely for professional fees to prepare U.S.-origin applications filed in 2012.

2. Filing fees have varied over time. Although fees are now $1,600,[99] through 2012 they varied between $1,250 and $1,260. I will assume $1,250 for each of 268,782 U.S. origin applications. This suggests total filing fees paid for U.S. origin applications filed in 2012 of 268,782 applications × $1,250 per application equals $0.336 Billion solely for U.S. filing fees.

3. Attorney's fees to respond to office actions vary greatly by the type and complexity of the office action. For complicated actions, the fees can run $5,000 or even higher, but generally the sum is much less, and I will assume here $2,500

---

applications related to consumer electronic products or to mechanical tools, and $500 for a computer method on the Internet. Given inflation since the time of this note in 2011, I would say $500 is the more reasonable estimate today.

[99] The current filing fees are $1,600 for ordinary companies, but only $800 (that is, 50%) for "small entities", and only $400 (that is, 25%) for "micro entities". By "filing fees", I mean the sum total of all fees that must be paid upon filing an application, which includes "Basic filing fee — Utility", "Utility Search Fee", and "Utility Examination Fee". The U.S. PTO lists its current fees at *http://www.uspto.gov/web/offices/ac/qs/ope/fee010114.htm*. The rules for classification as a "small entity" or a "micro entity" are a bit complex, and beyond the scope of this book, but may be reviewed at *http://www.uspto.gov/web/offices/pac/mpep/mpep-9020-appx-r.html#ar_d1fc9c_19092_1c8*, Rule 1.27 for "small entity" and Rule 1.29 for "micro entity".

per office action.[100] In 2012, there were about 540,000 first office actions to utility applications.[101] These are not broken out by U.S. and non-U.S. origin, but a reasonable assumption is about 51.5% U.S. origin,[102] so assume 278,000 such actions.[103] Total cost is therefore estimated at $0.695 Billion.

4. Although issuance fees are now $960,[104] they ranged between $1,740 and $1,770 in 2012. I will assume an average issuance fee in 2012 of $1,750. According to PTO statistics, there were 121,026 U.S. origin patents granted in 2012.[105] Therefore, total issuance fees for U.S. origin patents in 2012 were $0.212 Billion.

5. To estimate total maintenance fees paid for U.S. origin patents in 2012, note that there were 85,068 such patents issued in 2000, 84,270 in 2004, and 77,502 in 2008. However,

---

[100] This is my personal estimate.

[101] "USPTO Performance and Accountability Report fiscal year 2012", p.26, Figure 11 at the top, available at *http://www.uspto.gov/about/stratplan/ar/USPTOFY2012PAR.pdf*, p.175, Table 1 (last viewed on November 15, 2014).

[102] Over the ten years 2003–2012, about 48.5% of U.S. applications were foreign origin, and 51.5% were U.S. origin. "U.S. Patent Statistics Chart Calendar Years 1963–2013", available at *http://www.uspto.gov/web/offices/ac/ido/oeip/taf/us_stat.htm* (last viewed on November 15, 2014).

[103] A more accurate estimate would include not just first office actions, but all subsequent actions as well. According to the PTO Fiscal Report for 2012, cited above, at p.26, Figure 11 at the top, there are 2.5 office actions before final disposition by issuance or abandonment. I have no statistics or rational method for estimating second and subsequent office actions, but I will say first, in its reports, the PTO places extreme emphasis on first office actions, which suggests that these really are the bulk of the effort and cost, and second, in the confirming analysis below based on total PTO cost, the classification of office actions as "first" or "second" is irrelevant.

[104] Again, these are the fees for ordinary companies. The fees for small entities are reduced by 50%, and the fees for micro entities are reduced by 75%.

[105] "U.S. Patent Statistics Chart Calendar Years 1963–2013".

renewal rates in each of those years were approximately 70%, 93%, and 96%, respectively.[106] At the end of 2012, renewal rates were $1,150 at year 4, $2,900 at year 8, and $4,810 at year 12.[107] The total rates paid in 2012 to renew U.S. utility patents may therefore be estimated at $0.599 Billion.

Let us summarize these results.

Table 3-1: R&D versus Costs in 2012 for U.S. Origin Patent Items

Nature of Cost	Estimated Investment
1. Professional fees to prepare application.	$3.361 Billion
2. Filing fees.	$0.336 Billion
3. Attorney's fees for office action.	$0.695 Billion
4. Issuance fees for patents.	$0.212 Billion
5. Maintenance fees for patents.	$0.599 Billion
TOTAL	$5.203 Billion
Total U.S. R&D in 2012	$447.000 Billion
Patent Investment/Total R&D	**1.16%**[108]

---

106 "How many U.S. patents were in force in 2012?", by Professor Dennis Crouch, PatentlyO Blog, May 4, 2012, *http://patentlyo.com/patent/2012/05/how-many-us-patents-are-in-force.html* (last viewed on November 15, 2014). I have estimated these percentages from the table in this comment. I cannot break out renewal rates between U.S. origin and non-U.S. origin, so I assumed that the general rates apply also to U.S. origin patents.

107 The rates are significantly higher now, but our estimate is for 2012. Also, again the maintenance fees listed are for ordinary companies, but the fees are 50% less for small entities, and 75% less for micro entities.

108 If all patents are patent applications in the U.S. belonged solely to "micro entities", all PTO fees — filing, issuance, and maintenance — would be reduced by 75%, and the ratio of "Patent Investment/Total R&D" would fall from 1.16% to about 0.97%. This assumption is ridiculous, of course, but the truth is that some patent items are filed and prosecuted by small entities and micro entities, so that the true ratio in Table 3-1 should fall somewhere

b. Second Analysis

This is a variation of the first analysis. Here, categories 1 and 3, professional fees, are as above. However, all of the fees payable to the PTO will be calculated as a group. In 2012, the PTO earned $2.4271Billion, of which 89.8%, or $2.1795 Billion, were from patents. There is no official breakout of revenue between U.S. origin and non-U.S. origin patent items, but let us use the number 51.5% for U.S items, based on the relative percentage of patent applications filed in the period 2003–2012. Therefore, total estimated payments to the PTO in 2012 for U.S. origin patent items is $2.1795 Billion × 51.5%, or $1.122 Billion. Let us summarize these results.

---

within the range of 0.97%–1.16%. The effect of small and micro entities has no impact whatever on the general conclusion. Further, "micro entity" status became available only in 2103, so it had no effect whatever on the 2012 numbers in Table 3-1. Further, patents of U.S.-origin issued to "small entities" in the five-year period 2009–2013 has consistently been 28%-29% every year, United States Patent & Trademark Office, "Performance and Accountability Report fiscal year 2013", available at *http://www.uspto.gov/about/stratplan/ar/USPTOFY2012PAR.pdf*, page 198, Table 11. If we were reduce all fees paid to the PTO by 15% (meaning a reduction of 50%/item × 30% of items issued to small entities), the total impact would decrease the final ratio from 1.16% to 1.13%, and again, the general conclusion is not impacted at all.

Table 3-2: R&D versus PTO Fees in 2012 for U.S. Origin Patent Items

Nature of Cost	Estimated Investment
1. Professional fees to prepare application.	$3.361 Billion
3. Attorney's fees for office action.	$0.695 Billion
2, 4, and 5: All fees to the PTO.	$1.122 Billion
TOTAL	$5.178 Billion
Total U.S. R&D in 2012	$447.000 Billion
Patent Investment/Total R&D	**1.16%**[109]

In sum, based on various views of payments to the PTO, the ratio of patent investment to R&D in the entire economy appears to be approximately 1.16%.

c. Third Analysis

The Brookings Institution is considered to be one of the top think tanks in the United States. It has a very strong reputation, its reports are frequently cited, and in fact its official motto is "Quality. Independence. Impact." In February, 2013, it published a report entitled, "Patent Prosperity: Invention and Economic Performance in the United States and its Metropolitan Areas".[110] This report states, at p.8, that since

---

[109] Again, if all patent items in the U.S. belonged solely to "micro entities", then the ratio in Table 3-2 would fall somewhere within the range of 0.97% — 1.16%, and again, this effect is not relevant to the general conclusion. Further, if fees paid to the PTO were reduced by 15% to account for the items issued to "small entities", the final ratio would fall from 1.16% to 1.12%, and the conclusion is not impacted.

[110] "Patent Prosperity: Invention and Economic Performance in the United States and its Metropolitan Areas", by Jonathan Rothwell, José Lobo, Deborah Strumsky, and Mark Muro, Brookings Institution, Washington,

1975, on average one patent has been granted for about $3.5 Million in R&D. Could this sum be translated into a ratio of patent cost to R&D investment? To calculate such a ratio, we would need to understand the total cost of obtaining and maintaining a patent, both under the prior PTO fees and under the current fee schedule.

Table 3-3: Cost of Patent Applications Versus R&D

Nature of Cost	Pre-2013 Fee Schedule	Current Fee Schedule
1. Fee to prepare application.	$12,500	$12,500
2. Filing fee to PTO.	$1,250	$1,600
3. Fees to answer office actions. (2.5 actions × $2,500/action).	$6,250	$6,250
4. Issuance fee to PTO.	$1,750	$960
5. Maintenance fees to PTO.	$8,860	$12,600
TOTAL COST	$30,610	$33,910
Brookings: R&D investment	$3,500,000	$3,500,000
Cost of Patent/R&D	**0.87%**	**0.97%**[111]

D.C, February, 2013, available at *http://www.brookings.edu/~/media/research/files/reports/2013/02/patenting%20prosperity%20rothwell/patenting%20prosperity%20rothwell.pdf* (last viewed on November 15, 2014).

[111]   If all patent items in the U.S. belonged to micro entities, the final ratio of "Cost of Patent/R&D" in Table 3-3 would fall from 0.97% to 0.64%. This is a bigger effect than that noted in Tables 3-1 and 3-2, due primarily to the massive increase in patent maintenance fees that occurred in 2013. Realistically, however, if we deduct, from the total cost of a patent, 15% of the fees paid to the PTO (in order to account for small and now micro entity status patent items), the final ratio would fall from 0.97% to 0.90%. These impacts can happen only going forward, and they are more than a bit speculative. The benchmark ratio for investment in patents, that is, 1% of R&D investment, still appears valid, and will not be impacted for ordinary companies, but might be reduced slightly for small and micro entities in the future.

A fully loaded investment for a patent, as a percentage of R&D, appears to be in the range of 0.9%-1.00%, based on the statement of the Brookings Institution.

d. Fourth Analysis

Parchomovsky and Wagner, in their law review article, "Patent Portfolios", cited in Chapter 1, take an approach similar to that of the Brookings Institution, but based on issued patents rather than on applications. They present a graph in which they show that within the period 1963–1999, the ratio of "Patents to U.S. Corporations per Million 1996 R&D Dollars" varied between 0.19 and .39, with an average of about 0.30.[112] This ratio of patents to R&D dollars can be directly translated into a ratio of patent dollars to R&D dollars.

Table 3-4: Cost of Issued Patents versus R&D

Assumed Cost	$30,000	$33,000	$36,000
Patent Ratio	0.30	0.30	0.30
Imputed	$9,000	$9,900	$10,800
R&D Investment	$1,000,000	$1,000,000	$1,000,000
$ Patent/$ R&D	**0.90%**	**0.99%**	**1.08%**

In short, reviewing fully loaded patent costs to R&D, based on an assumed 0.30 patent per $1M R&D, yields a ratio of patent investment to R&D in the range of 0.90%–1.08%.

---

112 Parchomovsky and Wagner in "Patent Portfolios", p.18, Figure 2, entitled, "The Rise in Patent Intensity". This Figure 2 is taken from the book, "*A Patent System for the 21ˢᵗ Century*", edited by Stephen A. Merrill, Richard C. Levin, and Mark B. Myers, National Academies Press (September 3, 2004).

e. Factors Impacting the Ratio for Specific Companies

The 1% benchmark is only the beginning. Every company should consider various factors that should increase or decrease the benchmark for that particular company. Most particularly, young companies, particularly startups in technology-intensive industries and with growing markets, must seriously consider raising the ratio far beyond 1%, perhaps even double that or more. These companies live on innovation — their reason for existence is that they have introduced an innovation that will shake up one or more current industries and perhaps develop an entirely new market. Moreover, some of the great ideas of these companies, that is to say, some of the greatest inventions they will make over their entire lives, will be made in the early days, when the technology is completely new. For these companies, invention, *and the protection of invention*, is everything.

Companies like this tend to be, unfortunately, resource-poor, not only in terms of limited cash to invest in patents or R&D, but also in the time resources of engineers and senior technical people. Outside patent professionals do what they can to reduce the time commitments of technical people at the company, but the patenting process inevitably eats up some engineering time, and an active patenting program will eat up much more time than a passive or non-existent patenting program. Although R&D and patents should work together, they are rather in conflict within resource-poor companies, and this is another of the dilemmas faced by startup companies. High-tech startup companies must invest significantly in patents at the very beginning, or risk serious loss of value down the road.

Mature companies, on the other hand, have more choices. These are companies with established technologies and markets, and important but moderate technical improvements. In some cases, markets are declining, and companies in the industry are shifting resources to other opportunities. In all of these circumstances, mature companies may apply the 1% benchmark, or even decrease it.

On the other hand, there are mature companies that invest significant resources in patents, for a number of reasons. They may use patents as a lead to new businesses, or to implement an aggressive patenting program — Qualcomm and IBM are examples of companies with relatively aggressive patenting strategies. They may continue to add patent value even as they deemphasize operating activities — Motorola is an example. They may invest heavily in patents as a defensive measure, to combat or deter others — this seems to be the case with Samsung, and with the defensive aggregators such as AST and RPX. Mature companies, in mature or declining markets, with static or slowly changing technologies, may reduce R&D and reduce patenting such that the 1% ratio is maintained, or they may reduce R&D and essentially terminate patenting, or they may continue to emphasize patents even as the product business declines.

In short, the 1% benchmark is useful, but should be examined in light of the specific circumstances of the company and of the patent strategy the company chooses to pursue.

It is important to understand that this benchmark, patent investment of 1.00% of total R&D investment for a technology oriented company, is a gross figure, and will vary by type of industry and company. In particular, it is expected that relatively more should be invested in newer industries with relatively high rates of growth, and relatively less in more mature, slower growth industries. However, even more important than the industry is the state of the company — in almost all cases, newer, less established companies should be investing more in patents than older, more established companies. These relationships may be summarized in Table 3-5 below.

Table 3-5: Patent Investment by Industry Versus Company

	NEW COMPANY	ESTABLISHED COMPANY
Market with Above Average Growth and Prospects	**Segment A:** New Company, Growth Market, Investment above 1% of R&D	**Segment D:** Established Company, Growth Market, Investment 1% of R&D or more
Average Market	**Segment B:** New Company, Average Market, Investment above 1% of R&D	**Segment E:** Established Company, Average Market, Investment 1% of R&D or less
Market with Below Average Growth and Prospects	**Segment C:** New Company, Established Market, Investment *much above* 1% of R&D (or disinvest in business)	**Segment F:** Established Company, Established Market, Investment *much below* 1% of R&D

Segments A and B require a new company, possibly a startup, to invest heavily in both technology and patents protecting the technology. If the new company in a technical field does not offer a significant technical innovation, then what is the reason for the company's existence? Both technology investment and patent investment should be significant.

Segment C is unclear. Why is the new company investing in a stagnant or dying market? If the new company intends to reinvigorate the market with a major new innovation, that is fine, but investment must be quite significant in order to shake up the industry. If there is no major new innovation — no paradigm shift or Technology Inflection Point — then the new company should probably get out of the field (if it entered previously) or avoid the market (if it has not yet entered).

Segment D requires an established company to keep up in an attractive market, or invest more heavily than average if the company wishes to solidify its position. Segment E is not particularly attractive — the established company can probably keep up with average or less than average investment in patents. Finally, Segment F is gradually fading, and the established company should probably be focusing its efforts in other markets.

f. Summary of Section 1 — Top Down Budgeting

Although information is partial and imperfect, and no ratio is exactly 1.00%, nevertheless a variety of analyses, based on information from the PTO, Battelle, the Brookings Institution, and Parchomovsky & Wagner, yield a ratio of patent investment to R&D for the entire economy in the range of 0.90% to 1.16%. This supports an assumption of the Top Down patent portfolio budgeting — an average company, prior to consideration of special factors, might invest the equivalent of 1% of its R&D budget in patents. This ratio is only the beginning. Various factors should cause the company to increase or decrease its investment of patents in relation to this benchmark. Startups, younger companies, companies in areas with strong and rapidly changing technology, companies in growing markets, and companies that plan aggressive market strategies, should increase the investment of patents above 1% of R&D. Conversely, more mature companies, in areas with relatively static technology, or in areas with declining markets, and companies that implement a hold or defensive strategy, may consider decreasing their patent investments below 1% of R&D. Nevertheless, as a starting point for Top Down budgeting, 1% of R&D is a reasonable benchmark.

2. Bottom Up Budgeting: Targeting a Result

In contrast to Top Down budgeting, Bottom Up targets a result rather than a cost. The company makes a conscious decision about what it needs, plans to achieve that, and estimates the cost required to achieve this result.

What kinds of "conscious decision about need" will drive the portfolio?

For example, a company feels it has breakthrough, or "seminal" inventions. These applications must be filed and prosecuted to issuance, regardless of other strategic or even financial considerations. Such patents are rare, but if they can be obtained they should be, and lack of resources must be overcome.

As a second example, there are threats of patent infringement lawsuits. A number of questions may be asked:

1. Generally, is the industry litigious?
2. Is there rapid technical development, and hence obsolescence of older technology? Industry players may be fighting for technology dominance and market share.
3. Is there much patenting by major players in the

industry? Extensive patenting activities by competitors may lead to litigation.

4. Is the company a market leader in terms of market share and profitability? That is very good for the company's product business, but potentially very bad for the company's exposure to patent litigation — the large, successful companies are the best targets for patent litigation, because such companies have money to pay patent damages, and their risk is much greater if the lawsuit is lost.

The risk of litigation is the expected cost of losing a patent lawsuit times the expected probability of being sued and losing the suit, that is, (Expected Cost) × (Probability of being sued × Probability of losing the case). Fear of patent litigation can be a powerful incentive for a company to develop a strong portfolio as a counter-threat against potential plaintiffs.

As a third example, if the company adopts an aggressive patent strategy, it will be required by the force of circumstances to invest heavily in patents.

a. Examples of Bottom Up Budgeting

Let's consider two example of Bottom Up budgeting — Check Point Software as a company that needed to patent its seminal inventions, and Qualcomm as a company that has consciously selected an aggressive patent strategy and has pursued this strategy without pause.

Example 1 — Check Point Software Technologies

Check Point is one of the pioneers in electronic firewalls. Its portfolio is discussed in Chapter 1. The company appears to have 69 issued patents, primarily in the U.S., but also in Canada, China, Europe, Germany, Japan, Singapore, and South Korea. The company appears to have in addition 60 patent applications, again primarily in the U.S., but also in Europe plus several PCT international applications. If we assume fully loaded costs of $30,000 for each patent, and $15,000 for each application, Checkpoint's total investment in patents through its entire life, from 1994 through mid-2014, was about $3 Million.[113]

What may we say about $3M as a total investment by a company like Check Point? Let's summarize the data first for the life of the company, through the period 1994–2013, and then only for the past five years, 2009–2013, because Check Point has boosted its investment in patents in the past five years.

Throughout its entire life, in the period 1994 — 2013, the company invested $857 Million in R&D to generate $10.1 Billion in revenues and $5.1 Billion in operating profits. We can therefore see that the total investment in patents equals about 0.35% of R&D, well below the technology benchmark rate of 1.00%. Check Point's ratio of R&D/revenue through

---

[113] Fully loaded costs are of course exaggerated here, since some patents have not expired, some applications have not been prosecuted to a final result, and PCT international applications based on national applications tend to cost much less than $20,000 (although even the $20,000 may be exceeded in some Asian countries due to heavy translation costs). Thus, the investment might be less than $3 Million. On the other hand, there are probably some applications that have not been published, and these would need to be added to the investment. Further, some patents were acquired through purchase of the companies Zone Labs in 2004, Nokia Security Appliances Division in 2009, and Liquid Machines in 2010. Part of the acquisition prices may relate to patents, but I have found no figures on this, and I cannot make any such allocation. For this kind of portfolio, with about 69 patents and 60 published applications, $3 Million is a reasonable estimate.

its life is about 8.46%, which is not unreasonable for a high-tech company, and its margin Operating Profit/Revenues is a very strong 50.75%, but these results lead to ratios for Patents/Revenues of 0.03% and for Patents/Operating Profit of 0.06%.[114] In gross terms, prior to any adjustment for special considerations, this absolute level of investment, 0.35% of R&D and well below 0.1% on revenues and on operating profits, is simply inadequate.

What about the special considerations that drive the benchmark for a particular company? Do they suggest that Check Point's benchmark ratio should be 1.00%, or higher, or lower?

1. Check Point is certainly not a young company, but neither is it mature, so no change in the benchmark level.
2. There continues to be very strong innovation in this industry, which argues for a benchmark greater than 1.00%.
3. The electronic security market generally and the firewall market in particular continue to grow at strong rates. Such growth argues for a benchmark greater than 1.00%.
4. Check Point was a pioneer in firewalls, and continues to be one of the leading companies in terms of market share. It income and profits are very healthy, and continue to grow. As a market leader in excellent financial condition, it is a prime candidate to be sued by competitors seeking market share, or smaller

---

[114] All financial information for Check Point Software is taken or derived from *http://www.checkpoint.com/corporate/investor-relations/earnings-history/index.html* (last viewed on November 15, 2014).

companies seeking a share of Check Point's profits. All of this information argues for a benchmark greater than 1.00%.

5. There has been litigation in the firewall industry, but certainly not near the levels seen in the cellular market. Either no impact on the benchmark rate, or a weak impetus to lower the rate.

In short, it would seem, at least on the face of things, that Check Point's benchmark for investment in patents should at least reach the general benchmark rate of 1.00%, and probably should be higher. Its true rate, of 0.35%, appears inadequate.

Has the situation changed specifically in the past five years? Check Point has generated almost 50% of its portfolio in the period 2009–2013, so perhaps for that period, it has invested an appropriate amount in patents. Here is a quick summary, comparing financial information with patent investment in these years, based again on $30,000 per patent and $15,000 per application, published in that year.

Table 3-6: Check Point Patent Investments 2009–2013

	2009	2010	2011	2012	2013	Totals 2009–2013	Totals 1994–2013
Revenue $000	1,352,309	1,097,868	1,246,986	1,342,695	1,394,105	6,433,963	10,126,975
R&D $000	83,094	95,682	102,675	103,317	112,763	497,531	856,612
Operating Profit $000	415,017	535,014	642,174	746,535	760,905	3,099,645	5,139,092
Patents $000	165	330	165	375	390	1,425	3,000
$Patents/ $Revenue	0.0122%	0.0301%	0.0132%	0.0279%	0.0280%	**0.0221%**	**0.0296%**
$Patents/ $R&D	0.1986%	0.3449%	0.1607%	0.3630%	0.3459%	**0.2864%**	**0.3502%**
$Patents/ $Op Profit	0.0398%	0.0617%	0.0257%	0.0502%	0.0513%	**0.0460%**	**0.0526%**

Check Point's patent investment in the period 2009–2013, based on published applications and patents, *is worse* by all measures than its average investment throughout its entire life, 1994–2013. It is true that patent investment has increased, but that has been more than offset by strong growth in revenues, R&D, and operating profit. For example, the investment in patents as a percentage of R&D was only 0.2864% in the period 2009–2013, as opposed to 0.3502% over the entire life of the company.

What, then, may be inferred about Check Point's patent strategy and patent budgeting?[115]

1. Check Point filed, prosecuted, and obtained in 1997 and 1998, respectively, two seminal patents. Its actions,

---

[115] All of these conclusions are my personal inferences, based on published information.

that is, filing and prosecuting early applications on its major innovations, are very typical of a high-tech startup company. This was well done.

2. There then followed a period, 1999–2004 inclusive, when almost nothing was done in patents. There were about 5 patent filings in total over this six-year period. This is not unusual for a company that has decided as part of its strategy to either ignore patents, or to patent solely ideas that happen to come up from time to time. In other words, this is one form of Bottom Up budgeting — no specific budget and no specific patent activity, but to file if a reasonable invention is made.

3. Check Point's patent activity has been much stronger in the period 2005–2013, especially in 2009–2013, but this activity is deceptive. In quantitative terms, there has been no real change, and patenting activity continues well below the 1.00% benchmark.

4. Check Point's two seminal patents expired in February, 2014, and therefore its portfolio now lacks both quality and quantity.

Example 2 — Qualcomm

Qualcomm is very different than Check Point, in that Check Point's basic patent strategy is to do nothing (or to do minimal patenting from time to time), whereas Qualcomm's clear strategy is to do everything possible in patenting, and to incur all expenses in time and effort, in order to create a patent portfolio that will dominate an industry. In both cases, apparently the initial focus is on what must be done rather than the cost, which is the essence of Bottom Up budgeting, but the resulting strategies are polar opposites.

The six criteria for judging a portfolio are, as noted in Chapter 1, fit with corporate strategy, coverage of technology and products, balance of quality and quantity, geographic balance, time balance, and special considerations. These are discussed in reference to Qualcomm in Chapter 1, but it would be useful to compare Qualcomm both to Check Point and to industry benchmarks, in order to understand what it means for a company to make a conscious decision to dominate a market with patents.

Table 3-7: Comparison of Check Point, Industry, and Qualcomm at June 30, 2014

	Check Point	Industry Standard	Qualcomm
R&D Intensity ($ R&D/$ Revenues)	9.4%	7%-8%	20.8%
Number of items in patent portfolio	129	(Not Relevant)	57,216
Estimated total investment in patents over entire life of the company	$3 Million	(Not Relevant)	$1.71 Billion
Patent Activity Investment ($ investment in patents/$ R&D)	0.35%	1.00%	5.71%
$ in Patents/$ Revenues	0.03%	0.07%–0.08%	1.19%

This picture is very clear. Although Check Point invests relatively heavily in R&D, its investments in patents are anemic. This is typical of a company that has chosen not to pursue patents actively, and to budget only for specific patents as they come up from time to time. In contrast, Qualcomm invests very heavily in R&D (in comparison to the industry), and invests not merely heavily but indeed massively in patents (again, in comparison to the industry). Although Qualcomm, like Check Point, appears to target results rather than costs, Qualcomm's entire focus is on technology dominance, and that appears to be Qualcomm's consistent focus since the company's founding in the mid-1980's.

c. Summary of Section 2 — Bottom Up Budgeting

In the end, a patent strategy must balance costs and results. In Bottom Up budgeting, the initial focus is on results, followed by costs. This is the opposite focus of Top Down budgeting.

Bottom Up budgeting can be the result of a conscious patent strategy, as in the case of Qualcomm. Bottom Up budgeting can also be the result of an absence of patent strategy, or a strategy to do as little as possible, as in the case of Check Point. Bottom Up budgeting may be used to implement any strategy, be it aggressive or defensive or minimal.

3. Competitive Budgeting: Targeting Costs and Results Based on the Competition

In Competitive Budgeting, a company targets its competitors. The company executes four steps.

First, the company selects a group of competitors to create competitive benchmarks for both patent investment and patent results.

Second, the company determines the patent results achieved by these competitors, and infers the implied investments which were required to achieve these results. If possible, the company collects financial information about the competitors to create benchmarks of patent investment and results relative to R&D investment and/or to revenues.

The patent results reviewed may relate to the entire effort of each competitor. The examples in this Chapter 3, presented below, include review of the entire portfolio of each competitor. Alternatively, the company may review competitor patent results by country, by product and service, by technology, or by some combination of country, product, and technology. Patent results are almost always available by country, at least for the U.S. and for the major economic leaders in Europe and Asia. Product and technology information is more difficult to acquire, and would require some judgment as to allocation of patent items among different product and technologies, but it could be done in at least an approximate way.

Third, based on the information from the second step, the company creates its own benchmarks. These may be competitive benchmarks based on the patent results achieved by the competitors, or on the patent investments made by the competitors, or on both the results and investments of the competitors.

The benchmarks may be for the entire portfolio of the company, or for specific countries, products and services, or technologies. One way to do such a breakout is to base it on the detailed patent results reviewed in the prior step. A second way is to use only complete portfolio information of competitors in order to generate average benchmarks, but then to alter these averages up or down according to the what the company perceives as its high priority geographic, product, or technology markets.

Fourth, the company creates its own budget for patents, which may be Top Down (that is, a certain amount allocated, which produces some number of patents) or Bottom Up (that is, a certain number of patent items are budgeted, which implies a certain financial commitment). As with every budgeting process, there is an iterative process between costs and results until the appropriate mix is obtained. Of necessity, a company's patent budget should indicate priorities among countries, products and services, and technologies, whether or not the competitive benchmarks are based on entire portfolios or detailed slices of the competitors' patenting activities.

In sum, Competitive Budgeting begins with an understanding of the competitors, and ends with a balance between the company's budgeted costs and expected results.

Competitive budgeting creates a benchmark based on the patent activities of competitors. In this sense, it is similar to the general benchmark for all technology companies, that is, patent investment equal to 1.00% of R&D investment. However, in Competitive Budgeting, the benchmark can be and usually is something different than 1.00% of R&D investment, and there are multiple possibilities for the benchmark group. Here are just a few of the groups which might be used by a company to create a competitive benchmark:

1. All companies in the economy, comparing total patent investment to total R&D. This benchmark was explained in Section I as "Top Down budgeting".

2. A benchmark based solely on information & communication technologies ("ICT") companies. This is of course a much narrower group than all companies in the economy, but it may be still be quite broad. There are a number of ways specifically relevant ICT companies may be identified. For example:

a. Companies that patent primarily within specific "technology centers" of the patent office.[116]

b. Patents with specific technology classification numbers may be used to identify companies of interest.[117]

c. Specific industries may be aggregated — for example, the IEEE Spectrum Patent Power Scorecard lists 17 segments, and analyzes the patent portfolios of twenty companies or other entities within each segment.[118]

---

[116] The technology centers of the PTO are 1600 Biology and Organic Chemistry; 1700 Chemicals and Materials Engineering; 2100 Computer Architecture, Software, and Information Security; 2400 Computer Networks, Multiplex communication, Video Distribution, and Security; 2600 Communications; 2800 Semiconductors, Electrical and Optical Systems and Components; 2900 Designs; 3600 Transportation, Construction, Electronic Commerce, Agriculture, National Security and License & Review; and 3700 Mechanical Engineering, Manufacturing, and Products. A company could, by preference, identify and compare companies in 2100, 2400, 2600, 2800, and 3700. Or perhaps the company would exclude 3700. Or perhaps the company would focus on one center, such as 2600 Communications.

[117] The three most prominent classification systems are the International Patent Classification ("IPC"), the U.S. Patent Classification ("USPC"), and the European Classification ("ECLA"). Any or all of these could be used to identify relevant companies to be included in a benchmarking analysis.

[118] The segments are (1) Aerospace & Defense; (2) Automotive & Parts; (3) Biotechnology & Pharmaceuticals; (4) Chemicals; (5) Communication/ Internet Equipment; (6) Communication/Internet Service; (7) Computer Peripherals & Storage; (8) Computer Software; (9) Computer Systems; (10) Conglomerates; (11) Electronics; (12) Government Agencies; (13) Medical Equipment/Instruments; (14) Scientific Instruments; (15) Semiconductor Equipment Manufacturing; (16) Semiconductor Manufacturing; and (17) Universities/Education/Training. Obviously, very many combinations are possible. A company wishing to create a very wide ICT benchmark might compare itself to the one-hundred sixty companies in groups (5)-(9), (11), and (15)-(16). A semiconductor company might review only the forty companies in groups (15) and (16).

3. The company could select only competitors active within a very narrow segment that is related closely to the company's activities.[119]

These are all variations of the same theme. In all cases, the same four steps will be executed, and in this order:

1. Select what the company believes is an appropriate group of competitors from which to create benchmarks of specific relevance to the company.
2. Determine the patent results and implied investments of these specific competitors.
3. Create benchmarks for investment and/or results, based on the activities of these competitors.
4. Plan the company's patent investments followed by patent results (Top Down budgeting) or plan the company's patent results followed by required investments (Bottom Up budgeting).

a. Examples of Competitive Budgeting

Two examples follow.

Example 1 — The Firewall Industry

Check Point provides an excellent example of how a competitive benchmark might be constructed and applied. There

---

[119] There are many possibilities. For example, each technology center of the PTO is comprised of multiple groups, any of which could be used by the company to create a benchmark sample. The classification systems can become very specific by company activity. As a second example, a company could select only the twenty companies in its particular IEEE Spectrum Patent Power Scorecard. Google, for example, has been placed within the segment "Communication/Internet Services", together with AT&T, NT&T, RIM, Siemens, Sprint Nextel, Yahoo!, and thirteen other companies.

are two reasons. First, it demonstrates some of the difficulties inherent in creating such a benchmark. Second, it answers a question that must be of interest to many companies — "Regardless of how strong or weak my portfolio may be, how do I stack up against the competition?" As we have seen, Check Point's portfolio is weak in an absolute sense, or in comparison to all technology companies, but how does Check Point rate in comparison to its closest competitors?

Step 1 — Select a Relevant Group of Companies:
Check Point does not appear in any of the 17 segments listed by IEEE Spectrum in its Patent Power Scorecard. However, in its 2013 Form 20-F filing with the Securities & Exchange Commission, Check Point has identified its 14 closest competitors.[120] Check Point could simply use these 14 companies as its benchmark group, but first Check Point should ask, "Do these 14 companies fall within one of the segments listed by IEEE Spectrum?" If so, perhaps that segment of twenty companies might be a better sample to use. Here are the 14 companies, and the segments of the IEEE Spectrum analysis into which they fall.

120 These companies are listed in Check Point's 2013 20-F annual report, available at *http://www.checkpoint.com/downloads/corporate/investor-relations/sec-filings/2013-20f.pdf*, p.7.

Table 3-8: Competitors in the Firewall Industry

Competitor Listed by Check Point	Segment from IEEE Spectrum Patent Power Scorecard
1. Cisco Systems	(1) Communication/Internet Equipment
2. FireEye	[Does not appear on the Scorecard.]
3. Fortinet	[Does not appear on the Scorecard.]
4. Hewlett-Packard	(2) Computer Systems
5. IBM	(2) Computer Systems
6. Juniper Networks	(1) Communication/Internet Equipment
7. McAfee (acquired by Intel in 2011)	(3) Semiconductor Manufacturing (Intel)
8. Microsoft	(4) Computer Software
9. Palo Alto Networks	[Does not appear on the Scorecard.]
10. SonicWall (acquired by Dell in 2012)	(2) Computer Systems (Dell)
11. Sourcefire (acquired by Cisco in 2013)	(1) Computer/Internet Equipment (Cisco)
12. Symantec	(4) Computer Software
13. Watchguard Technologies	[Does not appear on the Scorecard.]
14. Websense	[Does not appear on the Scorecard.]

In short, of the 14 companies considered by Check Point to be its closest competitors, 3 appear on the IEEE Spectrum Patent Power Scorecard as "Communication/Internet Equipment", 3 appear as "Computer Systems", 1 appears as "Semiconductor Manufacturing", 2 appear as "Computer Software", and 5 do not appear on the list. Of these four segments, "Semiconductor Manufacturing" appears irrelevant, while "Communication/Internet Equipment" and "Computer Systems" appear relevant but are heavily hardware-oriented while Check Point is heavily software-oriented (although Check Points does sell some hardware together with its software). "Computer Software" would seem to be the most relevant segment, but it is extremely broad, including many activities that are of little relevant to Check Point, such as database management (Oracle is on the list), pdf software (Adobe is on the list), and digital media (AOL is on the list). In conclusion, no particular segment from the IEEE Spectrum is a perfect fit to Check Point's business.

Different benchmarking groups could then be selected. Such groups could be larger, or smaller, than the 14 companies identified by Check Point in is 2013 20-F filing. Here are just a few of the possibilities:

Table 3-9: Possibilities for a Firewall Industry Benchmark Group

Possibilities	Source	Number of Companies	Advantage(s)	Dis-advantage(s)
(1) Original sample	Check Point's 2013 20-F Report	14	Clear and relevant	May be too small
(2) Closest segment plus original sample	IEEE Computer Software segment; and Check Point's 2013 20-F Report	About 30	Broader sample	Less relevant to Check point
(3) All four IEEE segments with a close competitor, plus others on Check Point list	IEEE for Internet Equipment, Computer Systems, Computer Software, Semiconductor Mfg; and Check Point's 2013 20-F Report	85	Very broad sample	Low relevance to Check point

Possibilities	Source	Number of Companies	Advantage(s)	Dis-advantage(s)
(4) All eight IEEE segments in ICT, plus others on Check Point list	IEEE four segments above, plus the segments Internet Services, Computer Peripherals & Storage, Electronics, and Semiconductor Equipment; and Check Point's 2013 20-F Report	165	Extremely broad sample	Very low relevance to Check Point (approaches entire ICT industry)
(5) Group A Check Point competitors	Check Point's 2013 20-F Report at p.7	8	Extremely relevant	Could be too small to be meaningful

The original group of 14 companies, all identified by Check Point as important competitors, seems to be a good choice, assuming however that relevant information is available for these companies. Options (2), (3) and (4) above are more inclusive, but less directly relevant to Check Point. Option (5) above was defined by Check Point in the 20-F filing, in which the company divided its main competitors into two lists that I call "Group A" and "Group B". Group A includes eight companies — Cisco, Fortinet, Juniper Networks, McAfee, Palo Alto Networks, SonicWall, Sourcefire, and WatchGuard. These companies seem to compete in Check Point's main business. The other six companies, in Group B, are said to compete "with respect to specific products we [Check Point] offer". It would be possible to select a relatively small group of only the 8 companies in Group A, assuming again that sufficient information is available about these 8 companies.

Although five options are presented above, and many other options are possible, let us select here the original 14 companies because they have been identified by Check Point as its closest competitors, and because this is a reasonably large but not unmanageable sample size.

In all cases, the selection of specific companies for the benchmark group is an extremely important factor in performing Competitive Budgeting of patent investment.

Step 2 — Determine the patent results and implied investments of these competitors:

Patent information is readily available for all of these 14 companies. Financial information is available for 12 of the companies. Two of the companies provide very little public information about their finances — SonicWall, originally a private company and acquired by Dell in 2012; and Watchguard Technologies, which has been a private company since 2006. The benchmarks will therefore exclude these two, and will be based on data from the remaining 12 companies.

Check Point's patent position in relation to the companies it considers its closest competitors may be summarized in a table.

Table 3-10: Check Point Portfolio versus Portfolios of Competitors

	Total Patent Items* at 6/30/2014	2013** Revenue $M	2013** R&D $M	Ratio 2013** R&D /2013** Revenue	Total Patents/ 2013** Revenue $M	Total Patents/ 2013** R&D $M
Check Point Software	145	$1,394	$113	8.1%	0.1040	1.2859
Cisco Systems	22,988	$48,600	$5,942	12.2%	0.4730	3.8687
FireEye	42	$162	$66	40.9%	0.2600	0.6360
Fortinet	404	$615	$103	16.7%	0.6569	3.9353
Hewlett-Packard	103,454	$112,298	$3,135	2.8%	0.9212	32.9997
IBM	248,919	$99,751	$6,226	6.2%	2.4954	39.9806
Juniper Networks	3,212	$4,669	$1,043	22.3%	0.6879	3.0796
McAfee (Sold to Intel in early 2011)	1,817	$2,065	$344	16.7%	0.8800	5.2821
Microsoft	83,954	$77,849	$10,411	13.4%	1.0784	8.0640
Palo Alto Networks	44	$396	$62	15.8%	0.1111	0.7042
Sourcefire (Sold to Cisco in July, 2013)	86	$223	$42	18.6%	0.3855	2.0688
Symantec	4,002	$6,906	$1,012	14.7%	0.5795	3.9545
Websense (Went private 2013)	133	$361	$63	17.5%	0.3679	2.1009
AVERAGES (Mean)	36,091	$27,330	$2,197	15.84%	0.6923	8.304
AVERAGES (Median)	1,817	$2,065	$344	15.80%	0.8800	3.9353

	Total Patent Items* at 6/30/2014	2013** Revenue $M	2013** R&D $M	Ratio 2013** R&D /2013** Revenue	Total Patents/ 2013** Revenue $M	Total Patents/ 2013** R&D $M
How Does Check Point Compare? (mean)	0.4% of the mean patent portfolio	5.1% of mean 2013 revenue	5.1% of mean annual 2013 R&D	51.15 of mean (2013 R&D/ 2013 Revenue)	15.0% of mean (patent items/ 2013 revenue)	15.% of mean (patent items/ 2013 R&D)
How Does Check Point Compare? (median)	8.0% of median patent portfolio	67.5% of median 2013 revenue	32.8% of median annual R&D	51.3% of median (2013 R&D/2013 revenue)	11.8% of median (patent items/ 2013 revenues)	32.7% of median (patent items/ 2013 R&D)
How Does Check Point Compare? (ranking)	Tied with Websense for 9th of 13	8th of 13	8th of 13	11th of 13	Tied with Palo Alto Networks for last place	11th of 13
CONCLUSIONS in comparison to the main competitors	Much smaller patent portfolio than those of competitors	Among the focused and smaller companies, close to average	Very low level of investment in R&D compared to smaller competitors	Very low level of investment in R&D relative to revenue	Extreme under-invest-ment in patent portfolio	Extreme under-invest-ment in patent portfolio

[*: "Patent items" include every U.S., European, German, and Japanese patent and patent application, plus every PCT international application filed with WIPO. No attempt has been made to subtract out applications that were later issued as patents, and for that reason the total numbers of patent items listed here are expected to be the slightly higher than the actual numbers of discrete items.]

[**: All figures are 2013, except McAfee is 2010 (prior to its purchase by Intel in 2011), Sourcefire is 2012 (prior to its purchase by Cisco in 2013), and Websense is 2012 (prior to its going private in 2013).]

This Table presents a gloomy picture for Check Point. Specifically on the comparative data, it does badly. Look at the last three columns of Table 3-10 toward the bottom. Check Point ranks 11th of 13 companies in R&D as a percentage of revenue, it is tied for last place in patent investment relative to revenue, and it ranks 11th of 13 in patent investment relative to R&D. If we were to ask the question, "Despite Check Point's general weakness in patents, is its position reasonable in relation to its competitors?", the clear answer would be no. Although Check Point's investments in R&D are poor in comparison to the competition, its investments in patents are much worse.

However, perhaps it is the case that Check Point is increasing its patent investments in recent years, in order to redress the terrible balance against the company. Table 3-11 shows Check Point's investments in patents relative competitors within the last three calendar years, 1/1/2011 to 12/31/2013.

Table 3-11: Check Point versus Competitors in the Period
2011–2013**

	2011–2013 Patent Items*	2011–2013 Revenue $M	2011-2013 R&D $M	2013–2013 R&D $M/ 2011–2013 Revenue $M	Total Patents/ 2011–2013 Revenue $M	Total Patents/ 2011–2013 R&D $M
Check Point Software	33	$3,984	$319	8.0%	0.0083	0.1034
Cisco Systems	6,006	$137,879	$17,253	12.5%	0.0436	0.3481
FireEye	27	$279	$90	32.3%	0.0969	0.3005
Fortinet	178	$1,582	$247	15.6%	0.1125	0.7197
Hewlett-Packard	12,485	$359,900	$9,788	2.7%	0.0347	1.2755
IBM	43,689	$311,174	$18,786	6.0%	0.1404	2.3256
Juniper Networks	1,487	$13,482	$3,171	23.5%	0.1103	0.4689
McAfee** (Sold to Intel in early 2011)	179	$3,992	$667	16.7%	0.0448	0.2684
Microsoft	22,656	$221,515	$29,265	13.2%	0.1023	0.7742
Palo Alto Networks	21	$740	$122	16.5%	0.0284	0.1715
Sourcefire (Sold to Cisco in July, 2013)	32	$519	$94	18.1%	0.0616	0.3422
Symantec	1,672	$19,826	$2,843	14.3%	0.0843	0.5881
Websense** (Went private 2013)	40	$1,058	$172	16.3%	0.0378	0.2321
AVERAGES (Mean)	6,808	$82,764	$6,371	15.1%	0.0697	0.6091
AVERAGES (Median)	179	$3,992	$667	16.7%	0.0616	0.3481

	2011–2013 Patent Items*	2011–2013 Revenue $M	2011-2013 R&D $M	2013–2013 R&D $M/ 2011–2013 Revenue $M	Total Patents/ 2011–2013 Revenue $M	Total Patents/ 2011–2013 R&D $M
How Does Check Point Compare? (mean)	0.48% of mean patent portfolio	4.8% of mean annual revenue	5.0% of mean annual R&D	53.0% of mean (R&D/ revenue)	12.3% of mean (patent items/ revenue)	17.0% of median (patent items/ R&D)
How Does Check Point Compare? (median)	18.4% of median patent portfolio	Almost the same as the median annual revenue	47.8% of median annual R&D	47.9% of (median/ revenue)	13.5% of median (patent items/ revenue)	29.7% of median (patent items/ R&D)
How Does Check Point Compare? (ranking)	Tied for 10th with Sourcefire	8th of 13	8th of 13	11th of 13	LAST PLACE	LAST PLACE
CONCLUSIONS for the period 2011–2013	Slightly worse in overall patent items	No significant change in revenue ranking	No significant change in R&D ranking	No significant change in R&D to revenues	Competitive ranking patents to revenues has worsened	Competitive ranking patents to R&D has worsened

[*: Same definition of "patent item" as in prior Table 3-10 All patent items are for the years 2011–2013.]
[**: Financial information is 2009–2010 for McAfee, and 2010–2012 for Websense.]

It is now possible to draw two conclusions regarding Check Point's competitive position with regard to patents. This information will then be used to create benchmarks for Check Point.

First, as a percentage of revenue, Check Point has under-invested in R&D relative to competition. Check Point does better only than its much larger competitors, Hewlett-Packard and IBM, whose absolute levels of R&D investment are much higher than Check Point's, but whose R&D intensity relative to revenue is low. More important, perhaps, is that in comparison to the relatively smaller independent players in the industry — FireEye, Fortinet, Juniper Networks, Palo Alto Networks, and Websense — Check Point's levels of R&D investment are very poor.

Second, Check Point's under-investment in R&D would suggest that Check Point has probably under invested in patents as well, and that is indeed the case. However, Check Point's under-investment in patents is worse than its under-investment in R&D, such that in comparison to its main competitors, Check Point's total investment in patents in the period 2011–2013 appears to be dead last as a percentage of both revenues and R&D. In reality, two of the weakest competitors in patents, FireEye and Palo Alto Networks, appear to be increasing their investments in patents in recent years, leaving Check Point in last place for the period 2011–2013.[121]

---

[121] In some cases, the state of a company's patent investments may suggest the state of the company's financial status. Relatively light investment may suggest financial weakness in the company, whereas relatively heavy investment might suggest financial strength of the company. However, this inference is useful primarily for private companies rather than public companies. Public companies must, in any case, publish their financial results. The financial state of a public company should be clear from its pubic information, so inferences from patent investment are hardly necessary. Here, for example, Check Point's patent investments have been relatively light, but its revenue growth has been excellent in the period 2007–2013, as shown in Table 1-2, and its published financial statements show a consistently high profit margin on sales. For a profitable company that, in the period 2007–2013, generated more than $7.5 billion in revenues and invested over $700 million in R&D, total patent investment of about $3M is simply very low, and does not reflect the company's financial state.

Step 2 requires both a review of patent results and implied investments. The patent results appear in Tables 3-10 and 3-11 above. What can we say about the financial investments required for these results?

Certain assumptions are required to fill gaps in knowledge, and to prevent the process from becoming complicated to no end. In particular, let us assume that the investment by a company in any year is equal to a fully loaded cost of $30,000 for each U.S. patent, and $15,000 for every other patent item including U.S. applications, European patents and applications, German patents and applications, Japanese patents and applications, and PCT international applications filed with WIPO. The assumed costs for U.S. patents and U.S. applications are reasonable. The assumed costs for other patent items are reasonable given an assumption that U.S. corporations almost always file first in the U.S., and then move on to non-U.S. counterpart filings. Since much of the main work has been performed in the U.S. case, the non-U.S. case should cost less.

With these assumptions, and using publicly available information about patent filings and financial results, we can now determine how much money Check Point and its main competitors have invested in patents throughout the three-year period 2011–2013, inclusive.

Table 3-12: Patent Investments of Check Point and Competitors 2011–2013

	Total Patent Items in Period	U.S. Patents	Other Patent Items	Total Patent Investment $M*	Patent Investment as % of Revenues in the Period	Patent Investment as % of R&D in the Period
Check Point Software	33	21	12	$0.8	0.0203%	0.25%
Cisco Systems	6,006	3,084	2,922	$136.4	0.0989%	0.79%
FireEye	27	12	15	$0.6	0.2100%	0.65%
Fortinet	178	91	87	$4.0	0.2550%	1.63%
Hewlett-Packard	12,485	4,296	8,189	$251.7	0.0699%	2.57%
IBM	43,689	19,586	24,103	$949.1	0.3050%	5.05%
Juniper Networks	1,487	865	622	$35.3	0.2617%	1.11%
McAfee (for 2009–2010)	179	105	74	$4.3	0.1067%	0.64%
Microsoft	22,656	8,610	14,046	$469.0	0.2117%	1.60%
Palo Alto Networks	21	11	10	$0.5	0.0649%	0.39%
Sourcefire	32	13	19	$0.7	0.1300%	0.72%
Symantec	1,672	1,121	551	$41.9	0.2113%	1.47%
Websense (for 2010–2012)	40	14	26	$0.8	0.0765%	0.47%
AVERAGES (mean)	6,808	2,910	3,898	$145.8	0.1555%	1.34%
AVERAGES (median)	179	105	74	$4.3	0.1300%	0.79%
How Does Check Point Compare? (mean)	Much less	Much less	Much less	Much less	Check Point is 13.1% of the mean investment	Check Point is 18.7% of the mean investment

	Total Patent Items in Period	U.S. Patents	Other Patent Items	Total Patent Investment $M*	Patent Investment as % of Revenues in the Period	Patent Investment as % of R&D in the Period
How Does Check Point Compare? (median)	Much less	Much less	Much less	Much less	Check Point is 15.6% of the median investment	Check Point is 31.7% of the median investment
How Does Check Point Compare? (ranking)	Tied for 10th with Sourcefire	9th of 13	12th of 13	Much less	LAST PLACE	LAST PLACE
CONCLUSIONS for the period 2011–2013	Worse in overall patent items		Check Point concentrates more on U.S. patents	Check Point's dollar investment lags	Very weak investment in the period 2011–2013	Very weak investment in the period 2011–2013

[*: Assumes U.S. patents × $30,000 plus other patent items × $15,000.]

With this Table 3-12, both the patent results and implied patent investments have been determined and presented. Step 2 is finished.

Step 3 — Create benchmarks for investment and/or results:

In competitive patent budgeting, each company must create its own benchmarks based on several factors:

1. Competitive Activity: The patent results and patent investments for Check Point's main competitors are displayed above. They show very serious under-investment in patents by Check Point, in comparison to every one of 12 key competitors.

2. Industry and Market Factors: As noted, factors such as young company, new technology, strong technology-intensity in the industry, growing market, and others, suggest that the benchmark should be higher than an average 1.00% benchmark for technology companies in general. Indices can be made for these factors, but the key consideration is the company's perception of these factors.

3. The Company's Strategy: To date, Check Point's apparent strategy has been to write two excellent patents in the early days, and then to engage in patents only to the minimal extent required. The company may continue its relative disengagement from patents, or it may choose another approach. For example, the company could decide to at least match competitive investment in patents in recent years — this would require the company to boost its investment from 0.25% of R&D to a sum in the area of 0.79%-1.34% of R&D. In other words, the company would have to increase patenting activity by 200% to 400%, implying a total annual investment of at least $1.0M-$1.5M as opposed to the current level.

Alternatively, the company may decide that it wishes not only to match current levels of investment, but in fact to close the gap in the accumulated levels of investment from past years. However, this would require an investment of at least $20M, and realistically probably much more. For Check Point, this sum would be about 6% of its annual R&D budget. Such a sum may indeed be invested, but almost certainly not in one year, and not exclusively on in-house inventions. Other companies invest much more than $20M per year in patents, and in fact companies such as Qualcomm and IBM do invest at this level as a percentage of R&D, but Check Point has no tradition for doing this. Realistically, the closing of the patent gap would require a multi-year program, including both increased investment in-house and the purchase of relevant patents from outside parties.

A third approach would be for the company to become a leader in patents, just as it has been a leader in products and services for firewall protection. Given the history and current status of the company, this approach is hypothetical only, but it could be done.

In 2013, Check Point had a 55% profit margin, generating $761M in pre-tax operating income. Its cash flow position is even stronger, generating $811M in cash from operating activities in 2013. Check Point has the financial resources to implement any strategy it wishes in regards to patents, but the company needs to make a conscious decision to select and implement a strategy.

The benchmark, based either on planned results or planned investment, will follow from Check Point's view of the competition, industry & market factors, and the company's strategy. In this industry, an investment in patents of 1% of annual R&D would be about average. Check Point may decide, for reasons discussed, to raise the benchmark beyond 1%. Conversely, the company may continue to invest at the level of about 0.25%, but this would be merely a continuation of a policy of neglect.

Step 4 — Plan the company's patent investments, then desired results (Top Down), or plan the company's desired results, then the required investments (Bottom Up).

The benchmark, whether based on investments or results, is only a gross figure. Specific decisions would need to be made about where to invest, when, and for what products and technologies. Many of these details could be driven by Check Point's understanding of its competitors, including in particular both geographic areas and products emphasized by competitor patent filings.

A budget would be completed, driven either by a level of investment comfortable to the company (Top Down approach) followed by expected patent results, or driven by desired patent results (Bottom Up approach) followed by expected costs. Both investments and results will be compared, both in the planning and the implementation, to the activities of Check Point's main competitors.

In the example given, data and benchmarks are created for the overall patent portfolios of Check Point's key competitors. Information could be collected, and benchmarks created, (1) by specific country; (2) by one or more specific products; (3) by specific technologies; and/or for (4) issued patents versus pending (and published) applications. Public data is certainly available for category (1), at least in many major countries, and public data also exists for published applications (although not for unpublished applications) in category (4). Categories (2) products and (3) technologies would require an allocation of competitor patent items among various products and technologies — this allocation may be done by technical experts, or by automated allocation using specific search words, or by automated allocation using various technology classification numbers.[122] Although benchmarks may be created for various

---

[122] Patents are categorized by both U.S. patent classification numbers and International Patent Classification numbers. Either or both sets of classification numbers can be used to allocate competitor patents into different product and technology categories. The classification numbers attached to patent items are not perfect, however, and are certainly not customized for the purpose of a company's detailed review of its competitors' portfolios.

slices of the portfolio (by specific countries, technologies, or products and services), sliced benchmarks are not created in the examples presented here.

Example 2 — The Electronic Signature Industry

The patent portfolio of Silanis Technology was presented and discussed in Chapter 1. Silanis operates in an area which is sometimes called "the electronic signature industry", and which provides authentication of electronic documents. The business is sometimes referenced as an example of a "Software as a Service" (or "SaaS") kind of business.[123]

This industry is a good candidate for a second example of competitive patent budgeting, because the industry is much different from Check Point's firewall industry, and the problems of competitive analysis are very different in these two industries. We will again go through the budgeting process, step by step.

Also, review of competitor patents by technical experts is markedly superior to an automated review by search words or by classification numbers, but expert review is also much more expensive than automated review. Each company must decide, when it reviews competitor patents, which kind of review is warranted in each situation.

[123] I am by no means an expert in this business. My crude understanding is that "electronic signature" is the sending of an electronic message in which the sender intends to be bound in some way, legally or financially or morally, by the message. Such a signature may be encrypted according to various digital algorithms. SaaS is a growing type of business model in which software is not sold, but rather services are enabled to users, who pay either a fixed fee per time or a usage fee. In SaaS, substantially all of the operative software is hosted by the service provider, which implies, necessarily, that the customer's "client device" is "thin", whereas the server is "fat". In other words, the fat server executes most of the system operations, not the thin client. This short description of the electronic signature industry is all that is required for present purposes.

Step 1 — Select a Relevant Group of Companies:

It is possible, based on a variety of publicly available reports, to identify the following companies as being both members of the electronic signature industry[124] and apparently the companies most relevant for comparison of patent investments:[125]

---

[124] The following sources, among others, help identify possible candidates for inclusion in the benchmark group and provide the general background information in Table 3-13: (1) Table of six companies in the e-signature business, *www.g2crowd.com/categories/e-signature*; (2) The web site *www.crunchbase.com* for general information on many private companies; (3) The seventeen-page report by Craig Le Clair of Forrester Research, entitled, "E-Signatures, Q2 2013", available at *https://274a0e7125acf05720ef-7801faf96de03497e5e-0b3dfa5691096.ssl.cf2.rackcdn.com/ForresterWaveeSignature.pdf*; and (4) The membership listing of the Electronic Signature & Records Association, available at *http://www.esignrecords.org/?page=ESRAmembers*, although some of these companies provide supporting services rather than digital or electronic signatures. All of these sources were last reviewed by me on November 15, 2014.

[125] In today's Internet world, the accumulation of a list of possible candidates is usually not difficult. The problem, however, is to winnow out the irrelevant and distracting in order to produce a high-quality list. Here, for example, there are 29 companies listed as members of the Electronic Signature & Records Association, but clearly some of these are not solution providers, and a selection must be made. In creating the list of competitors in Table 3-13, I picked the companies that appeared to me to be the most relevant. However, I do not work in this business. An entity in the business, such as Silanis Technology, would likely create a different and probably superior list of competitors for comparison of patent investment.

The goal of the example presented here is not to identify the specific strengths or weaknesses of Silanis, but rather to demonstrate how a private company, active in a field with many other private companies, might plan its patent investments in comparison to other companies in the industry. This example of Silanis Technology is much different from the first example of Competitive Budgeting, which was the firewall industry, because the firewall industry is almost all public companies whereas the electronic signature industry is almost all private companies (or in one case a division of a public company where business-specific information is difficult to obtain).

Table 3-13: Members of the Electronic Signature Industry

Company	Status	Available Information
1. AlphaTrust	Private company.	Founded 1999.
2. Ascertia	Private company.	Founded 2001. 30 employees. Based in the UK.
3. AssureSign	Private company.	Founded 2008. 60 employees.
4. DocuSign	Private company.	Founded 2003. $210M in total funding to date. Rumored to have valuation of $1.6B at March, 2014. Employee growth from 100 in 2012 to 700 at 03/2014. Rumored to have $40M in sales 2012, $110M-$120M in 2014.
5. EchoSign (acquired by Adobe)	Private company (acquired by public company Adobe in 2011).	Founded 2005. $9M in funding before purchased by Adobe in 2011. Adobe announced expected annual sales in 2012 of at least $50M, and expected annual sales in 2014 of at least $160M.
6. eSettlement Solutions	Private company.	Founded 2008. Niche player — only real estate transactions, and focused on Maryland/District of Columbia/ Virginia.
7. RightSignature	Private company.	Founded 2009. No apparent outside funding.
8. RPost	Private company.	Founded 2000. $2.9M in funding. Involved in at least 20 lawsuits for patent infringement or declaratory judgment of non-infringement.
9. Sertifi	Private company.	Founded 2005. 11 employees. Annual revenue estimated at $5M-$10M.
10. Signiant	Private company.	Founded 2000. 75 employees. $10M in funding.
11. SIGNiX	Private company.	Founded 2002. $2.8M in funding. Subsidiary of ProNVest, Inc., a financial advisory firm apparently unrelated to digital commerce or electronic signatures.

Company	Status	Available Information
12. Silanis Technology	Private company.	Founded 1992. Was public on AIM UK. Went private in June, 2013. H1 2012 revenues of $3.3M and R&D of $2.8M, compared to H1 2011 $7.3M revenue and $1.9M R&D.[126] 100 employees.

Unlike Check Point's firewall industry in which all of the main competitors were public companies, here all of the companies are private. It is true that EchoSign is now part of the public company of Adobe Systems, which does make a difference as is discussed below, but that fact does not help identify information specifically for the electronic signature industry. Silanis' former status on the AIM London Stock Exchange provides only a limited amount of financial information. To determine the parameters of the industry and the appropriate group of companies for patent benchmarks is very challenging.

There are two separate problems.

First, it is not clear which companies are really within the industry. Should eSettlement Solutions appear on this list at all? RPost Holdings provides "secure email", of which digital signatures appear to be a small part — should it appear on this list? There are many other companies that also provide encryption or other data security products or services. They are not on the list above, but should they be? Although the boundaries of this business are a bit blurred, and almost all

---

126 Financial information for Silanis covering the period January 1, 2012 — June 30, 2012, from a press of September 5, 2012, entitled, "Silanis Intl SNS Interim Results", available at *http://www.bloomberg.com/bb/newsarchive/aOmgOCN6MNdg.html* (last viewed on November 15, 2014).

the main participants are private companies, it is likely that Silanis Technology and other players in the industry have a clear understanding of who the major competitors are. For outsiders trying to evaluate this industry, identifying the players is a serious problem, but perhaps not such a difficulty for companies in the field.

Second, even if it were possible to identify the participants in the industry, how could they be reviewed to determine benchmarks for (R&D/revenue), (patent investment/revenues), and (patent investment/R&D)? Financial information for these private companies is simply not public. Pieces of data, such as those listed above for number of employees or level of investment, might help solve the first problem — identity of participants in the industry — but they cannot help create financial benchmarks for patent investment.

In these circumstances, there is no alternative but to look directly at the patent information of the involved parties to see if a benchmark can be created. Patent information for issued patents and published applications is always available, irrespective of the status of the company as large or small, public or private.[127]

---

[127] To the best of my knowledge, every issued patent, in every country, must be disclosed and publicly available. However, this is not true of ownership interest in patents. For ownership interest, the availability of public information about patents depends on two assumptions:

First, that the patent has been formally assigned to the owner. In some countries, assignments of patents must be recorded with the patent office. In other countries, assignment is not required, but enforcement by an assignee can occur only if the assignment is first recorded. In the United States, recordation of assignment is always voluntary, which means, in essence, that if an assignment has not been recorded, the assignment is not of public record and could not be used in the way suggested here to create a patenting benchmark. It is my experience that corporations overwhelmingly demand

Step 2 — Determine the patent results and implied investments of these competitors

In a case where there is little public information about companies in the industry, patent benchmarks must be based almost exclusively on patent information rather than on a combination of patent and financial information. For the portfolios of the various benchmarking candidates, I have reviewed the U.S. patents, the U.S. patent applications, the European patent items, the German patent items, the Japanese patent items, and the PCT international applications.[128] I have also reviewed patent litigation activities of the various companies. Table 3-14 shows the results of these reviews:

---

recordation of patent assignments, but I am not aware of any study to that effect.

Second, that an assignment is recorded, and that the party listed as the "assignee" is the true party in interest. This is not always the case. Corporations sometimes create straw entities to hold patent interests, and in this way to hide the true ownership. There are various reasons for this. For example, a company may not want to disclose its interest in particular patents in order to hide its strategy, or to prevent a run up in the prices of specific patents. In my experience, operating companies, such as those listed here, do not usually hide their identity as the owner in interest, but again, I have no study to confirm this.

Nevertheless, these two assumptions are reasonable because, in my estimate, the great majority of operating companies record assignments, and do so by listing the true owners in interest. That is not true of pending applications, however. In most of the world, applications are disclosed only 18 months after their priority date, and in the United States an option exists to prevent any disclosure of the application prior to its issuance as a patent. In general, therefore, for creating patent benchmarks, the use of published patents and patent ownership by operating companies provides excellent information, and the use of published applications and ownership of applications provides reasonable but imperfect information.

128 These patent items were reviewed using the web site *www.freepatent-sonline.com*.

Table 3-14: Patent Portfolios in the Electronic Signature Industry

Company	Patent Portfolio	Comment(s)
1. AlphaTrust	0 patent items.	
2. Ascertia	0 patent items.	
3. AssureSign	1 U.S. patent, number US 8,612,763. Estimated investment = $30,000.	Long and complicated independent claims which probably would not catch any possible infringer.
4. DocuSign	7 U.S. patents; 16 U.S. applications; 7 European patent items, and 18 PCT international applications = 48 patent items. Estimated investment = $825,000.	(1) Mixed quality: 2 patents with good claims, 5 patents with moderate to weak claims. Some patents have heavy forward citations (but not the ones with the best claims). (2) The portfolio is heavily oriented toward the United States. (3) 3 of 7 patents acquired from other parties. (4) DocuSign has filed patent infringement lawsuits against Health Applications, RPost, Sertifi, and Yozen.

Company	Patent Portfolio	Comment(s)
5. EchoSign (acquired by Adobe)	EchoSign: 6 U.S. patents (including 3 assigned to Adobe); 1 U.S. applications (1 assigned to Adobe) = 7 patent items. Estimated investment = $195,000. — — — — — — — Adobe at 6/30/2014: 2,274 U.S. patents; 1,561 U.S. applications; 377 European patent items; 127 German patent items + 128 Japanese patent items; 233 PCT international applications = 4,700 patent items. Estimated investment = $105M.	EchoSign's portfolio (including the four items assigned to Adobe Systems) has patents which range from moderate to very good. For its size, it is relatively high-quality. However, it is entirely U.S., and it is very small. By itself, this portfolio could not be used aggressively to generate revenues or market share. Also, EchoSign's portfolio is inadequate for defense, due to the portfolio's small size and the fact that a market leader with $100M+ in sales is an attractive target for both competitors and patent monetizers. However, the portfolio is backed by the resources of Adobe Systems — any lawsuit could be fully contested, and Adobe could buy any patents required to counter-sue another company. In sum, despite its small size and lack of non-U.S. items, this portfolio, together with the backing of Adobe, is probably adequate for defensive purposes.
6. eSettlement Solutions	0 patent items.	
7. Right Signature	3 U.S. applications; 2 EP applications; 2 PCT international applications = 7 patent items. Estimated investment = $105,000.	All patent items filed on October 20, 2010. No issued patents, so no right to sue. The published applications have very long and complicated independent claims which probably would not catch any possible infringer.

Company	Patent Portfolio	Comment(s)
8. RPost	20 U.S. patents; 25 U.S. applications; 6 European patent items; 2 German patent items; 2 Japanese patent items; 4 PCT international applications = 59 patent items. National filings include 2 in Australia, 7 in Asia (China, India, Korea); 21 in Europe (Austria, Belgium, Switzerland, Denmark, France, Ireland, Italy, Luxembourg, Netherlands, Spain, UK), 2 North American (Canada, Mexico) = 32 patent items. Total patent items = 59 + 32 = 91. Estimated investment = $1.665M.	(1) In relation to the rest of the industry, a relatively large portfolio, with geographic coverage on four continents. (2) Patent strength is very mixed. Some of the patents appear, on their face, to be relatively strong, but some are moderate or weak. (3) Patents are focused very heavily on all aspects of email, including electronic signatures as they relate to email. (4) Over the past five years, RPost has been engaged in at least 27 patent lawsuits — suing at least twenty-seven companies in twenty-two lawsuits, being sued in at least four lawsuits for declaratory judgment of non-infringement, and being a defendant in at least one patent lawsuit.* The costs of pursuing such litigation easily exceed the total cost of building RPost's patent portfolio, although litigation costs may be reduced by contingency arrangements with attorneys, and offset by licensing revenue RPost expects to gain.
9. Sertifi	0 patent items.	
10. Signiant	4 U.S. patents; 1 U.S. application = 5 patent items. Estimated investment = $135,000.	Long and complicated independent claims which probably would not catch any possible infringer.
11. SIGNiX	2 U.S. patents; 1 U.S. application = 3 patent items. Estimated investment = $75,000.	Long and complicated independent claims which probably would not catch any possible infringer.

Company	Patent Portfolio	Comment(s)
12. Silanis Technology	6 U.S. patents; 3 U.S. applications; 11 European Patent items; 5 German patent items; 10 PCT international applications, 3 Canadian patents; 12 Canadian applications = 50 patent items. Estimated investment = $1.04M.	The earliest patent, US 5,606,609, very strong, acquired from Scientific-Atlanta in 2000, but expired in September, 2000 (so may be used to obtain damages, but may not be used to obtain an injunction against any infringer). The other patents are of moderate quality, all focused on verifying and transferring documents.

[*: Most of RPost's lawsuits are reported in the RPost web site, at *http:// www.rpost.com/about-rpost/intellectual-property/infringement-actions* (last viewed on November 15, 2014). Other lawsuits are discoverable by a general search using the terms "RPost" and "patent infringement". Over the period 2009–2014, RPost has been involved in patent litigation against Adobe Systems, AOL, Canada Post Corporation, Comprova, Constant Contact, DocuSign, EchoSign, Epsilon Data Management, ExacTarget, Experian, Farmers Insurance, Globalpex, GoDaddy.com, Goodmail, Infogroup, Innovapost, j2 Global, Pointofmail.com, Privasphere, ReadNotify, Responsys, RightSignature, StrongMail Systems, Swiss Post, Symantec, Trend Micro, Trustifi, Vocus, Yahoo!, and Zix Corporation. There may be others as well, but these are the ones I can identify. Some of these lawsuits have settled, some are ongoing as of November, 2014. RPost is engaged in additional litigation alleging trademark infringement and false advertising under the Lanham Act.]

Can patent benchmarks be created from the information in Table 3-14, despite the absence of any reliable financial information? Note first that that the 12 companies fall into three natural groups.

- Group 1 includes companies with no patents or patent applications. These companies, AlphaTrust, Ascertia, eSettlement Solutions, and Sertifi, are simply irrelevant for purposes of patent benchmarking.

- Group 2 includes companies with portfolios that are both small and lacking in the kind of "breakthrough patents" that could either create great value or pose a threat to competitors. These companies, AssureSign, RightSignature, Signiant, and SIGNiX, have patents or applications that are few in number and for the most part irrelevant.
- Group 3 includes companies with significant patent portfolios. Each of these companies, DocuSign, EchoSign, RPost, and Silanis, is unique and must be considered individually.

DocuSign is one of the leaders in the product market, with total investment of over $200M, a reputed market value of $1.6 Billion, and sales for 2014 estimated to be over $100M. It has a patent portfolio of about 48 items, at a total investment of a bit less than $1M by my estimate. Almost 50% of its portfolio is in the United States, and it is noteworthy that in 2013 it acquired 3 of its 7 U.S. patents, in fact the 3 of its patents with the earliest priority dates. The company is not particularly litigious, but it has sued on occasion. DocuSign was involved in two patent infringement suits against RPost — in one of these suits, DocuSign was the defendant, and in the other it was the plaintiff. The overwhelming impression is that DocuSign wishes to concentrate on the product side, and invested in patents, both in the portfolio and in lawsuits, as a support for its product strategy. The corporate strategy is market dominance, and the patent strategy is a defensive portfolio to prevent disruption of the corporate strategy.

EchoSign is also a product leader, with sales for 2014 estimated to be over $150M. Its patent portfolio appears to be relatively high-quality, but it is simply too small to make a difference in this industry. Either for aggressive or defensive purposes, EchoSign's patent portfolio was simply inadequate for a product leader. This changed in 2011, when Adobe bought EchoSign. Not only does EchoSign have its 7 U.S. patent items, at a total investment of about $200,000, but it also has the backing of Adobe — a public company with over $4B in annual sales, and a patent portfolio of about 4,700 items, including over 3,800 United States patents items. EchoSign is now in an outstanding defensive position. The EchoSign business has a few reasonably good patents, access to many more, ability to purchase additional patents, and the resources required to defend against a lawsuit. Although Adobe and EchoSign have also been sued by RPost, patent litigation should not be an overwhelming concern for EchoSign. When a company becomes a product leader but a patent follower, the company has reached a decision point. One option is to sell the company for a good price to a larger concern that can take on the weight of patents and patent litigation. I have no knowledge of Adobe's motivation to buy EchoSign, nor do I know why EchoSign agreed to be sold, but two of the effects are that Adobe acquired a broader product line[129]

---

[129]　In its Annual 2011 10-K Report, Adobe stated, at p.11:

"Another aspect of our document services strategy is targeting the market of electronic signatures used to sign contracts. In fiscal 2011 we acquired EchoSign, a provider of on-demand, web-based, electronic signature solutions. Utilizing a simplistic model that doesn't require scanning software, signature pads or digital certificates, EchoSign is used to sign nearly one million contracts per month. We intend to integrate EchoSign's solution into our offerings, and it will be a cornerstone for how we grow our document services, cloud-based revenue in fiscal 2012. In addition, by making the cloud-based EchoSign capabilities available to millions of Adobe Reader users, we believe we can substantially grow the awareness of our solution in the broader contract delivery and

and EchoSign removed any significant concern about patent litigation.

For purposes of patent benchmarking, EchoSign is not particularly helpful. The company had an inadequate portfolio, and redressed the problem not by patent investment, but rather by alliance with a larger entity. If Silanis chooses to sell itself to another company in the industry, EchoSign would be a good model, but otherwise, EchoSign's portfolio is not a good signal to Silanis.

RPost presents an entirely different picture than that of either DocuSign or EchoSign. It is similar to DocuSign in that it has invested heavily in patents. I estimate about $1.665M invested in its patent portfolio, resulting in about 91 patent items, about half of which are in the United States, and the rest spread throughout Asia, Australia, Canada, Europe, and Mexico. However, RPost is radically different from DocuSign in that RPost's entire existence appears to be centered on its patents rather than its products. The company's first patent infringement lawsuit seems to be have been initiated in September, 2009, and since that time it has filed more than twenty lawsuits alleging patent infringement, trademark infringement, and false advertising. I find no evidence of product sales or any evidence of an emphasis on products.[130]

---

signing market particularly where paper and overnight express mailing continues to be used."

Clearly a broad product line was the main reason for Adobe's purchase of EchoSign. Adobe probably was not attracted by EchoSign's small patent portfolio, and in fact, the absence of a significant portfolio might have lowered the price Adobe paid.

[130] I cannot and do not say that no such evidence exists for RPost product sales, only that I cannot find any. It is clear that RPost has at least some products. Forrester Research, in its review entitled, "E-Signatures, April, 2013",

On the other hand, RPost's emphasis, at least over the past few years, appears to be patent licensing rather than product sales. In an Internet interview published on September 26, 2011, Mr. Zafir Khan, the CEO of RPost, was asked, "What is the competitive landscape for this company?", and he answered,

> "We have 35 patents that have been granted in 21 countries. Our patents are early dated, and we believe they give us the broad claim in the market we focus on, **legal proof for email**, that extends into different business- or email-related transactions involving electronic signatures and encryption. Certainly there are competitors trying to enter the market today, and there are competitors on the fringes of the market as well." (Boldface emphasis in the original)[131]

There is not, in this definition of "competitive landscape", any discussion of specific technologies, specific products, market niches, or similar aspects of what is typically considered to be corporate strategy or "competitive landscape". The whole emphasis in this quote, and in the rest of the interview, is on obtaining compensation for the company's early R&D efforts and innovations. This approach is neither product-oriented nor jointly product & patent oriented. RPost, through this statement and particularly through its actions over the past five years, appears to be very heavily patent-oriented. Perhaps this is the reason it has built a portfolio of 91 items, much larger than either of its nearest competitors, DocuSign

discusses the RPost E-Signature Services at pp.8, 11, and 13, but this product was released in 2002, and no sales data are provided in the Forrester review.

[131] "How to Build a Strong IP Portfolio: rPost CEO Zafar Khan (Part 5)", interview by Sramana Mitra, One Million by One Million Blog, available at *http://www.sramanamitra.com/2011/09/26/how-to-build-a-strong-ip-portfolio-rpost-ceo-zafar-khan-part-5/* (last viewed on November 15, 2014).

(48 items) and Silanis (50 items). Its advantage in U.S. patent items is even greater — 45 U.S. items for RPost versus 23 for DocuSign and 9 for Silanis.

Silanis is different from the other three major patent-holders in this industry. Silanis appears to have at least some outstanding products. In the Forrester Research Report for Q2, 2013, at p.11, the Silanis products e-Sign Enterprise, e-SignLive, and e-Sign Desktop, are ranked #1 for e-signature capture, #2 for current features (second only to the DocuSign's "Enterprise Edition"), tied for #1 with DocuSign for strategy, and #2 for market presence (second only to DocuSign). According to this review, again at p.11, Silanis' main problem seems to be not a product deficiency, but rather an absence of "global support". If this problem had been addressed, then Silanis, according to the information presented by Forrester Research, would have been #1 in current features and #1 overall.

However, despite apparent product excellence, it is not clear that Silanis is succeeding in the product market. Its last reported sales, $3.3M for the first half of 2012, are anemic in comparison to the expected $100M+ sales for DocuSign and EchoSign/Adobe in 2014. Silanis has reported 100 employees, a figure that apparently has not changed in several years, but this is not a figure commensurate with tens of millions of dollars in annual sales, certainly nothing to compete with the triple digit sales expected of DocuSign and EchoSign.[132] Or

---

[132] Silanis is profiled, together with many other Canadian companies, by the Canadian Advanced Technology Alliance, in a report entitled, "Canadian Advanced Security Industry — Industry Profile 2003", available at *http://www.cata.ca/files/PDF/pssf/rapport_canada.pdf* (last viewed on November 15, 2014). The report states, at p.150, that Silanis has 65 employees and annual revenues within the range of $5M — $25M. This was in 2003. However,

consider a comparison by investment. More than $200M has been invested in DocuSign, of which the most recent round is $85M in March, 2014.[133] EchoSign is now part of a public corporation with a $4B annual turnover. How could Silanis possibly match the resources that are now being poured by DocuSign and EchoSign into the electronic signature business?

On the patent front, Silanis has had a reasonably sized portfolio of 50 items. In the United States, the portfolio is a bit small, at 6 patents and 3 applications. The true concern, however, is Silanis' recent drop in patent quality. Silanis has 6 U.S. patents, of which 5 are moderately strong, in some

---

according to another report of the Canadian government, the number of employees at Silanis as of April 9, 2013, was 35. *http://www.ic.gc.ca/app/ ccc/srch/nvgt.do?lang=eng&prtl=1&sbPrtl=&estblmntNo=123456179276&p rofile=cmpltPrfl&profileId=2056&app=sold* (last viewed on November 15, 2014). In other words, it would appear that the number of Silanis employees has shrunk by almost 50% in the decade 2003–2013. Silanis itself, however, states that it a "growing team of nearly 100 employees..." Silanis Technology web site, *https://www.silanis.com/about-us/profile-history* (last viewed on November 15, 2014). Totals of 65 employees in 2003, 35 in 2013, and almost 100 in late 2014, demonstrate the problem — using number of employees as a proxy for sales is inherently unreliable. However even if we assume that the number of employees has risen from 65 in 2003 to 100 in 2014, the growth in employees has been quite moderate for a market that is booming. If 65 employees generated $5M — $25M in 2003, then analogously "almost 100" employees in 2014 might generate annual sales in the range of $8M — $38M. This range does not seem unreasonable, especially the upper part of the range which suggests perhaps as much $400,000 sales per employee per year. The problem, however, is that from a competitive point of view, even the upper range of $38M is dwarfed by the expected sales of both DocuSign and EchoSign/Adobe.

133 "DocuSign gets $85 million more in investments", by Coral Garnick, The Seattle Times, March 4, 2014, available at *http://seattletimes.com/html/ businesstechnology/2023044164_docusignfundingxml.html* (last viewed on November 15, 2014).

cases perhaps a bit more than that. Silanis' sixth U.S. patent, US 5,606,609, entitled, "Electronic Document Verification System and Method", is an outstanding patent, probably the single best patent in this industry. However, on September 19, 2014, this patent expired solely due to the passage of time. Silanis may still seek patent damages for infringement of this outstanding patent, but Silanis cannot obtain an injunction preventing infringement. The deterrence value of this patent has dropped dramatically, and with it, the strength of Silanis' entire U.S. patent portfolio has also fallen. Silanis has not in the past used its patents for offense. Rather, the portfolio has been used for deterrence. RPost has sued many players in the industry, including DocuSign, EchoSign, Adobe, and RightSignature, but to the best of my knowledge RPost has not sued Silanis.

The last piece missing from this review of the portfolios of DocuSign, EchoSign, RPost, and Silanis, is the time line for these portfolios. Are these companies increasing their patent investments, decreasing them, or maintaining past levels?

For EchoSign, the answer is clear. Its entire portfolio consists of 6 issued U.S. patents and 1 pending U.S. application. Three patents were issued in 2011, the application was published in 2012, and thee patents were issued in 2013. Very little has been invested in patents, and all of it within the past few years. It is not clear that anything has been invested in 2014.

For Silanis, the story is also quite simple. Of a total of 50 identifiable patent items, the company obtained 2 European patents and 1 German patent in 2009, 2 Canadian patents in 2010, 1 U.S. patent in 2012, and nothing in 2011, 2013, or 2014. In other words, within the five-and-a-half years of 2009 to mid-2014, the company obtained 6 patent items, or about 12%

of its entire portfolio. At the same time, the company's best U.S. patent US 5,606,609, expired in September, 2014. This is a picture of a company that is allowing its portfolio to degrade over time, simply by failing to invest. This could be part of a strategic decision, or could simply reflect a lack of available resources.

The stories of DocuSign and RPost are completely different. Both of these companies are investing significant resources in patents, although again for totally different purposes — DocuSign for defensive deterrence, RPost to generate revenues and possibly market share. Here is a review of DocuSign's recent patent results, starting with mid-2014 at the top and continuing with full year results for each of the years 2013 through 2009, respectively.

Table 3-15: DocuSign's Patent Results 2009 to Mid-2014

	US Patents	US Applications	European Patent Items	PCT International Applications	TOTAL THIS YEAR	% of Portfolio This Year	Cumulative Percentage of Portfolio
2014	1	1	3	0	5	10%	10%
2013	3	6	2	9	20	42%	52%
2012	1	0	2	0	3	6%	58%
2011	0	1	0	4	5	10%	69%
2010	0	1	0	3	4	8%	77%
2009	0	2	0	2	4	8%	85%
2009–2014	5	11	7	18	41	85%	
Total in Portfolio	7	16	7	18	48		
% of This Category	71%	69%	100%	100%	85%		

DocuSign has created 85% of its portfolio in the past 5.5 years. In the past eighteen months, from January, 2013, through mid-July, 2014, DocuSign has created 52% of its entire patent portfolio, including most of its U.S. patents and half of its PCT international applications. This is a company that has dramatically increased its investment in patents. Is this increase related to RPost's lawsuit against DocuSign in June, 2011? Does it reflect a strategic decision by DocuSign to protect its market share as it fights for the #1 position? Different motivations may be inferred, but these facts speak loudly.

By comparison, we can compare RPost's patent achievements in the period 2009–2014, coinciding with the first patent infringement lawsuit filed by RPost in September, 2009, and continuing through its most recent activity.

Table 3-16: RPost's Patent Results 2009 to Mid-2014*

	US Patents	US Apps.	European Patent Items	German Patent Items	Japanese Patent Items	PCT Internat'l Apps.	TOTAL THIS YEAR	% of Portfolio This Year	Cumulative Percentage of Portfolio
2014	2	3	0	0	0	0	5	8%	8%
2013	5	4	0	0	0	0	9	15%	24%
2012	4	3	1	0	1	0	9	15%	39%
2011	3	4	0	0	0	0	7	12%	51%
2010	3	3	1	0	0	0	7	12%	63%
2009**	2	1	0	0	1	1	5	8%	71%
2009– 2014	19	18	2	0	2	1	42	71%	
Total in Portfolio	20	25	6	2	2	4	59		
% of This Category	95%	72%	33%	0%	100%	25%	71%		

[*: This Table reflects RPost's activity only in these categories, that is, the U.S., Europe, Germany, Japan, and PCT. These categories represent 59 patent items in total, which is 65% of RPost's entire portfolio. RPost has also filed thirty-two national counter-parts in seventeen different countries in Asia, Australia, Europe, and North America, but these are not included in the review above.]

[**: The two U.S. patents in 2009 were acquired from another party in that year. They were both filed and issued much earlier, but became relevant for RPost only upon acquisition.]

Like DocuSign, RPost has invested heavily in patents, generating 71% of its entire portfolio in the period 2009–2014. Like DocuSign, RPost has invested heavily in U.S. patents, creating almost its entire U.S. portfolio within this time frame, and creating more than 50% of its U.S. patents in the last three years alone. It is worth noting that although RPost was founded in 2000, it obtained its first patent in 2007, acquired its next two patents from an outside party on August 6, 2009, and initiated the first of its patent infringement lawsuits on September 14, 2009. The growth in RPost's patent portfolio has gone hand in hand with the growth of RPost's litigation efforts. If history be a judge, RPost's heavy and continuing investments in U.S. patents suggest that RPost's litigation efforts are likely to continue into the future. RPost's apparent corporate strategy is to monetize its R&D achievements through a licensing & litigation program.

All of the foregoing information about the patent portfolios of DocuSign, EchoSign, RPost, and Silanis, may be summarized in a table, and with this we will complete Step 2 in Silanis' process of benchmarking.

Table 3-17: Competitors in the Electronic Signature Industry

	Size of Portfolio (items)	Implied Investment in Portfolio	Geographic Focus	Current Activities (2009–2014)	Apparent Patent Strategy
DocuSign	48	$825,000	US-48%, Europe-15% Int'l Apps-37%	Heavy investment, especially U.S.	Defensive
EchoSign	7	$195,000	US — 100%	Very light; U.S. oriented	Defensive
RPost	91	$1,665,000	US-49%, Europe-32%, Asian-10%, Other-9%	Heavy investment, especially U.S.	Aggressive
Silanis	50	$1,035,000	US-18%, Europe-32%, Int'l Apps-20%, Canada-30%	Almost no activity	Unclear

Step 3 — Create benchmarks for investment and/or results:

On the basis of the information presented in Step 2, what should be a competitive benchmark for Silanis' future investments in its patent portfolio? This depends on the patent strategy to be selected, but let us review five options.

First, the company may choose to match the investments of its main competitors, particularly those of DocuSign and RPost. DocuSign obtained 3 patent items in 2012, 20 in 2013 (almost half of which were PCT international applications), and 5 in the first half of 2014 with an expected 10 for the year. In other words, about 33 in the period 2012–2014, or 11 patent items per year. RPost has obtained 9 patent items in 2012, 9 in 2013, and 5 in the first half of 2014 with an expected 10 for the year. In other words, about 28 in the period 2012–2014, or 9–10 patent items per year.

Simply to match DocuSign and RPost, Silanis would need to obtain about 10 patent items per year, and would need to invest about $200,000–$250,000/year in patents.

What about geography? DocuSign is heavily oriented toward the U.S., but it also continues to invest in European patents. RPost's investments appear to be even more heavily oriented toward the U.S. (although it may be continuing with national stage filings in Europe). At the same time, Silanis' overall portfolio is weak in the U.S., with only 9 U.S. items versus 23 for DocuSign and 45 from RPost. If Silanis does choose to increase its patent investment, it must file at least a significant portion of its filings in the U.S. In light of the expiration of Silanis' star patent, US 5,606,609, Silanis may wish to buy an outstanding patent to replace the expired star, but this might require a significant investment far beyond Silanis' total annual budget for patents.

A second possible strategy is for Silanis to catch up to the current investment rate of DocuSign and RPost, and also to make up for the ground lost over the past three years. This, however, would require obtaining up to 20 patent items per year over 3 years, at an annual investment within the range of $400,000-$500,000 per year. In other words, Silanis would need to match its total investment to date in patents, over the three year period 2014–2016. This is probably unrealistic, but it is an option.

A third possible strategy is go way beyond matching or even catch up. Rather, the company can become a monetizer of its own technology, similarly to what RPost has done. Silanis' products have been rated highly by Forrester Research, and presumably the products are based on superior technology. Since Silanis has already demonstrated in expertise in technology development, perhaps it should invest heavily in technology that it can later monetize. This would require very significant investment, and also a change in the mindset of Silanis executives from product-orientation to patent-orientation. The strategy may not be realistic, but it is an option.

A fourth possible strategy is to do nothing — that is, continue to pay renewal fees to maintain the current portfolio, but do not invest in new patents. To make a conscious decision not to invest is indeed a strategy, it appears to be what Silanis has been doing in recent years, and it would require only that Silanis continue its current approach. The benchmarking information is then not of direct use, but the information nevertheless gives Silanis a clear picture of what the main competitors are doing now and what they are likely to do at least in the near future.

A fifth possible strategy is for the company to simply cease being independent, and to sell the company at the best price possible. In other words, to adopt the same approach selected by EchoSign in 2011 when it sold itself to Adobe Systems. Silanis has good products, apparently good technology, and a reasonable patent portfolio — sale of the company at a good price may be a viable option. If this is the strategy, then probably no further investment should be made in patents, and the information in Step 2 will not be of direct relevance to Silanis.

If sale of the company is planned, an alternative strategy would be to maximize potential patent protection through new applications, but at the lowest possible cost. Probably the best approach would be to file one jumbo application, including all inventions for which Silanis has not yet sought patent protection. The jumbo application would be a Provisional Patent Application, in which the inventions are described but the filing costs are very low and there are few formalities for preparation or filing. If the company is slated for sale within a year, a jumbo Provisional Patent Application including all of the company's not yet patented inventions may be an excellent strategy to maximize the company's value during the critical period during which potential buyers are performing due diligence.

These possible strategies for Silanis Technology may be summarized in a table.

Table 3-18: Possible Patent Strategies for Silanis Technology at Mid-2014

Strategic Options	Investment Requirement	Likelihood of Selection
1. Match the investments of DocuSign and RPost.	$200,000/year	Possible (if Silanis has the resources).
2. Match DocuSign and RPost, plus make up lost ground.	$400,000/year	Unlikely (given the recent record).
3. Become a monetizer of technology. Grow both R&D and the patent portfolio.	Much more than $400,000/year.	Very unlikely.
4. Only maintain the current portfolio, but do not add to it.	Probably $50,000/ year, perhaps less.	High possibility.
5a. Sell the company, with its products, technology, and patents, for the best price. No further investment in patents.	Again $50,000/year or less to maintain the portfolio.	Unknown (depends on corporate strategy).
5b. Sell the company, but first file a jumbo PPA including all of the company's not yet patented inventions.	The cost set forth in 5a above, plus a few thousand dollars to prepare a jumbo PPA.	Unknown (depends on corporate strategy)

The main competitors in the electronic signature industry are private companies that do not publish financial information. Therefore, benchmark ratios based on sales, R&D, and patent activity, cannot be determined. However, issued patents are always published, and information for pending applications is usually available. On the basis of only patent information (no financial information), benchmarks for investment and patent results can be selected by Silanis, but the selection depends on the corporate strategy Silanis chooses to pursue.

Step 4 — Plan the company's patent investments, then desired results (Top Down), or plan the company's desired results, then the required investments (Bottom Up):

This book began with a statement that effective patent strategy must depend upon and further the corporate strategy of the company. Once a corporate strategy is selected, patent benchmarking can be performed, the patent strategy may be selected, and a specific patent plan may be created with Top Down or Bottom Up budgeting. The general process was explained already in Example 1 — Check Point.

In this Example 2, the main question is, "What should be Silanis' corporate and patent strategies?" Let us review the strategies of the main competitors.

Table 3-19: Corporate and Patent Strategies in the Electronic Signature Industry

Company	Apparent Corporate Strategy	Apparent Patent Strategy
DocuSign	Dominate the product market.	Strong defensive portfolio.
EchoSign	Dominate the product market.	Moderate defensive portfolio, but backed up by a large public company.
RPost	Monetize early technology.	Strong aggressive portfolio; initiate licensing & litigation program.
Silanis	Not clear.	Not clear.

Silanis' growth in personnel appears to have been very gradual over the last decade, despite a rapidly growing market. The last published financial report presents very weak sales. Silanis' products and technology appear to be outstanding, but where does the company go from here? How can the company match the resources of one competitor, DocuSign, that received recently an $85M investment, or the resources of another company, EchoSign, that is now a division of a $4B public company? The patent strategy supports the corporate strategy, and not vice versa. Once the fundamental questions of corporate strategy are answered, a supporting patent strategy may be formulated, but not before.

b. Summary of Competitive Budgeting

With have looked at two very difficult industries in order to emphasize that Competitive Budgeting can be performed even in different circumstances. In both examples, the four steps are executed: (1) Selecting a relevant group of competitors; (2) Determining patent results and implied investments for these competitors; (3) Creating benchmarks for the company's patent investments and/or patent results; and (4) Planning the company's patent investments and/or results. In the relatively public firewall industry, information is readily available, and specific benchmarks may be determined. In the relatively private electronic signature industry, complete and updated financial information about competitors is almost impossible to obtain, but patent information is still available, and inferences may be drawn about the overall patent investments and geographic patent investments of these competitors. In both cases, a Competitive Budget can be generated.

4. Hybrid Budgeting: Balancing Costs, Results, and Competitors

As explained in the Introduction to Chapter 3, the use

of any of Top Down, Bottom Up, or Competitive Budgeting methods is very uncommon in their pure forms. Rather, almost all companies use some kind of hybrid approach, perhaps with a particular emphasis on one of the three aspects of cost (Top Down), patent results (Bottom Up) or competitive position (Competitive Budgeting.)

It is practically certain that the costs (read "planned investments") will be an important factor, so Top Down budgeting is likely to play a role in almost all budgeting schemes. Most companies, however, plan also for the results they wish to achieve, at least according to flexible targets, so Bottom Up is also frequently employed. In my experience, the Competitive Budgeting approach is much less common, and is employed more by companies interested in and sophisticated about patenting, rather than by the average corporation.

Of all possible hybrid combinations, probably the most commonly used is Top Down cost budgeting together with Bottom Up results budgeting. Competitive Budgeting may or not be added. If Competitive Budgeting is added, the goal may be either to match competitors (presumably to achieve an acceptable defensive position) or to build a superior portfolio (potentially to generate value either by obtaining licensing revenue or by driving competitors away from a particular market).

Conclusion to Chapter 3

The process of budgeting for an excellent patent portfolio is not rigid. Any of three basic methods can be used by companies. These three methods are Top Down budgeting, Bottom Up budgeting, and Competitive Budgeting. In addition, Hybrid Budgeting may be used, which is a combination of two or all three of the other methods. Table 3-20 summarizes and compares these four methods.

Table 3-20: Methods to Budget Patent Activity in a Company

	What is budgeted?	Main criteria for budgeting
1. Top Down Budgeting	Cost/Investment in patents	Available resources or investment to a general benchmark (typically patent investment/ R&D or patent investment/ revenue).
2. Bottom Up Budgeting	Patent items to obtain	Perceived need, based on both the company's R&D intensity and its chosen patent strategy.
3. Competitive Budgeting	Either cost or patent items to obtain	Either available resources or perceived need, specifically in comparison to what major competitors have done.
4. Hybrid Budgeting	Some combination of cost/investment, results, and competitive position	Depends upon which of the three other methods are used in the hybrid combination.

Each method is legitimate, and each method is actually employed by technology companies. Whichever of the methods is selected, a balance must be achieved between investments and expected results. This balance is achieved iteratively.

(1) There is a target, either in results (patents and applications) or in costs/investments.

(2) The opposite element is estimated (that is, targeted results will require an estimate of costs, or a targeted

level of investment will generate an estimated number of patents).

(3) The comparison will require at least one adjustment, and perhaps multiple adjustments, until acceptable levels of patent results and patent investments have been budgeted.

In all cases, the ultimate plan will include a balance between patent investments and patent items to be obtained. This balance is at the heart of the company's patent strategy. In all cases, the patent strategy must match and advance the corporate strategy. Therefore, in all cases, the corporate strategy must be determined first, and will set guiding parameters for the patent strategy.

Chapter 4

Summary

Chapter 4 summarizes key ideas presented in the preceding chapters. These key ideas include basic concepts of defining patent portfolios in Chapter 1, of creating excellent patent portfolios in Chapter 2, and of budgeting for patent investment in Chapter 3. The key ideas in Chapter 4 are presented in Question & Answer Format, grouped according to logical topics.

Topic 1: Basic Characteristics of an Excellent Patent Portfolio (Questions 1–10)

Topic 2: Managing the Patent Portfolio (Questions 11–14)

Topic 3: Budgeting for Patents (Questions 15–19)

Topic 4: Special Topics
a. Technology Inflection Points (Questions 20–22)
b. Patent Aggregation (Questions 23–27)
c. Patent Evaluation (Questions 28–30)

Topic 1: Basic Characteristics of an Excellent Patent Portfolio

Q1: What is a "patent portfolio"?

It is a group of patent items (meaning both issued patents and pending applications) that are owned or controlled by a single entity or person. There are two basic kinds of groups of patent items, one in which the patent items *do not* address the same general technical issue, and the other in which the patent items *do* address the same general technical issue. Portfolios with items unrelated to a common technical issue are only portfolios in the same that they are commonly owned or controlled. Thus, one can say, "IBM's patent portfolio", meaning tens of thousands of patent items on many unrelated subjects. This kind of portfolio, of unrelated items, is relevant when an entire company is being sold, or when all of the patents of a company are being sold, but otherwise a portfolio of unrelated items is not of much use.

This book is about the second kind of portfolios, that is, portfolios in which all of the patent items address a single technical issue. There may be different aspects of the same issue, but it is still the one issue. By its definition, the patents in one "Patent Family" will typically address a single technical issue, but a portfolio of related items may also include multiple patent families.

Q2: What are the differences between an individual patent and a patent portfolio?

Some people look on a portfolio as a kind of "super-patent", meaning a single patent but having many more claims that an individual patent. This view is correct in one sense, but also limited. A portfolio has two very significant advantages over a single patent. Every patent is judged by the validity of its claims, the scope of its claim coverage, and discoverability (also called "detectability") of infringement by outside parties. A single patent is *always* vulnerable to invalidation — either of the entire of patent, or of some or all of the patent's claims. In any patent litigation, a defendant will do everything it can to invalidate or render unenforceable the claims asserted by the patentee, and these actions may succeed. However, a defendant's chance to invalidate all of the claims in a large group of patents is much weaker — one, or two, or a few patents may always survive. Thus, a portfolio of patents is much more resilient than a single patent, no matter how good the patent may be. Second, the claims of a single patent will have a certain scope of claim coverage, but the claims of multiple patents related to the same technical issue are almost certain to have a greater scope of claim coverage than that of the single patent.

These two advantages, greater resilience against invalidity attacks, and greater scope of claim coverage, mean that in almost all cases a portfolio is superior, generally far superior, to a single patent.

Q3: How is a patent portfolio judged?
Six factors are considered:

(1) Fit with corporate strategy: If the portfolio does not contribute to the company's goals as determined by the corporate strategy, then the portfolio is misdirected.

(2) Coverage of key technologies and markets: The company determines its key technologies and markets, and requires that patents in the portfolio be directed to covering these technologies and markets. The portfolio may also have specific patent items directed at the products or technologies of specific competitors.

(3) Appropriate balance of quality and quantity in patent items.

(4) Appropriate geographic balance.

(5) Appropriate time balance.

(6) Special considerations for this portfolio: Strong or

weak market growth, the company's relative competitive position in the market, and the patent actions of competitors, are examples of "special considerations".

Q4: What kind of balance between quality and quantity would be expected in an excellent portfolio?

Table 4-1 below summarizes the expected balance between quality and quantity.

Table 4-1: Comparison of Quality and Quantity in Patents

Type of Patent	As Classified in Table 2-2 (wind energy)	As Discussed in this Book	Expected Impact on the Portfolio	Expected Percentage in the Portfolio
High-value	"High"	Breakthrough patents — — — — Seminal patents — — — — Very valuable patents	Creates most of the value in the portfolio	1% of the entire portfolio (varying from about 0.5% to about 2.0%)
Valuable	"Medium High"	Valuable patent	Creates most of the remaining value of the portfolio, but substantially less than 50% of the total value	10% of the entire portfolio (varying from about 7% to about 12%)
Low-value	"Medium" — — — "Low"	Supporting	Creates a minority of value, either by coverage of minor improvements ("Medium") or solely by adding to the bulk quantity of the portfolio	90% of the entire portfolio (varying from about 86% to about 92%)

In general, the great majority of value will come from the "high-value patents", which have been called in this book, in descending order of value, "breakthrough patents" (representing Technology Inflection Points or other paradigm shifts), "seminal patents" (meeting certain criteria including, among others, heavy citation by others in the industry), and "very valuable patents" (which create much value but do not meet the criteria of the first two kinds of patents). These are typically about 1% of all the patents in a portfolio.

Most of the remaining value is created by the "Medium High" or "valuable" patents, comprising roughly 10% of the total patents in the portfolio.

The great bulk of patents, about 90%, are "supporting". The wind energy study distinguished between "Medium" patents, which seems to cover minor improvements, and "Low" patents which appear to have no relevance but which contribute to the overall bulk quantity of the portfolio. In the wind energy study, about 50%-70% of the patents were "Medium" (meaning value beyond mere quantity), and about 20%-40% were "Low" (meaning no contribution other than sheer bulk). I cannot judge the allocation between patents that cover minor improvements and those that make no contribution beyond body count, but I agree completely that "supporting" patents comprise about 90% of a typical excellent portfolio.

Q5: Is there a conflict between achieving quality of patents in a portfolio and quantity of patents in the portfolio?

There is indeed inherent tension between quality and quantity in the management of patent portfolios, although such tension is not necessarily irresolvable. Many companies, particularly large companies in established industries, tend to put an emphasis on quantity of patent items. Quality is also very important, but judgments will be made to a large degree based on quantity. Many companies, particularly small and startup companies in rapidly changing industries, will put an initial emphasis on quality, and only later will these companies bulk up on quantity (or not at all if the startup fails).

There are, however, companies that have resolved the tension by promoting, during the same time period, both quality and quantity of patents in the portfolio. Google and Apple, cited in Chapter 2 and particularly in Tables 2-5, 2-6 and 2-10, are currently in the midst of a very strong process of increasing quality and quantity simultaneously. If current trends continue, Google and Apple will be leaders in both patent quality and patent quantity by 2017.

Q6: Is there a conflict between building a portfolio in-house and buying patents from outside parties?

No, there is no such conflict. Building and buying are two methods of achieving the same goal, which is to obtain an excellent patent portfolio. There are advantages and disadvantages to each approach, as illustrated in Table 2-9. Generally, building is much cheaper and has greater flexibility to include or exclude various topics from the portfolio. Generally, buying is much quicker (since it takes effect immediately upon acquisition) and has greater certainty of outcome (since the issued patents and their prosecution histories are known at the time of purchase). Many companies build their own portfolios. Broadcom and Silanis Technology are examples in Chapter 2 of companies that supplemented their portfolios by buying valuable patents.

The two methods, building and buying, are not in conflict, but must be managed together to achieve the goal. Nevertheless, there are companies that have a feeling of "Not

Invented Here", meaning they have a bias in favor of their own inventions and a bias against buying patents developed by others. The NIH attitude has weakened in recent years, as we have witnessed strong patent purchases by many leading companies.

Q7: What is a "patent thicket"?

It is a particular kind of patent portfolio in which multiple aspects of the same general invention are covered. The intensity of a patent thicket creates very serious problems for competitors wishing to produce and sell products or services in the market covered by the portfolio. To invalidate all of the relevant claims is almost impossible, and to avoid the claim coverage of all aspects of the invention is also very difficult. An example of a patent thicket appears in Chapter 1, Example 3 — Fuji Photo Film.

A patent thicket exists in a particular country (based on patents issued in that country) and at a particular point in time (which is to say, the time at which the owner of the thicket enforces the patents against infringers). To create a thicket in multiple countries would require the patentee to file and prosecute patents in each country. To maintain the thicket over time would require the patentee to manage the time balance of the patent thicket.

Q8: What are the main considerations in determining whether a portfolio has geographic balance?

There are four major factors:

(1) Importance of the market: Discussed in Q9 below.
(2) Cost: Each country has its own fees for filing applications, for maintenance of pending applications (for which European countries often charge but

the U.S. does not), for issuance of patents, and for maintenance of issued patents. There are also costs for preparing applications in each country, even if a national application is based upon the filing in another country. Translation costs can be very expensive. In short, expected costs are a major consideration in the achievement of geographic balance.

(3) Enforceability of the patent: If a patent would not be enforced in a particular country, then there is no point in trying to obtain the patent in that country. This is relevant in two respects:

    a. There are some types of patents that would be enforced in some countries, but not in others. The enforcement of so-called "software patents" is a very controversial topic today in the legal world, but at least as of the current writing, patents on software may still be obtained and enforced in the United States. Such patents might not be obtainable in Europe, and are probably beyond any hope in Asian countries. The likely conclusion is that software patents should be pursued only in the United States. Therefore, "geographic balance" of a portfolio would not require software patents in non-U.S. markets, and in fact *would require the company NOT to file* such patents outside of the U.S.

    b. There are some countries that have a reputation for refusing to enforce the patents of non-nationals. The People's Republic of China has such a reputation. This attitude may be changing, but at least as of now it is unclear that any Chinese patent held by a non-Chinese national will be enforced in the PRC. If the company is interested in current enforceability of its patents, "geographic balance" may suggest that the company not pursue patents in the PRC. (The company may still file in the PRC on the assumption, or perhaps in the hope, that the situation will change in the future.)

(4) Timing: Patents filed earlier tend to issue earlier. This suggests that a company should file first in the countries of greatest importance. Priority dates may still be maintained, but nevertheless the most important countries will receive the earliest protection. Also, the country of first filing almost always sets the basic structure and tone of the application — subsequent filings, in other countries, are usually translations or minor adaptations of the original filing. In short, the order in which geographic balance is achieved is also important.[134]

Q9: *Which country or countries should be part of the geographic balance?*

For a country that considers itself an international player in a technology market, coverage in the U.S. is almost mandatory. The U.S. is likely to be the biggest single market for the products and services covered by innovation, the U.S. is likely to be one of the major players in the development of the technology, and the consequences of patent infringement (both by

---

[134] Issues of timing always come up sooner or later, but it may be important whether the decisions must be made "sooner" or "later". A PCT international application may be filed to push off geographic filing decisions for up to 30 months, and this delay is indeed one of several reasons that people file PCT applications.

injunction and by damages) are almost certainly more severe in the U.S. than in any other country.

Many companies also file in their home countries, usually in order to deter lawsuits against them in these markets. The patents are considered to buy peace of mind.

Companies sometimes file in countries of major market importance. This protects both the company and its downstream customers. Companies sometimes file in the home countries of specific competitors, but this makes sense only if these are very important competitors and only if the company believes that the home courts of such companies will penalize infringers of patents owned by non-nationals. I have noted above the Chinese attitude to enforcement of patents by non-Chinese against Chinese companies. Would a Finnish court be willing to assess hundred of millions of dollars in damages against Nokia? Would a Dutch court order Philips to shut down a product line that infringed the patent of a non-Dutch national?[135]

------

135   Perhaps ironically, *national* chauvinism is *international* in character. In the initial lawsuit between Apple and Samsung, an American jury awarded Apple $1.049 Billion and awarded Samsung $0 in its countersuit. "Apple Inc. v. Samsung Electronics Co., Ltd.", wikipedia, available at *http://en.wikipedia. org/wiki/Apple_Inc._v._Samsung_Electronics_Co.,_Ltd.* (last viewed on November 15, 2014). Some people feel this award is the result of pro-American bias by an American jury. See, e.g., "New Findings Show Foreman Had Bias In The Apple vs Samsung Lawsuit", by Brad Ward, September 26, 2012, available at *http://thedroidguy.com/2012/09/new-findings-show-foreman-had-bias-in-the-apple-vs-samsung-lawsuit-37142#FMLVEeotoWuZChAp.97* (last viewed on November 15, 2014). Many people raised the question of national bias, and certainly this has been Samsung's view. See, e.g., "Samsung Claims Juror Bias in Apple Patent Lawsuit", Inquisitr, November 9, 2012, *http://www.inquisitr.com/393177/samsung-claims-juror-bias-in-apple-patent-lawsuit/* (last viewed on November 15, 2014). In short, it would appear that national bias knows no national bounds.

Q10: *What are the main considerations for achieving time balance in a patent portfolio?*

There are two aspects of time balance that are critically important. The first is continuity of coverage. The second is divestment to free resources in order to achieve the first aspect.

Companies exhibit many kinds of time patterns in their patent portfolios. One frequent pattern is shown in the example of Check Point in Chapter 1. The company very early on filed and prosecuted two outstanding patents. It then had almost no patent activity for seven years (1998–2004), and activity has picked up somewhat recently (2010-present) but not enough to compensate for its early gap in activity. This pattern is not unusual. A variation appears in the example of Silanis Technology in Chapter 1, in which the company did almost nothing in its early life (1992–1999), exploded with significant filing and a major purchase (2000–2003), and is now watching the portfolio deteriorate as patents expire over time. Neither of these companies has achieved a time balance in its portfolio. In contrast, Qualcomm, another example presented in Chapter 1, engaged actively in patents at its founding in the mid-1980's, and has not only continued but intensified its patenting activity over the years.

Continuity of coverage over time is critically important. If a hole in the coverage of a portfolio is discovered, the hole must be filled quickly. The only realistic way to do that is to buy a high-quality patent, which is exactly what Silanis did when it obtained US 5,606,609 in the year 2000.

Continuity is only one aspect of time balance. In addition, the company must divest of unneeded patent items over time, in order to free its resources for other patenting efforts. This may be done by abandoning unneeded applications, choosing not to pay maintenance fees on issued patents, or selling unneeded patent items to outside parties.

An unusual time consideration occurs when the company is going through a corporate event, particularly sale to another company, but also possibly a major investment in the company or a public offering. In anticipation of these events, the company may try to obtain priority filing dates for all the inventions not yet covered by past filings. One strategy is to file what is known as a "jumbo application", including descriptions of every such invention, whether or not the inventions are related to the same technical issue. Similarly, it is not critical to claim each such invention in the jumbo application, but each invention must be described in the jumbo application so that it may be claimed at a later date. Such "jumbo applications" are often Provisional Patent Applications (rather than the standard Non-Provisional Application), because preparation and filing costs tend to be much lower for Provisional Patent Applications (than for Non-Provisional Applications.).

Discussed above is the use of jumbo applications at major events in the life of a company. However, time balance for a startup company may also call for the filing of a jumbo application in the very early life of the company. A jumbo application costs much less, and may defer for months or even years filing and preparation costs of specific inventions. In order to reduce cost in the short-run, a startup company may file a jumbo application with two or more inventions in the same application. Over time, the inventions will be developed into standard applications, but the priority date is created and maintained from the jumbo application.

Topic 2: Managing the Patent Portfolio

Q11: *What is the main consideration for corporate and patent strategies?*

The most important consideration is that the patent strategy must match the corporate strategy, and contribute to the implementation of the corporate strategy. This may seem too obvious for words, but unfortunately patents are sometimes ignored altogether.

The main consideration has several implications:

First, there must be a corporate strategy, and it must address the question of patents. If there is no corporate strategy, then the company does not know where it is going, and the direction of the patents is the least of the company's problems. If there is a corporate strategy, but patents are totally ignored, then there is likely to be either severe under-investment in patents or misdirection in the investments for the patent portfolio.

Second, a patent strategy must be formulated, and it must call for supporting achievement of the goals set forth in the corporate strategy. The patent strategy may include targets for (1) technologies, markets, and products to be covered; (2) absolute size of the portfolio; (3) geographic balance; (4) time balance; and (5) the company's competitive position in both quantity and quality of patents.[136]

---

[136] Some people call these targets the patent "plan" rather than the patent "strategy". There is no point arguing over this terminology. The end goal is for the company to know what it must do with patents in order to advance the corporate strategy, and then to do that.

Third, the patent strategy must call for investment of the "right amount" of money and resources to achieve the necessary patent results. The "right amount" is discussed in Topic 3 below.

Q12: *What are the elements of a successful patenting program within a company?*

(1) Overwhelmingly, the key element is a "clear and well-understood commitment" by top management.

"Clear commitment" means that the company has a corporate strategy that addresses and gives guidance to the patent strategy. This commitment must be ongoing. Although top management is not required to be involved with every patent decision, top management must be aware of what is happening with patents and must change the direction of the patent strategy as that becomes required from time to time. In addition to understanding the quantity and geographic allocation of the patent portfolio, top management must be aware of the relative quality of the portfolio, and whether that quality is increasing or decreasing over time.

"Well-understood commitment" means that everyone in the company, not just top management or patent officers, but especially technical and product people, understands that patents are an integral part of the company's mission and activities. It may be the responsibility of the patent decision-makers or the patent drivers to deliver this message, but in whatever way it is delivered, the message is well-understood in the company.

(2) Clear criteria to measure success of the patenting activity. Discussed in Q14 below.

(3) Patent decision-makers, sometimes called "the Patent Committee", to create the patenting program, create the plan to generate patentable innovations, review innovations submitted by the engineers and technical people, select specific ideas for patenting, and oversee the patent process.

(4) A patent driver who is the point person to drive the program forward. The driver works with the Patent Committee, meets with and keeps in contact with the heads of technology development and the heads of project development, works with inventors, and sees to it that the inventions chosen by the Patent Committee are actually patented.

(5) Resolution of problems that will arise in the launch and management of the patent program. Serious problems will inevitably arise, but they can be resolved with appropriate attention, resources, and time.

(6) Sufficient time. The time required to create a successful and ongoing patent program depends greatly on the nature of the company, the corporate culture, and the intensity of the patenting efforts. For small or startup companies, the time frame is likely to be a few months to a year. For larger companies, full development may require 3–5 years. For companies whose corporate cultures are anti-patent, a change in cultural mindset is necessary, and that will likely require more than 5 years. Historically, many technical companies — particularly those that consider themselves "nimble", "young", and "directed toward 'really cool

products'" — have been anti-patent. Companies such as Google, Apple, and Microsoft, were at one time disdainful of patents, but that is no longer the case.

Q13: How can top management, or anyone for that matter, be aware of "the relative quality of the portfolio" at any particular point in time, let alone "whether that quality is increasing or decreasing over time"?

Patent quality is not some kind of esoteric mysticism, available only to the enlightened few. It is rather a discipline that can be understood and applied in a systematic manner. There are least four ways that patent quality in a portfolio can be determined and tracked, as shown in Table 4-2 below.

Table 4-2: Ways of Determining the Quality of a Patent Portfolio

	From Within the Company	By Outside Experts
Expert Review	Method 1: Expert review from within the company.	Method 2: Expert review by outside experts.
Automated Review	Method 3: Automated review according to the company's algorithm.	Method 4: Automated review by outside experts.

Method 1: Technology and patent experts can review the patent items. In my earlier book, **TRUE PATENT VALUE**, this is called "Expert Fundamental Analysis". It is very effective, but also costly. The out-of-pocket cost may be reduced by using internal experts, presumably full-time employees of the company. This internal review may be an entirely unstructured review, by saying to the experts, "Review these patents

according to your own discretion". At a minimum, of course, the review would include the VSD factors — **V**alidity of the patents, **S**cope of claim coverage, and **D**etectability of infringement. Or alternatively, the experts can be asked to apply specific criteria. For example, my earlier book, ***LITIGATION-PROOF PATENTS***, identifies the ten most common mistakes in ICT patents. The experts may be instructed to review the patents against these ten mistakes, in addition to other analyses performed.

Method 2: Expert review may be done by outside experts hired for this task. This is the preferred method when a major transaction is in the offing. For example, AOL hired a well-known patent firm to analyze its patents before the portfolio was sold to Microsoft for $1.056 Billion. Indeed, these experts improved the quality of the portfolio by additional filings and responses to office actions, before the portfolio was sold. This method is clearly the most expensive of the four methods, but it makes good sense in the right circumstances.

Method 3: Automated review according to criteria selected by the company, with relative weightings for the criteria also selected by the company. Automated review is discussed extensively in ***TRUE PATENT VALUE*** as "Proxy Fundamental Analysis". What might those factors be? The IEEE Patent Power Scorecard provides its own algorithm which is openly available on the Internet, and which may be applied as is or which may be modified according to the opinion of the company.

TPV lists an additional 15 factors, any of which may be applied in an automated review.[137]

Method 4: An automated review may be conducted by an outside consulting firm. A number of companies provided automated rating services for patents. These would include, for example, Innography, IPVision, OceanTomo, PatentRatings International, and Perception Partners. There are also specialized raters, who provide services for particular industries, such as Totaro & Associates for the alternative energy industry. An automated review may be performed according to solely the criteria of the consulting firm, or with various changes requested by the company.

It is vital for the company to understand the quality of its own portfolio, by whatever method or combination of methods are used. Further, the company must remain aware of the changing level of quality, and therefore quality reviews should be performed periodically. In addition, for the company to understand the "relative" quality of its portfolio, meaning relative to other companies, the company should also identify a few of its top competitors and perform some kind of review, probably a less intensive and less costly review, for at least a few of its top competitors.

Q14: What are the main principles of managing the patent portfolio?

First, coverage must be continuous, holes must be filled, and lower priority patent items must be divested to free

---

137   The 15 factors are listed in *TPV* at pp.68–70 and again at p.314.

resources for higher priority patenting. All of this is discussed above.

Second, there must be clear criteria for measuring the success (or failure) of the company's patent activities. What is the goal that must be achieved?

- If the goal is to generate revenue through patent licensing or litigation, how much revenue was achieved?
- If the goal is generate a certain number of patents in a specific country to cover product X, was the goal achieved?
- If the goal is to inhibit competitors from entering a specific product or technology market, was that goal achieved? Are there indications that competitors refrained from entry? Did competitors enter, and then receive prohibitory injunctions that caused them to withdraw, as happened in the Fuji Photo Film case cited in Chapter 1?

Specific criteria must be created. The criteria must be numeric to the extent possible, and in all cases the criteria must be capable of being measured and tracked over time.

Third, who is going to manage the patent portfolio? That is to say, where should the patent function be placed within the organization? Anyone with experience working in companies understands that this is a critically important question, vital to the success of the patenting effort. Should the patent portfolio be placed with the Legal Department, or with the Chief Technical Offer, or with the Vice President of Business Development, or with managers of the Strategic Business Units within the company, or with some combination of these (such as the Legal Department to obtain patents and the Business Development Department to generate revenue)? Each unit of the company will have its own outlook, its own goals, and its own emphasis. Placement of the patent responsibility is therefore a fateful decision for the success of the entire patent program.

Topic 3: Budgeting for Patents

Q15: What are the alternative methods to budget for patent investment?
There are four alternatives.

1. Top Down Budgeting.
2. Bottom Up Budgeting.
3. Competitive Budgeting.
4. Hybrid Budgeting: A combination of any two or all three of the foregoing.

Q16: What is "Top Down Budgeting" for patents?
This is a budgeting method by which the company first determines the amount of money it will devote to patenting activity. The company may then determine a target for number patent items to be derived from this budget — such a numerical target is fairly typical, although strictly speaking the method is completed upon determination of the total amount to be invested. In some implementations, the budget may be allocated among various geographic markets and/or among various technologies to be protected and/or among various products and services to be covered. Although this method may seem unscientific, it is very commonly employed.

The first and defining step of Top Down budgeting is

to determine how much should be invested in patents. Benchmarks are often used. One benchmark that may be used is 1% of R&D. This is a general benchmark that is based on various analyses such as the total amount invested in U.S.-origin patents per year versus the total annual R&D expenditures in the U.S., and the average number of patents granted per $1M of R&D dollars in the United States. This 1% figure must be customized for each specific company according to the state of that company (new or established), the growth prospects of the industry (above average, average, or below average), and the various patent strategies of the company (standard investment, or intent to shakeup the market with breakthrough patents), as reflected in Table 3-5.

Given that the 1% ratio is based upon (patent investment)/(R&D investment), are there other benchmarks that can be used? A fuller picture would add, at a minimum, the revenue results of the company. For example, a standard R&D investment as a percentage of sales for high-tech company in a relatively well established market might be 7% of revenues. In the last few years, Check Point, which is in the relatively technology-intensive and rapidly changing market for firewalls, has been investing about 9.4% of its revenues in R&D, with a range of 8.3%-11.3%.[138] These rates are well above the average investments of technology companies, but perhaps suited for a company such as Check Point in the industry in which it specializes. These figures suggest that Check Point invests strongly in R&D, but also highlight Check Point's very weak investments in patents. Check Point's investments in patents are about 0.35% of R&D in comparison to an industry

---

138 These results for Check Point are presented in Table 1-2, for the years 2007–2013.

standard of 1.00%, or in other words, and about 0.03% of revenues in comparison to an industry standard of about 0.07%.[139] By way of comparison, Qualcomm is an extremely heavy investor in R&D at about 20.8% of revenues in comparison to the industry standard of 7%, and an even stronger investor in patents, at 5.71% of R&D (in comparison to the industry standard of 1.00%) or 1.19% of revenues (in comparison to the industry standard of 0.07%).[140]

Patent investments could be compared also to profit figures. That is not typically done, because there are so many factors that impact profit, whereas the patent investments are intended to show relative emphasis in comparison to R&D or to top-line revenues. The profit figure is most relevant in order to determine if a company could devote more resources to patents if it chose to do so. Both Check Point and Qualcomm, for example, have had very healthy profit margins, so that their relative investments in patents do not appear to be related at all to financial constraints. See "Top Down Budgeting" in the Glossary.

Q17: What is "Bottom Up Budgeting" for patents?

This is a budgeting method by which a company first determines what kinds of patent activity results it needs, rather than the amount of money to be allocated to the patent budget. In the end, of course, a financial budget must be prepared, but the focus is on creating a certain kind of patent portfolio rather than on limiting the funds allocated to the activity. This form of budgeting is often used to create priorities in patenting activities.

---

139   These results for Check Point are presented in Table 3-7.

140   These results for Qualcomm are presented in Table 3-7.

This form of budgeting is based on the company's perception of its needs for patents. That perception will be affected by various factors which may be unique and special to an industry or to the company. For example:

- Is the industry characterized by heavy patent litigation? If so, the company needs more patents, and probably higher quality patents.
- Is there rapid technological development, and rapid technological obsolescence in the industry? If so, this, too, would likely drive a perception that more patents and great quality are needed.
- Are competitors patenting heavily? If so, the company should patent more to meet the competition.
- Is the company a market leader in terms of market share and profitability? There is certain kind of "patent jujitsu" in which the company's success in products and services is used against it. A market leader is a very attractive target for patent plaintiffs. Such a company has a large market share, so patent damages are likely to be high. Such a company has strong profitability, so it can afford to pay heavy patent damages. Patent plaintiffs are not particularly interested in suing small and unsuccessful (or "not yet successful") companies — plaintiffs prefer to sue people who can pay. A company that is a market leader should take this into consideration when setting its patent budget.

See "Bottom Up Budgeting" in the Glossary.

Q18: What is "Competitive Budgeting" for patents?

This is a budgeting method by which a company determines the patent investments of its major competitors, and then sets its own budget to achieve a desired competitive position. There are four steps to this method: (1) Determine the group of competitors from which benchmarks will be derived; (2) Determine the patent results from these competitors, and the patent investments which were invested to achieve these results; (3) Create benchmarks for patent results to be achieved, or amount to be invested, or both; (4) On the basis of the benchmarks, plan the company's investments, then results (or conversely, first results, then investments required to achieve the results).

A number of factors impact Competitive Budgeting, chief of which are the results and investments of competitors. In addition the nature of the industry (a young, dynamic industry calls for greater effort), and the nature of the company's strategy (which may to meet competition, catch up with competition, or shake up the industry with extraordinary investments in R&D and in patents). See "Competitive Budgeting" in the Glossary.

Q19: What is "Hybrid Budgeting" for patents?

Companies do not typically use any of Top Down, Bottom Up, or Competitive Budgeting in their pure forms. Rather, they usually combine two or three of these methods to come up with what the company believes is the best balance of investment, results, and competitive position. This combination is called "Hybrid Budgeting". See "Hybrid Budgeting" in the Glossary.

Topic 4: Special Topics

a. Technology Inflection Points

Q20: What is a Technology Inflection Point?

A Technology Inflection Point (or "TIP" for short) is a major change in a particular technology that will likely have a major impact on an existing industry, or that may create an entirely new industry with new technology that supplants an older industry with outdated technology.

Q21: How is a Technology Inflection Point related to patents?

A technology that can capture a TIP, with an early priority date, is likely to be extremely valuable. Such a patent may be a "breakthrough patent", which reflects the fact that it protects a "breakthrough invention" at the Technology Inflection Point.

Q22: What are the relationships between fundamental research, applied research, technology, products, and patents?

As reflected in Table 2-3, fundamental research creates new science, but these results are not patentable, because fundamental concepts of science are not patentable under 35 United States Code sec. 101.[141] On the other hand, the results of applied R&D, as opposed to the results of fundamental R&D, are certainly patentable. If the results are disruptive, in the sense that they have a major change on a technology or an industry, then they are likely to produce "high-value pat-

---

[141] See, e.g., *Alice Corporation v. CLS Bank*, Slip opinion 13-298, 573 U.S. _____ (decided June 19, 2014), at p.11, citing a long line of Supreme Court cases for the proposition that "laws of nature", "natural phenomena", and "abstract ideas", are not patentable under 35 U.S.C. sec. 101.

ents". If, for example, technical results create paradigm shifts at a Technology Inflection Point, then the protecting patents could be not just "high-value" but in fact "breakthrough", which is the most valuable category of patent. Other results of R&D, those which suggest gradual improvements products, will likely be captured by patents that are either "valuable" (but not "very valuable") or "supporting" (meaning they add a bit of value to a portfolio but cannot stand on their own).

b. Patent Aggregation

Q23: What is a "patent aggregator"?

It is a company or other entity that collects and administers multiple patents on the same subject. The aggregator may also own the patents, although that is not required. If the aggregator administers the patents of competing companies, the result is what is known as a "patent pool". Patents may be aggregated for either aggressive or defensive purposes.

Q24: What is an "aggressive patent aggregator"?

It is an aggregator that aggregates patents for aggressive purposes. In particular, patents are aggregated so that the aggregator may license the patents to outside parties. If the outside parties will not take a license, then the aggregator enforces the patents by launching patent infringement litigation against the outside parties. A "licensing & litigation program" is the essence of an aggressive patent aggregator. Examples of aggressive aggregators, listed in Table 2-7, include Acacia Research, Conversant IP Management, Innovatio IP, Intellectual Ventures, InterDigital, Rembrandt IP Management, Unwired Planet, and WiLAN.

Q25: What is a "defensive patent aggregator"?

It is an aggregator that aggregates patents for defensive purposes. In particular, patents are acquired so that they may not fall into the hands of parties that would seek to license or litigate them. The aggregator may sell the patents to friendly parties, or license the patents to various parties on a voluntary basis (and possibly for free), but no litigation program is initiated. The motivation of a defensive patent aggregator is completely different from the motivation of an aggressive patent aggregator. Examples of defensive aggregators, listed in Table 2-7, including AST, LOT Network, OIN, RPX, and Unified Patents.

Q26: What is a "patent pool"?

It is an aggregation of patents from competing companies on the same general topic. In theory, a patent pool may be for aggressive or defensive purposes, but in reality, when people speak of "patent pools", they mean only "aggressive patent pools". Indeed, a "defensive patent pool" is really no different than a "defensive patent aggregation".

The common meaning of "patent pool" is a pool of patents on the same subject, aggregated from different and competing companies, and intended to be licensed or litigated against third parties. All of the patents in the pool relate to some specific technical standard, and all of the patents must, by law, be evaluated by technical and legal experts and found to be "essential" to implementation of that technical standard.

Patent pools are relatively common in the ICT technology areas, particularly in computers and communication. They are discussed extensively in my earlier book, *TECHNOLOGY PATENT LICENSING: An International Reference on 21st Century Patent Licensing, Patent Pools and Patent Platforms.*

Q27: *You have said that an aggregator may also "own" the aggregated patents. How is that possible? The owner is no longer an aggregator.*

It is true that a company or entity that actually owns all the patents it controls is not technically an "aggregator", but in essence the company has been aggregating patents for its own purposes, and in that sense it is an aggregator. Take Intellectual Ventures, for example, a classic example of an aggressive aggregator. IV owns the patents it seeks to license or litigate. IV generates some of its patents in-house, but most of its patents have been purchased from other parties. As an owner, IV is not subject to the kinds of laws that fall on a patent pool administrator. The thing that makes IV a bit different is that many companies have invested in IV, and so they own shares in the corporation known as "Intellectual Ventures", but they do not own the specific patents that belong to IV. In terms of its efforts to aggregate, then license or litigate, IV is like any other aggressive aggregator.

RPX is an example of a defensive aggregator that owns the patents it aggregates. As a practical matter, however, since RPX does not assert or litigate patents against any party, it is irrelevant whether RPX owns or does not own the patents it aggregates. It is, in any case, a defensive aggregator.

c. Patent Evaluation

Q28: *How are patents evaluated?*

Three general factors are always considered, just these three, but always these three.

(1) Validity: Are the claims valid? In fact, is the entire patent valid? In many evaluation systems, if there

is serious doubt about the validity of the patent, or about important claims within the patent, the valuation will drop to zero and no further evaluation will be conducted. In that sense, this is a yes-no question in some evaluation systems. In other systems, serious doubt will lower the overall value of the patent, but will not destroy its estimated value completely. If a patent valuation does not address validity, that absence means that there is not an obvious problem with the validity of the patent or its claims.

(2) Scope of claim coverage: This is the main criterion for judging patents. If the scope of coverage is such that there is current infringement of some of the claims, or if infringement is expected in the "near future" (typically understood to be no more than 3 years, and sometimes less), then claim scope is considered to be good and the patent has value. If there is infringement now, but an infringer could design around the patent in order to avoid future infringement, then the claims have value for past damages, but the infringer may avoid an injunction, and therefore the value of the patent is reduced.

(3) Discoverability (or "detectability") of infringement: Usually this is not a problem except for specific kinds of patent claims such as manufacturing methods, or electronic circuits that are difficult perceive, or structures at the nano-scale. As with issues of validity, a serious problem of discoverability may greatly impact the value of the patent, but if the issue is not raised in an evaluation, the inference is that discoverability of infringement is unlikely to present any problem.

The three general factors noted above are captured in the acronym VSD. Some evaluation systems break out one or more of these general factors into multiple sub-factors, so that there may be 5, 10, or even more sub-factors, but all of these systems are refinements of the basic approach — in all cases, the three general factors must be considered. Some reviews are done by experts, in which case they may be called "EFA" reviews, short for "Expert Fundamental Analysis". Some reviews are performed in an automated manner, in which case they may be called "PFA", short for "Proxy Fundamental Analysis".

Q29: What is the meaning of "Expert Fundamental Analysis"?

First, it is review done by a technical or legal expert, rather than by a machine applying an algorithm. Second, the review is "fundamental" in the sense that it is trying to determine the internal quality of the patent, and not necessarily the monetary value of the patent in a licensing & litigation program. Monetary value is the ultimate test, but such value is based, at least in part, upon the internal quality of the patent, and no monetary value can be assigned unless the quality of the patent is assessed.

Q30: What is the meaning of "Proxy Fundamental Analysis"?

First, it is a review not by a technical or legal expert, but rather by a machine acting according to an algorithm. The machine is acting as a proxy for a human expert. Second, as indicated above, it is "fundamental" review, trying to determine the internal quality of the patent, which is a basis for monetary value.

Afterword

This book began with a quote from Abraham Lincoln's "Lecture on Discoveries and Inventions". Let us end with the same text.

President Lincoln listed four discoveries that he considered of great value to world history. These four are the discovery of writing, the discovery of printing, the discovery of America, and the introduction of patent laws.

A person could debate the members of this list. Perhaps one of these four discoveries should not be on the list? Perhaps another discovery should be added to the list? More important, however, is the specific reason for the inclusion of these four. President Lincoln said,

> "I have already intimated my opinion that in the world's history, certain inventions and discoveries occurred, of peculiar value, *on account of their great efficiency in facilitating all other inventions and discoveries*." (emphasis added by me)[142]

This really is the point of the patent system — patents provide the right and ability to secure temporary advantage

[142] "Lecture on Discoveries and Inventions", April 5, 1858, available at *http://www.abrahamlincolnonline.org/lincoln/speeches/discoveries.htm*, second to the last paragraph (last viewed on November 15, 2014).

by exposing the invention to public view. This temporary advantage is a major facilitator of new inventions and scientific discoveries, in two respects. First, it gives inventors strong financial incentive to invent and to patent their inventions. Second, it makes new inventions available to the public, initially under license from the patentee while the patent remains valid, and later, after the patent has expired, as part of the total information in the public domain.

This book has discussed three general topics:

(1) Quality of patent portfolios;
(2) Ways to create excellent patent portfolios; and
(3) Budgeting investments required to create excellent patent portfolios.

The overriding purpose of the book was to make a contribution to increasing the quality and value of patent portfolios. When individuals and companies create excellent patent portfolios, they fulfill the function of the patent system, and they also encourage additional inventions and discoveries by all other parties. However, patent portfolios that are weak create the opposite effect — they waste the time and resources of the patent generator and they threaten outside parties with litigation and liability for infringement of patents that do not catch anyone and that, in many cases, should never have been issued in the first place. Whereas a strong portfolio encourages innovation, a weak portfolio discourages innovation. The sole difference is the quality of the portfolio.

Appendix

List of Principles for Excellent Patent Portfolios

CORPORATE AND PATENT STRATEGIES: Corporate strategy must come before anything else. Patent strategy must follow and support corporate strategy.

Principle 1: ***A technology company must determine its strategy with regard to patents.***[143]

Principle 2: ***A good patent portfolio matches the strategic focus of its owner.***[144]

Principle 3: ***Invest the "right amount" in patents.***[145]

    3a. ***For a standard technology company, one possible rule is that the investment in patents should be about 1% of the amount invested in R&D.***

    3b. ***Set your patent investment with regard to the perceived patent investments of your key competitors.***

---

[143] See also *TPV*, 7-3-1 (Portfolio).

[144] See also *TPV*, 7-3-3 (Portfolio).

[145] See also *TPV*, 7-1-2 (Portfolio).

3c. *Compare patent costs to the likelihood of being sued, the possibility of losing the litigation, and costs either in financial damages or in being enjoined from selling products.*

CHARACTERISTICS OF AN EXCELLENT PATENT PORTFOLIO: Only a few characteristics determine the quality of a portfolio. These characteristics are (a) Fit with corporate strategy; (b) Coverage of key technologies and products; (c) Balance of quality and quantity of patents, one form of "mix" of patents; (d) Geographic balance; (e) Time balance; (f) Considerations specific and special to this portfolio.

Principle 4:   *Balance of quality and quantity.*[146]

Principle 5:   *Geographic balance.*[147]

5a. *Protection in the U.S. is critical.*

5b. *Protection in a home market is often appropriate.*

5c. *Other markets for geographic protection.*

Principle 6:   *Time balance.*[148]

MANAGING THE PATENT PORTFOLIO: Management must be active and ongoing. Holes in the portfolio must be identified and filled, the portfolio must be managed over time, criteria must be established for measuring the success of portfolio management, and the patenting function must be located with the organization such that patenting makes its

---

[146] See also *TPV*, 7-1-1 (Portfolio).

[147] See also *TPV*, 7-2-1 (Portfolio).

[148] See also *TPV*, 7-2-2 (Portfolio).

maximum contribution to achieving the corporate and patent strategies.

Principle 7:   ***Identify and fill holes in coverage.***[149]

Principle 8:   ***Time management, including divestment.***[150]

Principle 9:   ***Establish criteria for measurement.***

Principle 10:   ***Place the patenting function within the organization.***

---

[149]   *TPV* 7-2-3 (Portfolio) points out that the quickest way to fill a hole in a portfolio is to identify and then buy the missing patent protection. This method is also likely to be more expensive than the slower but less expensive method of internal patent building.

[150]   *TPV* 7-3-3 (Portfolio) states that if the goal is to maintain the strength of a portfolio, patenting activity must continue over time. Further, *TPV* 7-1-3 (Portfolio) explains that when some of the main drivers of value in a portfolio have expired, the company must make some fundamental decisions regarding what to do about the portfolio.

Glossary

(Including Acronyms)

Aggregation: See "Aggregator".

Aggregator: An entity that collects and administers multiple patents on the same subject. The most common examples are a Non-Practicing Entity, or "NPE", which aggregates patents to license or litigate, and a Defensive Patent Aggregator, or "DPA", which aggregates patents to keep them out of the hands of hostile parties. The administrator of a patent pool is not generally considered an "aggregator", but in fact, a patent pool is an aggregation of patents. Similarly, when a single company or entity "aggregates" patents, for whatever purpose, that company is generally not considered an "aggregator", although in reality the company is acting as one. See "Defensive Patent Aggregator", "DPA", "Non-Practicing Entity", "NPE", and "Patent Pool".

BCP: Acronym for "biotechnology, chemical, and pharmaceutical", representing the three technology areas based on applied chemistry and biology, which are fundamentally different from ICT. These areas are sometimes called "the unpredictable arts". Nano-technology, to the extent it may be manipulated by chemical processes, may belong in this group, or it may be classified in the ICT group. Compare with "ICT".

Bottom Up Budgeting: See "Budgeting for Patent Investment".

Breadth of Claim Coverage: The claims of a patent portfolio can be broad in either or both of two ways. First, the claims of a portfolio may cover a variety of embodiments or implementations of a single Point of Novelty. This may be called "claim mix" for a single PON, including, for example, structure claims, method claims, hardware claims, software claims, and others, for a single PON. Second, the claims of a portfolio may cover multiple Points of Novelty, but all related to the same general theme. The Fuji Film portfolio, discussed in Chapter 1, is an example. Claim breadth is created by the scope of the independent claims in the patents of the portfolio, whereas "depth of coverage" is created by the dependent claims. Compare with "Depth of Claim Coverage".

Breakthrough Patent: See Types of Patents by Value Contribution.

Budgeting for Patent Investment: There are at least four methods commonly used to budget for patent investment, in which the last method is a combination of two or more of the other methods.

> **Top Down Budgeting:** A method by which a company determines first the total budget it will devote to patenting activity. The company then allocates the budgetary amounts for patenting in specific countries, to cover specific products or services, and possibly by general areas of technology. The initial budget may be determined by the perception of the total amount of money available

for patenting in comparison to other activities, or by the amount perceived necessary to protect the company's products and services, or by the amount needed to protect the company from competitors. Some kind of formal benchmark measure may or may not be used. Although Top Down Budgeting is perhaps the least scientific of the various methods of budgeting for patent investment, it is nevertheless frequently used.

Bottom Up Budgeting: A method by which a company first determines what kind of patenting activity it needs, then determines and allocates the resources to meet the needs. May be based on the number of patent applications to be filed and prosecuted, or on the number of patents to be received, or on both. Will likely include activity by specific country, by specific product or service, and possibly by area of technology. This method in its purest form, in which cost is simply not a factor, is very uncommon, but the method is frequently used in a modified form in order to identify, prioritize, and fund what the company considers to be its most important patenting priorities.

Competitive Budgeting: As its name suggests, this method focuses on the patenting activity of close competitors, and attempts to meet competitive action in a way most suited to the company's overall strategy. The goal is to achieve a competitive patent position, either defensive or aggressive, that is acceptable to the company. When this method is used, competitive benchmarks are essential. The company first determines its most relevant competitors, then researches the published patent results of these competitors (very likely together with financial information about these competitors), creates competitive benchmarks for investment, and finally forms a budget for its own patenting activity.

Hybrid Budgeting: A mixing of cost, results, and competitive position, to determine the company's budget for patenting activity. As a practical matter, every investment made by a company must be concerned with results, costs, and competitive position. Total focus on one activity to the total exclusion of the other two factors is not realistic. A balance of some sort must be achieved, and Hybrid Budgeting is one way of achieving the balance. Although the initial focus may be primarily on one of the three factors, the budgeting process is iterative to yield ultimately what the company believes is appropriate weight to each of the three factors. In a sense, every budgeting process is a hybrid, since compromises must always be made. In its purest form Hybrid Budgeting tries to give approximately equal weight to each of the three factors, rather than emphasizing or de-emphasizing any of the factors. In an alternative form, one or two factors may be emphasized in comparison to significant de-emphasizing of the other factor(s). As examples, (1) competition may be downplayed, as the company seeks to balance perceived needs with the resources perceived to be available; or (2) the company's sole goal may be to match competition, so that the budget is set by a competitive benchmark; or (3) the company may seek to implement an aggressive patent strategy, so that targeted results take precedence over the other factors.

Citation of One Patent by Another Patent: "Citation" by a patent is what happens when one patent makes reference to another patent. Evaluators of a specific patent often review either or both of (1) the number of citations made by that patent to earlier patents (which are called "reverse" or "backward" citations) and (2) the number of citations received by that patent (which are called "forward citations", because they are forward in time from the cited patent).

Assume two patents, X which is earlier in time, and Y which is later in time. Y cites patent X. Therefore, patent Y why has made a "backward citation" to patent X (also called a "reverse citation"), because patent Y is citing backward in time. Also, by this same citation, patent X has received a "forward citation" from patent Y, because the citation is forward in time from patent X.

If a single company or entity owns both patents X and Y, then the citation is a "backward self-citation" from Y, or a "forward self-citation" to X. Conversely, if patents X and Y are owned by different entities, then the citation is a "backward non-self citation" from Y, or a "forward non-self citation" to X.

Claim Mix: One way of judging the quality of a group of patents such as a portfolio is by seeing if there is a "claim mix", also called "claim diversity". There are different forms of "claim mix". In the context of a patent portfolio, this often means the balance between a few high-quality patents and a mass of moderate to lower quality patents. "Claim mix" may also mean the types of claims in a patent or in a patent portfolio, such as the mix between structure claims and method claims, "client-side" claims and "server-side" claims, "hardware claims" and "software claims", and others. This kind of mix is more often used for the claims in either one patent or a small group of patents, but it could be applied to the entire portfolio. Generally, greater "mix" or "diversity" means that the portfolio is stronger in its claim validity and scope of claim coverage. A greater claim mix in a portfolio is often associated with higher quality and higher value for several reasons: (1) because the portfolio may capture multiple inventive concepts related to the same general invention; (2) because each inventive concept can be captured in multiple ways; (3) because the overall scope of claim coverage, represented by both number of inventive concepts and the coverage per concept, can be greater; (4) because the claims in the portfolio are much more resistant to invalidation at trial — that is, claim validity is stronger; and (5) because ultimately, a strong mix of claims in multiple patents increases the chance of creating a "patent thicket", which is a very strong position for a patent holder. See also "Client-side Claim", "Dependent Claim", "Independent Claim", "Patent Thicket", "Server-side Claim", "VSD".

Claim Parallelism: This is a particular kind of claim mix in which a single Point of Novelty is protected by multiple types of claims, and in which the mix is achieved by using the same claim structure and same claim terminology in method, apparatus, and component claims of the same patent. When done properly, claim parallelism provides very strong protection for a single Point of Novelty. However, claim parallelism requires the same terminology in the various kinds of claims. If different terminology is used, the parallelism is lost, and maximal protection is not obtained.

Client-side Claim: Most communication systems have a "client side", sometimes called customer premises, consumer site, mobile station, the home, etc., and a server side. For ICT system and method claims, it is important that you know whether each element of a claim is on the client side or the server side. There is a rule of patent law that direct infringement of a patent claim requires that *only one party* (not two) perform all the elements in the claim. If one claim has both client-side elements and server-side elements, that claim violates this rule and is therefore in danger of being unenforceable. Compare with "Server-side Claim".

Competitive Budgeting: See "Budgeting for Patent Investment".

Cultivating Patents: This is one of three processes by which a corporation or other entity converts innovations into patents. In cultivating, the corporation or entity deliberately develops and patents concepts that it considers to be technological "breakthroughs". Cultivating is a planned process in which the dominant role is filled by patents. The patents may be accompanied by R&D which typically follows the patents, and which, together with the patents, may be the basis of a new business within the company. In some forms of cultivating, there is no R&D, or the R&D is minimal. In such forms, the objective may be aggressive (that is, to generate money from the patents), or defensive (that is, to prevent others from obtaining and asserting patents against a market). In this book, cultivating patents is called Model III, and is the newest form by which various entities build patent portfolios. Compare "Gathering Patents" and "Matching Patents".

Defensive Patent Aggregator ("DPA"): A company or other entity that aggregates patents primarily to keep them out of the hands of potentially hostile parties. See "Aggregator". Compare with "Non-Practicing Entity".

Dependent Claim: A "dependent claim" is a claim that depends on an earlier claim. Each dependent claim will refer to the earlier claim at the very start. For example, "2. Claim 1, further comprising…", is dependent claim #2, which depends on earlier claim #1. A dependent claim includes all of the elements in the claim depended on, plus the added element in the dependent claim. The scope of the dependent claim is necessarily narrower than the claim on which it depends. The dependent claim never comes to life, that is, it does not become operative as a practical matter, unless the claim on which it depends has been rendered invalid or unenforceable. Compare "Independent Claim".

Depth of Claim Coverage: The degree to which a patent, or a patent portfolio, may lose its independent claims, but still retain good scope of coverage through its dependent claims. In every patent, the scope of claim coverage is determined by the independent claims. Similarly, the scope of coverage for a portfolio is determined by the independent claims of the patents in that portfolio. If independent claims were never invalidated by the PTO, or the courts, or the International Trade Commission, then the only claims in a patent should be its independent claims. However, in the real world independent claims are sometimes invalidated. Therefore, patents include dependent claims that become active when the independent claims are invalidated. These dependent claims give the patent, or the portfolio, depth of coverage, meaning the relative strength of the patent or portfolio to maintain its scope of coverage when independent claims have been invalidated. Compare "Breadth of Claim Coverage".

Discoverability of Infringement: Also called "detectability of infringement". See "VSD".

DPA: Acronym for "Defensive Patent Aggregator".

Gathering Patents: This is one of three processes by which a corporation or other entity converts innovations into patents. In gathering, the corporation or entity patents innovative concepts that happen to pop up. The gathering process is serendipitous rather than planned. In this book, it is called Model I of patent generation, and it is probably the oldest method of creating patents. Compare "Cultivating Patents" and " Matching Patents".

Hybrid Budgeting: See "Budgeting for Patent Investment".

ICT: Acronym for "information & communication technology", with patents typically featuring electronic or mechanical structures or methods, and which tend to be based on applied physics. The group includes computers, electronics, and communication systems, including hardware and software. This group also includes mechanical patents, and also medical device patents (e.g., implants, tools). Material science patents, particularly those in nanotechnology, are sometimes grouped in ICT. Compare with "BCP".

Independent Claim: A claim that does not depend on any earlier claim is called "independent". An independent claim will not refer to an earlier claim. An independent claim includes only the elements in that claim itself and, when correctly drafted, includes a single Point of Novelty, although each PON may be expressed through multiple independent claims. Compare with "Dependent Claim".

Innovative Concept: See "Point of Novelty".

Inventive Concept: See "Point of Novelty".

Jumbo Application: See "Types of Patent Applications"

Matching Patents: This is one of three processes by which a corporation or other entity converts innovations into patents. In matching, the corporation or entity deliberately develops and patents concepts that match its R&D effort. Matching is a planned process in which the dominant role is R&D rather than the patents. In this book, matching patents is called Model II, and it is a well established process by which companies build patent portfolios to support R&D efforts. Compare "Cultivating Patents" and "Gathering Patents".

Manual of Patent Examining Procedure ("MPEP"): A lengthy manual published by the U.S. patent office and describing all of the laws and regulations used in the examination of patent applications in the United States. Sometimes called "the patent examiner's Bible", but it is also used extensively by patent attorneys and patent agents. As of March, 2014, the 9th Edition of the MPEP had been published and was in force.

MPEP: Acronym for "Manual of Patent Examining Procedure".

Method Claim: This is a patent claim that describes the way something is done, or the manner in which something is achieved. Every method claimed in a patent is carried out by one or more structures, which may be claimed in the patent as "structure claims". Compare "Structure Claim".

Non-Practicing Entity: A company or other entity that aggregates patents primarily to assert them in a licensing & litigation program against possible infringers. The entity is "non-practicing" in the sense that it does not actually implement the methods or produce the products which are the subjects of the aggregated patents. The term "Non-Practicing Entity" is neutral. A pejorative term for the same concept is "patent troll". See "Aggregator". Compare with "Defensive Patent Aggregator".

Non-Provisional Application ("NPA"): See "Types of Patent Applications".

NPA: Acronym for "Non-Provisional Application". See "Types of Patent Applications".

NPE: Acronym for "Non-Practicing Entity".

Parallelism: See "Claim Parallelism".

Patent Activity Intensity: A measure of the degree to which a company or entity invests in patents. One way to measure patent activity intensity is to compare the resources invested in patents over time to the total investment in R&D over the same period. Patent activity intensity is one aspect of an entity's financial commitment to patents, as reflected in the equation (R&D intensity) × (patent activity intensity) = (\$ invested in R&D/revenue) × (\$ invested in Patents/\$ in R&D) = (\$ invested in Patents/revenue). Compare "R&D Intensity".

Patent Family: A group of patent items that are all related through one chain of priority. Most typically, there is a single application that serves as a "daddy" of many continuations applications, all claiming priority through the daddy application. Very commonly, the daddy application is also a "granddaddy" application, in which there are continuations applications from the continuation applications. There is no limit to the number of generations that may rely upon the original patent application. All of the applications in such a group of patent items are considered to be part of the same patent family. Further, if patent items are pursued in multiple countries, they are all considered part of the same patent family as long as they all share a common chain of priority.

Patent Item: As used in this book, a "patent item" is either an issued patent or a pending patent application. There are several references in the book to "patent items", by which is meant all of the patents and applications of a particular company.

Patent Pool: Multiple patents, owned by multiple competitors and aggregated into a single group for joint licensing or litigation, are described as being in a patent pool. A patent pool typically is formed around a written technical standard, and patents admitted to the pool must be, by law, "essential" to implementation of the standard. Because entry into a patent pool follows evaluation by technical and legal experts who have determined that the patent is indeed "essential" to the standard, presence in a pool is one sign of potential value in the patent.

Patent Portfolio: A group or collection of two or more patent items (meaning patents and/or patent applications) that are owned or controlled by the same entity, and that are "related" in the sense that they are directed at the same technical subject or problem. Some people use this term to include all of the patents and applications belonging to a company, whether or not these patent items relate to one or multiple subjects or problems. If, however, the patent items relate to multiple subjects or problems, it would be more accurate to say that the company owns several portfolios

Patent Strategy: The targeted results and targeted investments for patents planned by a company to support its corporate strategy. The "results" will include the intended patents and patent applications to be obtained in specific geographic areas, and over a specific period of time. The patent and applications may be obtained by patenting in-house ideas or by buying patents from external sources. A good patent strategy will support the overall corporate strategy.

Patent Thicket: A type of patent portfolio that creates great value for the patent owner and significant problems for competitors. A group of patents working together to protect various aspects of the same general invention. Generally owned and administered by one company, but may also be administered (and not owned) by a single entity such as a patent pool administrator, an NPE, or a DPA. Patent pools, NPE aggregations, and DPA aggregations, are generally not thought of in the industry as "patent thickets", but in reality that is what they are. See "Aggregator", "Defensive Patent Aggregator", "Non-Practicing Entity", and "Patent Pool".

Point of Novelty ("PON"): This is the part of the claim that is new, for which a particular patent claim was allowed by an examiner. In every independent claim, there should be a single PON. A claim may have multiple Points of Novelty, but if it does, then the claim is narrower in scope than it might have been. It happens sometimes during the prosecution process that the patent office allows a claim for a Point of Novelty that was not intended or expected by the applicant. In the end, however, every patent claim must have at least one Point of Novelty. A single patent may cover only one invention, but that invention may have multiple Points of Novelty, and hence the patent may have multiple PONs. The PON is sometimes called "innovative concept" or "inventive concept", and these terms are acceptable provided there is no confusion — there may be multiple innovations in a single patent, all of which are related to the overall invention.

PON: Acronym for "Point of Novelty".

PPA: Acronym for "Provisional Patent Application". See "Types of Patent Applications".

Provisional Patent Application ("PPA"): Often called simply "Provisional". See "Types of Patent Applications".

R&D Intensity: A measure of the degree to which a company or entity invests in R&D. One way to measure R&D intensity is to compare the resources invested in R&D over time to the total revenues generated by the company over the same period. R&D intensity is one aspect of an entity's financial commitment to patents, as reflected in the equation (R&D intensity) × (patent activity intensity) = ($ invested in R&D/revenue) × ($ invested in Patents/$ in R&D) = ($ invested in Patents/revenue). Compare "Patent Activity Intensity".

Scope of Claim Coverage: See "VSD".

Seminal Patent: See "Types of Patents by Value Contribution".

Server-side Claim: Most communication systems have a "client side" and a "server side", the latter sometimes called head end, network operations center, network control, etc. For ICT system and method claims, it is important that you know whether each element of a claim is on the client side or the server side. There is a rule of patent law that direct infringement of a patent claim requires that *only one party* (not two) perform all the elements in the claim. If one claim has both client-side elements and server-side elements, that claim violates this rule and is therefore in danger of being unenforceable. Compare with "Client-side Claim".

Structure Claim: This is a patent claim for a certain arrangement of physical items or elements. There are several types of structure claims, including claims for systems, claims for a product (sometimes called a "machine" or a "device"), and claims for components of a product (such as a circuit, a sub-assembly, etc.). A structure claimed in a patent may support one or more methods, which may be claimed in the patent as "method claims". Compare "Method Claim".

Supporting Patent: See "Types of Patents by Value Contribution".

Technology Inflection Point ("TIP"): A TIP is a major change in a particular technology. It is possible, in some cases, to anticipate where and what the changes are likely to be. Major changes occur where (1) a change in approach can remove or lessen a major weakness or bottleneck, and thereby have great impact on the performance of existing technology, or (2) an entirely new technology supplants the old technology, with major effect — this is sometimes called a "paradigm shift".

TIP: Acronym for "Technology Inflection Point".

Top Down Budgeting: See "Budgeting for Patent Investment".

Types of Patent Applications:

> **Jumbo Application:** An application that has at least two, and potentially many more than two, inventions in the written description. The purpose of a jumbo application is to get the inventions filed, after which they may be pursued in multiple NPAs while maintaining the early priority date of the original filing. The filing of a jumbo application, with many inventions described but not all claimed, is one technique that is used to build a large portfolio with an early priority date for all of the patent items.
>
> Note that there are at least two alternative definitions of "jumbo application", neither of which are intended here:
>
> (1) A patent with a lengthy written description. MPEP 608.01 Specification, para. 6.31, states, "This paragraph is applicable to so-called 'Jumbo Applications' (more than 20 pages, exclusive of claims)." *http://www.uspto.gov/web/offices/pac/mpep/s608.html* (last viewed on November 15, 2014.).
>
> (2) A Non-Provisional Application with more than 20 claims. See, e.g., "Jumbo Patents on the Decline", by Dennis Crouch, January 17, 2104, available at *http://patentlyo.com/patent/2014/01/jumbo-patents-on-the-decline.html* (last viewed on November 15, 2014), in which it is stated, "[the decline in jumbo applications] is largely due to fee increases instituted in 2004 that make it cost prohibitive to file a large number of claims".

I do not mean either the number of pages in the written description, or the number of claims. I mean only that the patent deliberately includes multiple inventions. The description may well run to more than 20 pages, but that is not a requirement of what I mean by a "jumbo application". The application may also include more than 20 claims, but that certainly is not a requirement, and in fact defeats the purpose of filing to give an early priority date to many inventions, while pursuing the various inventions in later filed continuation applications.

Non-Provisional Application ("NPA"): This is an ordinary application, subject to standard rules of the U.S. patent office for ordinary applications. It is the kind of application that people typically mean when they say, "patent application". It must conform to the formal rules of the patent office, and it incurs standard fees for filing an ordinary application. The term "NPA" encompasses a first filed ordinary application, continuation applications, continuation-in-part applications, and divisional applications. Compare with "Provisional Patent Application".

Provisional Patent Application ("PPA"): This is a special form of application that exists only in the United States. Material must be submitted as part of the application, but there are no formal rules for what must be submitted or the form in which the material may be submitted. Filing fees are drastically less than the comparable fees for filing a Non-Provisional Application. The PPA is valid for only one year from the date of filing. If a Non-Provisional Application based on the PPA is filed within that one-year period, the NPA may claim priority back to the date on which the PPA was filed. If no NPA is filed within that period, then the PPA automatically expires at the end of the year and without any disclosure by the patent office. A PPA *cannot* result in a patent, but can serve as a priority date for a later filed NPA that may result in a patent. Compare with "Non-Provisional Application".

Types of Patents by Value Contribution:

Breakthrough Patent: A patent that covers a truly unique invention, and that is likely to present a paradigm shift in an industry or even the creation of an entirely new industry. A breakthrough patent often covers or describes a Technology Inflection Point. The value of a breakthrough patent comes not primarily from the patent's placement in a portfolio, but rather from the subject of the patent itself. Breakthrough patents can add tremendous value to portfolios, but they are very rare. There are many portfolios, including even excellent portfolios, that do not have any breakthrough patent.

Seminal Patent: One type of high-value patent that may form a basis for an excellent patent portfolio. A "seminal patent" has certain characteristics that can make it of fundamental importance in a particular industry. These characteristics are:

(1) early priority date; (2) hundreds of forward non-self citations; (3) addresses a major technical problem, or contributes significantly to a technology area; and (4) has sufficiently broad scope to cover a significantly sized market.

Seminal patents are uncommon, but not as rare as

breakthrough patents. Since by its definition a seminal patent covers a large market, it can create great value. Compare "Breakthrough Patent" and "Very Valuable Patent".

Very Valuable Patent: A patent that is highly rated according to a VSD analysis, but for one reason or another does not rise to the level of a "seminal patent" (perhaps because it lacks strong forward non-self citations). In particular, a very valuable patent, like a seminal patent, covers a large market, meaning that there is likely significant infringement of the patent. The breakthrough patents, seminal patents, and very valuable patents, taken together, are likely to comprise only 1% of the patents in a large portfolio, but are likely to generate more than 50% of the financial value of that portfolio. See also "Seminal Patent".

Valuable Patent: A valuable patent is one that has some infringement, or that is expected to be infringed in the near future, but that does not meet the criteria of a "Very Valuable Patent" (and of course not of a "Seminal Patent" or a "Breakthrough Patent"). A valuable patent adds value particularly when it is part of a portfolio. By itself, such a patent is likely vulnerable to designaround, or to attack on claim validity, or to other actions by potential infringers trying to avoid liability. Valuable patents may comprise 10% of the total number of patents in a typical portfolio (or let us say within a range of 5% — 15% of all the patents in the portfolio). Such patents add value to the portfolio, but less than half the total value of the portfolio.

Supporting Patent: A patent that may or may not add value as part of a portfolio, but which almost certainly would add no value by itself. This patent might or might not be infringed now or in the future. It may cover a relatively minor or less important feature of a system, product, or method, or perhaps the patent may be easily designed around by potential infringers. In almost all portfolios of significant size, supporting patents will comprise the great bulk of the patents, perhaps as many as 90% of all the patents in portfolio. These patents add only minor value, but they are useful in those cases in which parties compare the relative sizes of portfolios to estimate the relative values of the portfolios.

Validity of Claim: See "VSD".

Valuable Patent: See "Types of Patents by Value Contribution".

Very Valuable Patent: See "Types of Patents by Value Contribution".

VSD: Acronym for "**V**alidity of claim, **S**cope of claim coverage, and **D**iscoverability (or **D**etectability) of infringement". The strength of an individual claim depends on exactly three factors: (1) whether that claim would be validated at trial, (2) the extent to which the claim is infringed now or will be infringed in the future, and (3) the ability of the owner of the patent to discover (or detect) infringement of the claim. Similarly, the strength of an entire patent depends on the validity of all the claims, the scope of claim coverage, and the ability to discover infringement. Similarly, the strength of an entire portfolio depends upon the validity of claims for the patents in the portfolio, the market coverage of all the claims in all the patents, and the ability to discover infringement of various claims in the portfolio. When professional evaluators review a single patent or a portfolio, they will always consider the three factors in VSD. See "Patent Portfolio".

Bibliography

Adobe Systems, Incorporated, Form 10-K Report for 2011, available at *http://www.adobe.com/aboutadobe/invrelations/pdfs/ FY11_10-K_FINAL_Certified.pdf.*

Alice Corporation v. CLS Bank, slip opinion 13-298, 573 US ____ (decided June 19, 2014).

Argento, Zoe, "Killing the Goose, The Dangers of Strengthening Domestic Trade Secrets in Response to Cyber-Misappropriations", *16 Yale Journal of Law & Technology 172–235* (2014), available at *http://yjolt.org/sites/default/files/ KillingTheGoldenGoose.pdf.*

Battelle Memorial Institute, "2014 Global R&D Funding Forecast", December, 2013, available at *http://www.rdmag.com/sites/ rdmag.com/files/gff-2014–5_7%20875×10_0.pdf.*

Broadcom Corporation v. Qualcomm, Inc., 543 F.3d 683 (Fed. Cir. 2008).

Broadcom Corporation v. Qualcomm Incorporated, "In the Matter of Certain Baseband Processor Chips and Chipsets, Transmitter and Receiver (Radio) Chips, Power Control Chips, and Products Containing Same, Including Cellular Telephone Handsets", U.S. International Trade Commission ("ITC") Case No. 337-TA-543.

Canada, Government of, "Industry Canada: Aerospace and Defence, Silanis Technology, Inc., Company Information",

April 9, 2013, available at *http://www.ic.gc.ca/app/ccc/srch/nvgt.do?lang=eng&prtl=1&sbPrtl=&estblmntNo=123456179276&profile=cmpltPrfl&profileId=2056&app=sold.*

Canadian Advanced Technology Alliance, "Canadian Advanced Security Industry: Industry Profile, 2003", 2003, available at *http://www.cata.ca/files/PDF/pssf/rapport_canada.pdf.*

Canadian Intellectual Property Office, *http://www.cipo.ic.gc.ca/eic/site/cipointernet-internetopic.nsf/eng/Home.*

Classen, H. Ward, "Creating an Intellectual Property Program: The Initial Steps", Webinair offered by Innography, Inc., June 24, 2014, available at *https://www.innography.com/learn-more/practitioners-guide-to-creating-an-ip-strategy.*

Check Point Software Technologies, Ltd., Form 20-F annual report for 2013, available at *http://www.checkpoint.com/downloads/corporate/investor-relations/sec-filings/2013-20f.pdf.*

Check Point Software Technologies, Ltd., summary of historical financial results for fiscal years 2009–2013, *http://www.check-point.com/corporate/investor-relations/earnings-history/index.html.*

CHI Research, Inc., "Small Serial Innovators: The Small Firm Contribution to Technical Change", February 27, 2003, prepared for the U.S. Small Business Administration, Office of Advocacy, available at *http://archive.sba.gov/advo/research/rs225tot.pdf.*

Crouch, Dennis, "How Many US Patents are In-Force?", PatentlyO Blog, May 4, 2012, available at *http://patentlyo.com/patent/2012/05/how-many-us-patents-are-in-force.html.*

Crouch, Dennis, "Jumbo Patents on the Decline", PatentlyO Blog, January 17, 2014, available at *http://patentlyo.com/patent/2014/01/jumbo-patents-on-the-decline.html.*

Crunchbase, "Silanis Technology", *http://www.crunchbase.com/organization/silanis-technology.*

Electronic Signature & Records Association, membership roster available at *www.esignrecords.org/?page=ESRAmembers*.

Epperson, Ron (of Intellectual Energy, LLC), and Kassaraba, Myron (of Pluritas, LLC), "Clean Tech Trends — Intellectual Property & Transactions", published in *les Nouvelles: Journal of the Licensing Executives Society*, June, 2014, at pp.88–95. See also Totaro & Associates.

Free Patents Online, *www.freepatentsonline.com*. Extensive database of patents and applications in the United States, Europe, Germany, and Japan, as well as PCT international applications.

Fuji Photo Film Co., Ltd. v. Achiever Industries, Ltd. (and twenty-six other defendants), "In the Matter of Certain Lens-Fitted Film Packages", U.S. International Trade Commission ("ITC") Case No. 337-TA-406.

Fuji Photo Film Co., Ltd., v. Jazz Photo Corp. et al., 394 F.3d 1368 (Fed. Cir. 2005).

G2Crowd, performance grid for Adobe EchoSign, AssureSign, DocuSign, RightSignature, Sertifi, and Silanis e-SignLive, available at *https://www.g2crowd.com/categories/e-signature*.

Garat, Renaud (of Questel IP Business Intelligence), "PATENT EVALUATION: Building the tools to extract and unveil intelligence and value from patent data", presentation at LES Moscow, May, 2014, available at *http://les2014.org/bundles/files/presentation/W23_Garat.pdf*.

Garnick, Coral, "DocuSign gets $85 million more in investments", The Seattle Times, March 4, 2014, available at *http://seattletimes.com/html/businesstechnology/2023044164_docusignfundingxml.html*.

Gertner, Jon, *The Idea Factory: Bell Labs and the Great Age of American Innovation*, (Penguin Press, New York, 2012).

Goldstein, Larry M., *Litigation-Proof Patents: Avoiding the Most Common Patent Mistakes*, (True Value Press, Memphis, Tennessee, 2014).

Goldstein, Larry M. *True Patent Value: Defining Quality in Patents and Patent Portfolios*, (True Value Press, Memphis, Tennessee, 2013).

Goldstein, Larry M., and Kearsey, Brian N., *Technology Patent Licensing: An International Reference on 21st Century Patent Licensing, Patent Pools and Patent Platforms*, (Aspatore Books, a division of Thomson Reuters, Boston, Massachusetts, 2004).

Green, Jay, and Shankland, Stephen, ""Why Microsoft spent $1 billion on AOL's patents", CNET, April 9, 2012, available at *http://www.cnet.com/news/why-microsoft-spent-1-billion-on-aols-patents/*.

Hallenbeck, Jim, "The Nortel Six — $4.5 Billion Peace of Mind?", Patents4Software Blog, July 18, 2011, available at *http://www.patents4software.com/2011/07/the-nortel-six-%E2%80%93-4-5-billion-peace-of-mind/*.

Hardiman, Jean Tarbett, "3-D printing creates custom knee replacements", The Washington Post, August 23, 2014, available at *http://www.washingtontimes.com/news/2014/aug/23/3-d-printing-creates-custom-knee-replacements/?page=all*.

Hicks, Dianna, and Hegde, Deepak, "Highly innovative small firms in the markets for technology", Georgia Tech Research Corporation, 2005, available at *https://smartech.gatech.edu/bitstream/handle/1853/24060/wp4.pdf*.

IEEE Spectrum Patent Power Scorecards. For 2013, *http://spectrum.ieee.org/at-work/innovation/patent-power-2013*, and for 2012, *http://spectrum.ieee.org/at-work/innovation/patent-power-2012*.

IFI Claims® Patent Services, "IFI CLAIMS˙ 2013 Top 50 US Patent Assignees", January 16, 2014, available at *http://www.ificlaims.com/index.php?page=misc_top_50_2013&keep_session=1800844745*.

Inquisitr, "Samsung Claims Juror Bias in Apple Patent Lawsuit", November 9, 2012, available at *http://www.inquisitr.com/393177/samsung-claims-juror-bias-in-apple-patentlawsuit/*.

Intellectual Asset Magazine Blog, "Google's evolution from IP refusenik to major patent owner continues", June 10, 2014, available at *http://www.iam-magazine.com/blog/detail.aspx? g=963240a0-e700–4a99-a676-c34e00f00c79.*

Intellectual Property Owners Association, "Top 300 Organizations Granted Patents in 2013", June 6, 2014, available at *http://www. ipo.org/wp-content/uploads/2014/06/2013-Top-300-Patent-Owners_5.9.14.pdf.*

Krassenstein, Eddie, "Man Compares His $42,000 Prosthetic Hand to a $50 3D Printed Cyborg Beast", 3DPrint.com, April 20, 2014, available at *http://3dprint.com/2438/.*

Le Clair, Craig, "The Forrester Wave™: E-Signatures, Q2 2013", Forrester Research, April 29, 2013, available at *https:// 274a0e7125acf05720ef-7801faf96de03497e5e0b3dfa5691096.ssl. cf2.rackcdn.com/ForresterWaveeSignature.pdf*

Lincoln, Abraham, "Lecture on Discoveries and Inventions", delivered April 6, 1858, in Bloomington, Illinois, available at *http:// www.abrahamlincolnonline.org/lincoln/speeches/discoveries. htm.*

Matsumoto, Craig, "Broadcom Picks a Peck of Patents", LightReading, December 26, 2002, available at *http://www.lightreading.com/ ethernet-ip/broadcom-picks-a-peck-of-patents/d/d-id/587217.*

Merrill, Stephen A., Levin, Richard C., and Myers, Mark B., editors, "*A Patent System for the 21st Century*", National Academies Press (2014).

Millstein, Seth, "3D-Printed Robot Self-Assembles When Heated, So the Robot Apocalypse Just Became Inevitable", Bustle.com, May 26, 2014, *www.digitaltrends.com/cool-tech/ mit-researchers-developed-3d-robots-self-assemble-heated/*

Mitra, Sramana, "How to Build a Strong IP Portfolio: rPost CEO Zafar Khan", September 28, 2011, and particularly Part 5, available at *http://www.sramanamitra.com/2011/09/26/how-to-build-a-strong-ip-portfolio-rpost-ceo-zafar-khan-part-5/.*

Parchomovsky, Gideon, and Wagner, R. Polk, "Patent Portfolios", *University of Pennsylvania Law Review*, Vol. 154., No. 1, pp.1–77 (2005), available at *http://papers.ssrn.com/sol3/papers.cfm?abstract_id=582201*.

Paris Convention for the Protection of Industrial Property (1883).

Patent Cooperation Treaty (1970).

Peplow, Mark, "Cheap battery stores energy for a rainy day," Nature. com, January 8, 2014, available at *http://www.nature.com/news/cheap-battery-stores-energy-for-a-rainy-day-1.14486*

Qualcomm 10-K annual reports, available at *http://investor.qualcomm.com/sec.cfm?DocType=annual*.

Quinn, Gene, "The Cost of Obtaining a Patent in the US", IPWatchdog®, January 28, 2011, available at *http://www.ipwatchdog.com/2011/01/28/the-cost-of-obtaining-patent/id=14668/*.

Randewich, Noel, "Qualcomm CEO see opportunity in data center server market," Reuters, January 6, 2014, available at *http://www.reuters.com/article/2014/01/06/us-ces-qualcomm-idUSBREA0510U20140106*.

Rothwell, Jonathan, Lobo, José, Strumsky, Deborah, and Muro, Mark, "Patent Prosperity: Invention and Economic Performance in the United States and its Metropolitan Areas", Brookings Institution, February, 2013, available at *http://www.brookings.edu/~/media/research/files/reports/2013/02/patenting%20prosperity%20rothwell/patenting%20prosperity%20rothwell.pdf*.

RPost Holdings, Inc., *www.rpost.com*, and especially the list of infringement actions at *http://www.rpost.com/about-rpost/intellectual-property/infringement-actions*.

RPX Corporation, Registration Statement (Form S-1), (Sept. 2, 2011), *http://www.sec.gov/Archives/edgar/data/1509432/000119312511240287/ ds1.htm.*]

Schmidt, Robert N., Jacobus, Heidi, and Glover, Jere W., "Why

'Patent Reform' Harms Small Business", IPWatchdog®, April 25, 2014, available at *http://www.ipwatchdog.com/2014/04/25/why-patent-reform-harms-innovative-small-businesses/id=49260/.*

Silanis International, "Silanis Intl Ltd SNS Interim Results" for the first half of 2012, September 5, 2012, Bloomberg News, available at *http://www.bloomberg.com/bb/newsarchive/aOmgOC-N6MNdg.html.*

Statute of Monopolies (1624).

Takahasi, Dean, "IBM reveals its top five innovation prediction for the next five years", VB News, December 16, 2013, available at *http://venturebeat.com/2013/12/16/ibm-reveals-its-top-five-predictions-for-the-next-five-years/.*

Talmud, Babylonian, *Tractate Ta'anit*, page 23a.

Totaro & Associates, *http://www.totaro-associates.com*, a consulting firm with particular expertise in intellectual property within the wind energy industry, cited in Epperson, Ron, and Kassaraba, Myron, "Clean Tech Trends".

Totaro & Associates, "Global Wind Innovation Trends Report: Q3, 2014", parts available at *http://media.wix.com/ugd/ba1f58_536 96aacea22418b8621e386f9963c03.pdf*, or the entire report may be purchased at *http://www.totaro-associates.com/#!landscape/c1qms*

Totaro & Associates, "Reduction of Cost of Energy Through Innovation", 2013, summarized at *http://www.totaro-associates.com/#!ip-landscape/c1k7h*, and posted in full at *http://media.wix.com/ugd/ba1f58_3e4296160be0621aae30878bdc11c066.pdf*

Twain, Mark, *Life on the Mississippi* (1883). Viewed at *http://www.markwareconsulting.com/miscellaneous/mark-twain-on-the-perils-of-extrapolation/.*

United States Code, Title 35, section 101, on subjects that are patentable.

United States Constitution (1787).

United States Design Patents
    Des. 345,750, "Single use camera", original assignee is Fuji Photo Film Co. of Japan.
    Des. 356,101, "Single use camera", original assignee is Fuji Photo Film Co. of Japan.
    Des. 372,722, "Camera", original assignee is Fuji Photo Film Co. of Japan.

United States Patent & Trademark Office, *www.uspto.gov*. The authoritative source for patents and applications filed in the United States, including prosecution histories, records of assignment, and other information.

United States Patent & Trademark Office, "Fee Schedule", listing the current fees for both patent and trademark applications, available at *http://www.uspto.gov/web/offices/ac/qs/ope/fee010114. htm*.

United States Patent & Trademark Office, "Jumbo Applications", MPEP 608.01, Specification, paragraph 6.31, available at *http:// www.uspto.gov/web/offices/pac/mpep/s608.html*.

United States Patent & Trademark Office, "Patent Rules", listing Rule 1.27 for "small entity" status and Rule 1.29 for "micro entity" statues, available at *http://www.uspto.gov/web/offices/ pac/mpep/mpep-9020-appx-r.html#ar_d1fc9c_19092_1c8*.

United States Patent & Trademark Office, "Performance and Accountability Report Fiscal Year 2013", available at *http://www. uspto.gov/about/stratplan/ar/USPTOFY2013PAR.pdf*.

United States Patent & Trademark Office, "Performance and Accountability Report fiscal year 2012", available at *http://www. uspto.gov/about/stratplan/ar/USPTOFY2012PAR.pdf*.

United States Patent & Trademark Office, Patent Technology Monitoring Team ("PTMT"), "U.S. Patent Statistics Chart

Calendar Years 1963–2013", July 24, 2014, available at *http:// www.uspto.gov/web/offices/ac/ido/oeip/taf/us_stat.htm.*

United States Reexamination Patent RE 34,168, "Lens-fitted photographic film package", original assignee is Fuji Photo Film Co., Ltd., of Japan.

United States Utility Patents

US 6,469, "Buoying Vessels Over Shoals", original assignee is Abraham Lincoln.

US 4,833,495, "Lens-fitted photographic film package", original assignee is Fuji Photo Film Co., Ltd., of Japan.

US 4,855,774, "Lens-fitted photographic film package", original assignee is Fuji Photo Film Co., Ltd., of Japan.

US 4,884,087, "Photographic film package and method of making the same", original assignee is Fuji Photo Film Co., Ltd., of Japan.

US 4,954,857, "Photographic film package and method of making the same", original assignee is Fuji Photo Film Co., Ltd., of Japan.

US 4,972,649, "Photographic film package and method of making the same", original assignee is Fuji Photo Film Co., Ltd., of Japan.

US 5,063,400, "Lens-fitted photographic film package", original assignee is Fuji Photo Film Co., Ltd., of Japan.

US 5,235,364, "Lens-fitted photographic film package with flash unit", original assignee is Fuji Photo Film Co., Ltd., of Japan.

US 5,361,111, "Lens-fitted photographic film unit with means preventing unintended actuation of pushbuttons", original assignee is Fuji Photo Film Co., Ltd., of Japan.

US 5,381,200, "Lens-fitted photographic film unit", original assigned is Fuji Photo Film Co., Ltd., of Japan.

US 5,408,288, "Photographic film cassette and lens-fitted photographic film unit using the same", original assigned is Fuji Photo Film Co., Ltd., of Japan.

US 5,436,685, "Lens-fitted photographic film unit whose parts can be recycled easily", original assignee is Fuji Photo Film Co., Ltd., of Japan.

US 5,606,609, "Electronic document verification system and method", original assignee is Scientific-Atlanta, subsequently acquired by Silanis Technology.

US 5,606,668, "System for securing inbound and outbound data packet flow in a computer network", original assignee is Check Point Software Technologies, Ltd.

US 5,657,317, "Hierarchical communication system using premises, peripheral and vehicular local area networking, original assignee is Norand Corporation, subsequently acquired by Broadcom Corporation.

US 5,682,379, "Wireless personal local area network", original assignee is Norand Corporation, subsequently acquired by Broadcom Corporation.

US 5,835,726, "System for securing the flow of and selectively modifying packets in a computer network", original assignee is Check Point Software Technologies, Ltd.

US 6,359,872, "Wireless personal local area network", original assignee is Intermec IP Corporation, subsequently acquired by Broadcom Corporation.

US 6,374,311, "Communication network having a plurality of bridging nodes which transmit a beacon to terminal nodes in power saving state that it has messages awaiting delivery", original assignee is Intermec IP Corporation, subsequently acquired by Broadcom Corporation.

US 6,389,010, "Hierarchical data collection network supporting packetized voice communications among wireless terminals and telephones", original assignee is Intermec IP Corporation, subsequently acquired by Broadcom Corporation.

US 6,583,675, "Apparatus and method for phase lock loop gain control using unit current sources", original assignee is Broadcom Corporation.

US 6,714,983, "Modular, portable data processing terminal for use in a communication network", original assignee is Broadcom Corporation.

US 6,847,686, "Video encoding device", original assignee is Broadcom Corporation.

Venetian Statute of 1474, also known as the "Venetian Statute on Industrial Brevets (1474)", in which the French word "brevets", short for "brevets d'invention", means literally "certificates of invention", and is translated as "patents".

Ward, Brad, "New Findings Show Foreman Had Bias In The Apple vs Samsung Lawsuit", The Droid Guy, September 26, 2012, available at *http://thedroidguy.com/2012/09/new-find-ings-show-foremanhad-bias-in-the-apple-vs-samsung-lawsuit-37142#FMLVEeotoWuZChAp.97.*

Wikipedia, "Apple Inc. v. Samsung Electronics Co., Ltd.", available at *http://en.wikipedia.org/wiki/Apple_Inc._v._Samsung_Electronics_ Co.,_Ltd.*

Wikipedia, definition of "patent portfolio", available at *http://en.wikipedia.org/wiki/Patent_portfolio.*

Index of Tables

1-1: R&D and Patent Investment by Stage of Company 37

1-2: Revenue and R&D Summary for Check Point
Software 46, 172 n.21, 229 n.138

1-3: Check Point Software's Patent Portfolio 46

1-4: Silanis Technology's Patent Portfolio. 52

1-5: Fuji Photo Film's U.S. Patent Portfolio in 1999 . . .59

1-6: Revenue and R&D Summary for Qualcomm 61

1-7: Snapshots of Qualcomm's Patent Portfolio 63

1-8: Qualcomm Equipment, Service, and Licensing
Revenues and Profits. 65

1-9: The Portfolios of Check Point, Silanis, Fuji
Photo, and Qualcomm. 70, 71

2-1: Three Models of Patenting Activity in a Company . 75

2-2: Comparison of Patent Portfolios in the Wind
Energy Industry 80, 80 n.50, 81–83, 83 n.53, 212

2-3: Research, Science, Technology, Products, and
Patents. 96, 233

2-4: Patents in the Litigation Broadcom v. Qualcomm .96

2-5: Top 20 Recipients of U.S. Patents in 2013. . . . 99–101

2-6:   Predicted Top Generators of U.S. Patents 100, 101 n.71

2-7:   Preferred Modes of Patent Activity by Type of
        Company 103, 234, 235

2-8:   The Processes of Building and Buying Patents . . 105

2-9:   Advantages and Disadvantages of Building and
        Buying Patents 106, 214

2-10:   The Portfolios of Google and Apple on Quality
        and Quantity 115, 116, 117

3-1:   R&D versus Costs in 2012 for U.S. Origin Patent
        Items 140, 140 n.108, 141 n.108

3-2:   R&D versus PTO Fees in 2012 for U.S. Origin
        Patent Items 142, 142 n.109

3-3:   Cost of Patent Applications versus R&D 143, 143 n.111

3-4:   Cost of Issued Patents versus R&D 144

3-5:   Patent Investment by Industry Versus
        Company 147, 229

3-6:   Check Point Patent Investments 2009–2013 154

3-7:   Comparison of Check Point, Industry, and
        Qualcomm, at June 30, 2014 . .156, 156 n.139, 156 n.140

3-8:   Competitors in the Firewall Industry 163

3-9:   Possibilities for a Firewall Industry Benchmark
        Group 164

3-10:   Check Point Portfolio versus Portfolios of
        Competitors. 167, 169, 171

3-11:   Check Point versus Competitors in the Period
        2011–2013 . . . . .169, 170

3-12:   Patent Investments of Check Point and
         Competitors 2011–2013 . . . . 174, 175

3-13:   Members of the Electronic Signature
         Industry 180 n.124, 180 n.125, 181

3-14:   Patent Portfolios in the Electronic Signature
         Industry 184, 185, 188

3-15:   DocuSign's Patent Results 2009 to Mid-2014 . . . 196

3-16:   RPost's Patent Results 2009 to Mid-2014 198

3-17:   Competitors in the Electronic Signature Industry 199

3-18:   Possible Patent Strategies for Silanis Technology
         at Mid-2014 203

3-19:   Corporate and Patent Strategies in the Electronic
         Signature Industry 204

3-20:   Methods to Budget Patent Activity in a Company 207

4-1:   Comparison of Quality and Quantity in Patents . 212

4-2:   Ways of Determining the Quality of a Patent
         Portfolio 224

Index of Names and Subjects

1% rule of patent investing: 28, 29, 49, 64, 68, 81 n.51, 82 n.51, 83, 84 n.53, 135–143, 143 n.111, 144–149, 177, 212, 213, 229, 241, 262

35 United States Code sec 101 (patentability): See "United States Code".

394 F.3d 1368: See "*Fuji v. Achiever Industries* — Decision of the Court of Appeals".

A

Acacia Research: 103, 104, 234

Adobe Systems: 51, 56, 164, 181, 182, 186, 188, 190, 190 n.129, 191 n.129, 193, 194 n.132, 195, 202, 265, 267

aggressive aggregator: 21, 79, 79 n.47, 103, 104, 123 n.85, 234–236

***Alice Corporation v. CLS Bank*, slip opinion 13–298, 573 US ___ (decided June 19, 2014):** 35 n.21, 233 n.141, 265

Allied Security Trust (AST): 79 n.48, 103

AlphaTrust: 181, 185, 188

Amdocs: 121 n.84

AOL: 84 n.53, 164, 188, 225, 268

Apple: 74, 77 n.44, 79 n.46, 84 n.53, 99–101, 101 n.70, 102 n.71, 115–118, 214, 218 n.135, 224, 268, 265, 275, 277

applied R&D: 85, 85 n.54, 233

Argento, Zoe: 110 n.73, 265

Ascertia: 181, 185, 188

AssureSign: 181, 185, 189, 267

AT&T: 87, 98 n.66, 99, 101, 161 n.119

B

backward citation (also "reverse citation"): 125 n.91, 248

balance of quality and quantity: See "quality and quantity, mix of ".

Battelle Memorial Institute: 136, 137 n.96, 148, 265

BCP (biological, chemical, and pharmaceutical): 14, 34, 160 n.118, 244, 252

Bell Labs (AT&T Bell Labs): 87, 87 n.55, 267

Bottom Up Budgeting: 16, 17, 133–135, 149, 150, 155, 157, 159, 161, 177, 178, 204, 206, 207, 228, 230–232, 245, 246

breakthrough invention: 32, 37, 48, 77, 87, 91 n.60, 149, 233, 250

breakthrough patent: 75, 79, 82, 82 n.52, 85–87, 91, 94, 189, 212, 213, 229, 233, 234, 245, 261, 262

Broadcom Corporation: 95, 96, 96 n.65, 97, 98 n.66, 103, 214, 265, 269, 274–276

Broadcom v. Qualcomm — ITC Case 337-TA-543: 96, 265

Brookings Institution: 142, 142 n.110, 143, 143 n.110, 144, 148, 270

Build or Buy: 15, 40, 75, 94, 102, 106, 107

C

Canada: 47, 51, 52, 52 n.35, 53, 54, 151, 187, 188, 191, 193 n.132, 194 n.132, 187,188, 191, 195, 199, 265, 266

Canada Post Corporation: 188

Canon: 99, 100

Carter, Jeffrey L.: 10

CDMA: 61, 67, 69, 299

Check Point Software Technologies: 14, 41, 42, 45, 45 n.31, 46, 46 n.32, 47–51, 55, 62, 71, 77, 98 n.66, 109, 150–152, 152 n.114, 153–157, 161, 162, 162 n.120, 163–172, 172 n.121, 173–179, 182, 204, 219, 229, 229 n.138, 230, 230 n.139, 266, 274, 276–278

CHI Research: 109 n.73, 110 n.75, 266

Cisco Systems: 163, 165, 167, 168, 170, 174

citation of one patent by another: 110 n.74, 248

claim mix: 70, 245, 248, 249

claim parallelism: 31, 249,254

Classen, H. Ward: 121 n.84, 266

client-side claim: 248–250, 257, 258

Comcast: 98 n.66

commitment to patent program: 120–123, 129, 130, 222

Competitive Budgeting: 16, 17, 29, 49, 134, 135, 157–159, 161, 166, 171, 175, 176, 179, 180 n.125, 200, 205–207, 228, 232, 246, 247, 250

competitive position: 17, 27, 102 n.71, 134, 135, 171, 206, 207, 212, 221, 232, 247

Comprova: 188

Comverse Network Systems: 121 n.84

Constant Contact: 188

Consumer Electronics Show ("CES"): 91, 91 n.59

Conversant IP Management: 103, 234

Corcos, Paz: 10

corporate strategy: 14, 25–27, 39, 41, 44, 48, 53, 60, 62, 66, 67, 70, 71, 74, 105, 121, 156, 189, 192, 199, 203–205, 208, 211, 221, 221 n.136, 222, 241, 242, 256

criteria for success of patent program: 41–43, 123–125, 125 n.90, 125 n.91, 129, 223, 227, 243

Crouch, Dennis: 140 n.106, 259, 266

Cultivating patents: See "Model III".

D

defensive aggregator: 21, 50, 55, 69 n.42, 79, 79 n.48, 103, 104, 123 n.85, 146, 234–236, 244, 250, 252, 254, 256,

Dell: 163, 166

dependent claim: 13, 245, 249, 251, 253

depth of claim coverage: 13, 245, 251

DigitalOptics: 77 n.44, 115

discoverability of infringement (also "detectability" of infringement): 21–24, 24 n.30, 25, 210, 237, 252, 263

DocuSign: 54, 181, 185, 188, 189, 191–194, 194 n.132, 194 n.133, 195–201, 203–205, 267, 277

Dvorson, Natalya: 10

E

EchoSign: 56, 181, 182, 186, 188–190, 190 n.129, 191, 191 n.129, 193, 194, 194 n.132, 195, 199, 202, 204, 205, 267

Electronic Signature & Records Association ("ESRA"): 180 n.124, 180 n.125, 267

EMC: 84 n.53

Epperson, Ron: 79 n.49, 80 n.50, 83 n.53, 267, 271

Epsilon Data Management: 188

Ericsson: 84 n.53

eSettlement Solutions: 181, 182, 186, 188

European Classification ("ECLA"): 160 n.117

European Patent Office: 35, 38, 52

ExacTarget: 188

Experian: 188

Expert Fundamental Analysis ("EFA"): 124 n.86, 224, 238

F

factors to judge a patent portfolio: 48–50, 53–55, 60–61, 67–68, 71, 123, 156, 211–212, 242

Fairview Research: 98 n.67

Farmers Insurance: 188

Federal Circuit (Court of Appeals): 57, 96

FireEye: 163, 167, 170, 172, 174

Forrester Research: 180 n.124, 191 n.130, 192 n.130, 193, 201, 269

Fortinet: 163, 165, 167, 170, 172, 174

forward citation: 110 n.74, 110 n.75, 110 n.76, 125 n.91, 185, 248

forward non-self citation: 82 n.52, 110 n.76, 248, 262

FRAND licensing: 299

freepatentsonline search site for patents: 46 n.33, 184 n.128, 267

Fuji Photo Film: 14, 24, 42, 45 n.31, 56, 57, 59–61, 71, 99, 103, 215, 227, 245, 267, 272–274, 276

***Fuji v. Achiever Industries* — Decision of the Court of Appeals, 394 F.3d 1368 (Fed. Cir. 2005):** 57, 267

Fuji v Achiever Industries — ITC Case 337-TA-406: 57, 267

Fujitsu: 99

fundamental R&D: 84, 84 n.54, 85, 85 n.54, 233

G

Garat, Renaud: 125 n.91, 267

Garnick, Coral: 194 n.133, 267

Gathering patents: See "Model I".

General Electric ("GE"): 20, 99, 103

General Motors: 99, 101

geographic balance: 26, 27, 33–35, 37, 49, 54, 56, 60, 68, 70, 71, 113, 123, 156, 158, 178, 187, 199, 205, 211, 215–217, 221, 222, 228, 242, 256

Gertner, Jon: 87 n.55, 267

Globalpex: 188

Glover, Jere W.: 110 n.73, 270

GoDaddy.com: 188

Goldstein, Larry M.: 1, 2, 3, 268, 299

good concept: 86–88, 94, 131

Goodmail: 188

Google , Inc.: 75, 77 n.44, 99–101, 101 n.70, 102 n.71, 103, 114–116, 116 n.81, 117, 118, 161 n.119, 214, 224, 268, 277

Green, Jay: 84 n.53, 268

H

Hallenbeck, Jim: 84 n.53, 268

Hardiman, Jean Tarbett: 92 n.62, 268

Harvard College: 299

Harvesting patents: See "Model II".

Hegde, Deepak: 110 n.73, 268

Hewlett-Packard: 163, 167, 170, 171, 174

Hicks, Diana: 110 n.73, 268

HighTech-Solutions: 10

high-value patent: 82 n.52, 84 n.53, 85–87, 94, 213, 233–234, 261

Hitachi: 99

Hybrid Budgeting: 17, 134, 135, 205–207, 228, 232, 247, 252

I

i4i: 98 n.66

IAM Magazine: 84 n.53, 101 n.70, 269

IBM: 77 n.44, 79 n.46, 87, 88 n.56, 93, 99, 100, 103, 115, 121 n.84, 146, 163, 167, 170, 171, 174, 176, 210, 271

ICT (Information & Communication Technologies): 14, 23 n.9, 25, 31, 33, 34, 77 n.44, 114, 114 n.80, 115, 116, 117, 118, 124, 124 n.87, 137 n.97, 159, 160 n.118, 165, 225, 235, 244, 245, 250, 252, 258, 299

IEEE (Institute of Electrical & Electronic Engineering): 77 n.44, 96 n.65, 114, 115, 118, 124 n.90, 160, 161 n.119, 162–165, 225, 268

IEEE Spectrum: 77 n.44, 114, 115, 118, 124 n.90, 160, 161 n.119, 162–164, 268

IFI Claims Patent Service: 98 n.67, 268

independent claim: 13, 59, 125 n.91, 185–187, 245, 249, 251–253, 256

Infogroup: 188

Innography, Inc.: 121 n.84, 124 n.89, 226, 266

Innovapost: 188

Innovatio IP: 103, 104, 234

Inquisitr: 218 n.135, 268

Intel: 99–101, 163, 167, 168, 170

Intellectual Ventures ("IV"): 21, 79 n.47, 98 n.68, 103, 104, 234, 236

InterDigital: 98 n.68, 99 n.68, 103, 104, 234

Intermec: 96 n.65, 274

International Patent Classification ("IPC"): 160 n.117, 178 n.122

IPO (Intellectual Property Owners Association): 98, 98 n.67, 99, 111 n.77, 269

IPVision: 124 n.89, 226

IPWatchdog®: 110 n.73, 137 n.97, 270, 271

ITC (International Trade Commission): 23, 57–59, 95, 96, 107, 251, 265, 267

ITC Case 337-TA-406: See *"Fuji v. Achiever Industries"*.

ITC Case 337-TA-543: See *"Broadcom v. Qualcomm"*.

J

j2 Global: 188

Jacobi, Eli: 10, 121 n.84

Jacobus, Heidi: 110 n.73, 270

Japanese Patent Office: 35

Jazz Photo Corporation: 57, 267

Jepson claim (two-part claim): 36

jumbo application: 38 n.25, 109, 111, 202, 220, 253, 259, 260, 272

Juniper Networks: 163, 165, 167, 170, 172, 174

K

Kassaraba, Myron: 79 n.49, 80 n.50, 83 n.53, 267, 271

Kearsey, Brian N.: 3, 268

Kellogg School of Management: 299

Key Claim Term: 31

Khan, Zafar: 192, 192 n.131, 269

Krassenstein, Eddie: 92 n.61, 269

L

Lanham Act: 188

Le Clair, Craig: 180 n.124, 269

LES (Licensing Executives Society): 80 n.49, 80 n.50, 125 n.91, 267

les Nouvelles: **Journal of the Licensing Executives Society International:** 80 n.49, 80 n.50, 267

Levin, Richard C.: 144 n.112, 269

LG Electronics: 99, 100

License on Transfer Network ("LOT Network"): 103, 235

Lincoln, Abraham: 11, 11 n.2, 11 n.3, 119 n.83, 239, 239 n.142, 269, 273

Liquid Machines: 151 n.113

LITIGATION-PROOF PATENTS: Avoiding the Most Common Patent Mistakes: 3, 13, 23 n.9, 32, 94 n.63, 113 n.79, 124 n.87, 225, 267, 299

Lobo, José: 142 n.110, 270

M

Manual of Patent Examining Procedure ("MPEP"): 38 n.99, 253, 259, 272

Marzel, A.S.: 2, 10

Matching patents: See "Model II".

Matsumoto, Craig: 96 n.65, 269

McAfee: 163, 165, 167, 168, 170, 171, 174

Merrill, Stephen A.: 144 n.112, 269

method claim: 23, 35, 35 n.21, 58, 59, 89, 108, 138 n.98, 195, 237, 245, 248–250, 253, 258. 262, 273, 274

micro entity for PTO fees: 41 n.30, 138 n.99, 139 n.104, 140 n.107, 140 n.108, 141 n.108, 142 n.109, 143 n.111, 272

Micron Technology: 100, 101

Microsoft: 77 n.44, 79 n.46, 84 n.53, 98 n.66, 99, 101 n.70, 103, 115, 163, 167, 170, 174, 224, 225, 268

Millstein, Seth: 92 n.62, 269

Mitra, Sramana: 192 n.131, 269

mix of quality and quantity: See "quality and quantity, mix of ".

Model I — Gathering patents: 75, 76, 130, 250, 252, 253

Model II — Matching patents: 75–77, 79, 93, 119 n.82, 130, 250, 252, 253

Model III — Cultivating patents: 75, 77–79, 84, 88, 92, 93, 119 n.82, 130, 250, 262, 253

Mollenkopf, Steve: 91

Mosaid: 103

Motorola: 101 n.70, 146

MPEG-2: 21, 79 n.47

Muro, Mark: 142 n.110, 270

Myers, Mark B.: 144 n.112, 269

N

Nokia: 79 n.46, 151 n.113, 218

Nortel: 84 n.53, 268

Northwestern University: 299

NPA (Non-Provisional Application): 109, 220, 254, 259–261

NT&T: 161 n.119

O

OceanTomo: 124 n.89, 226

One percent rule of patent investing: See "1% rule of patent investing".

Open Invention Network ("OIN"): 103

P

Palo Alto Networks: 163, 165, 167, 168, 170, 172, 174

Panasonic: 99

parallelism: See "claim parallelism".

Parchomovsky, Gideon: 24 n.11, 111, 112, 114, 119, 144, 144 n.112, 148, 270

Paris Convention: 36 n.23, 270

patent activity intensity ($ Patent/$ R&D): 64, 64 n.38, 66, 68, 254, 257

patent aggregation: 11, 17, 21, 22, 50, 55, 69 n.42, 79, 79 n.47, 79 n.48, 102–104, 106, 123 n.85, 146, 209, 234–236, 244, 250–252, 254–256

patent assertion entity ("PAE", troll, Non-Practicing Entity, "NPE"): 78, 78 n.45, 244, 251, 254, 256

Patent Committee ("the decision-makers"): 125, 126 n.92, 128, 129, 222, 223

Patent Cooperation Treaty (PCT): 36 n.23, 38, 168, 173, 184–188, 196–198, 200, 217 n.134, 267, 270

patent evaluation: 17, 21, 22, 28, 31, 36 n.22, 82 n.52, 113, 125, 125 n.90, 125 n.91, 209, 235–238, 248, 255, 264, 267, 299

patent family: 20 n.6, 210, 254, 255

Patent Manager ("the driver"): 126–129, 222, 223

patent pool: 3, 21, 50, 77, 79 n.47, 123 n.85, 234–236, 244, 255, 256, 268, 299

Patent Power Scorecard: 78 n.44, 115, 124 n.90, 160, 161 n.119, 162, 163, 225, 268

patent strategy: 14, 25–28, 41, 55, 60, 65, 71, 74, 105, 121, 129, 134, 146, 150, 154, 155, 157, 189, 199, 200, 203–205, 207, 208, 221, 222, 229, 241, 242, 256, 278

patent thicket: 24, 56, 59, 215, 249, 256

PatentlyO Blog: 140 n.106, 259, 266

PatentRatings International: 124 n.89, 226

People's Republic of China (PRC): 35, 36, 36 n.22, 216, 217

Peplow, Mark: 91 n.60, 270

Perception Partners: 124 n.89, 226

Philips: 98 n.66, 218

Point of Novelty ("PON", innovative concept, inventive concept): 13, 20 n.6, 24, 25 n.11, 59, 73, 86, 87, 89, 93, 105, 129, 130, 245, 249, 252, 253, 256, 257

Pointofmail.com 188

PPA (Provisional Patent Application): 202, 203, 220, 257, 260, 261

Principle 1 (patent strategy): 25–27, 241

Principle 2 (strategic focus): 26, 27, 241

Principle 3 (invest the right amount): 6, 28–30, 241, 242

Principle 4 (balance quality and quantity): 26, 30–33, 242

Principle 5 (geographic balance): 26, 33–37, 242

Principle 6 (time balance): 26, 37–39, 242

Principle 7 (fill holes in coverage): 26, 39–40, 243

Principle 8 (time management): 26, 40, 41, 243

Principle 9 (criteria for measurement): 26, 41–43, 243

Principle 10 (placement in the organization): 26, 42–44, 243

Privasphere: 188

Proxy Fundamental Analysis ("PFA"): 124 n.88, 225, 238

PTO (U.S. Patent & Trademark Office): 46 n.33, 107, 111 n.78, 116, 116 n.81, 137, 138, 138 n.99, 139, 139 n.101, 139 n.102, 139 n.103, 140 n.108, 141, 141 n.108, 142, 142 n.109, 143, 143 n.111, 148, 160 n.116, 161 n.119, 251, 259, 272, 273, 277

Q

Qualcomm: 15, 33, 40, 42, 45 n.31, 61, 61 n.37, 62–64, 64 n.39, 65, 65 n.40, 66–69, 71, 75, 77, 77 n.44, 79 n.46, 91, 91 n.59, 91 n.60, 95, 96, 98 n.66, 99–101, 102 n.71, 103, 104, 115, 146, 150, 155–157, 176, 219, 230, 230 n.140, 265, 270, 276, 277

quality and quantity, mix of (also "balance of quality and quantity"): 26, 30–33, 48, 54, 60, 67, 69, 71, 83, 107, 120, 131, 156, 211–213, 242

Quality or Quantity — the conflict between the two: 15, 73, 107–120, 213–214, 277

Quinn, Gene: 137 n.97, 270

R

R&D intensity: 62, 64, 66, 156, 172, 207, 254, 257

Randewich, Noel: 91 n.59, 270

ReadNotify: 188

Rembrandt IP Management: 103, 234

Research in Motion (RIM): 84 n.53, 161 n.119

Responsys: 188

Ricoh: 99

RightSignature: 181, 188, 189, 195, 267

Rothwell, Jonathan: 142 n.110, 270

RPost Holdings, Inc.: 181, 182, 185, 187–191, 191 n.130, 192, 192 n.130, 192 n.131, 193, 195–201, 203, 204, 269, 270, 278

RPX Corporation: 21, 50, 69 n.42, 79 n.48, 103, 146, 235, 236, 270

S

Samsung (including both Samsung Electronics and Samsung Display): 79 n.46, 99, 100, 100 n.69, 101 n.70, 103, 146, 218 n.135, 268, 275

Schmidt, Robert N.: 110 n.73, 271

scope of claim coverage: 21, 22, 22 n.8, 24, 24 n.11, 25, 70, 82 n.52, 119, 210, 211, 225

Seiko Epson: 99

seminal patent: 82, 82 n.52, 85, 86, 94, 154, 155, 212, 213, 257, 261, 262

SEP (standard-essential patent): 33 n.18, 235, 255

Sertifi: 181, 185, 187, 188, 267

server-side claim: 248–250, 257, 258

Shankland, Stephen: 84 n.53, 268

Sharp: 98 n.66

Siemens: 80, 82, 98 n.66, 99, 121 n.84, 161 n.119

Signiant: 181, 187, 189

SIGNiX: 181, 187, 189

Silanis Technology: 14, 40, 45 n.31, 51–53, 53 n.36, 54–56, 71, 97, 98 n.66, 109, 179, 180 n.125, 182, 182 n.126, 183, 188, 189, 191, 193, 193 n.132, 194, 194 n.132, 195, 199–204, 214, 219, 265–267, 271, 274, 276, 278

small entity for PTO fees: 41 n.30, 111, 111 n.78, 138 n.99, 139 n.104, 140 n.107, 140 n.108, 141 n.108, 142 n.109, 272

Software as a Service ("SaaS"): 179, 179 n.123

SonicWall: 163, 165, 166

Sony: 84 n.53, 99, 100

Sourcefire: 163, 165, 167, 168, 170, 171, 174, 175

Sprint Nextel: 161 n.119

Statute of Monopolies (1624): 76 n.43, 271

Strategic Business Unit ("SBU"): 42, 44, 227

StrongMail Systems: 188

Strumsky, Deborah: 142 n.110, 270

Studio Paz: 2

Sughrue Mion, PLLC: 10

supporting patent: 75, 79, 82 n.52, 83, 85, 86, 94, 113 n.79, 213, 253, 258, 263

Supreme Court (U.S. Supreme Court): 35 n.21, 57, 233 n.141, 265

Swiss Post: 188

Symantec: 163, 167, 170, 174, 188

T

Takahasi, Dean: 88 n.56, 271

Talmud: 4, 4 n.1, 271

technical standard: 20, 33, 33 n.18, 67, 69, 235,

Technology Inflection Point ("TIP"): 15, 17, 32, 73, 84, 85, 88, 89, 89 n.57, 90, 91, 93, 94, 131, 148, 209, 213, 233, 234, 258, 261

TECHNOLOGY PATENT LICENSING: An International Reference on 21st Century Patent Licensing, Patent Pools and Patent Platforms: 3, 33 n.18, 79 n.47, 235, 268, 299

THE IDEA FACTORY: Bell Labs and the Great Age of American Innovation: 87 n.55, 267

THE PATENT QUALITY SERIES: 3, 13, 299

time balance (balance over time): 26, 27, 37–42, 45–47, 49, 50, 55, 59–61, 68, 70, 71, 73, 123, 124, 156, 196, 198, 215, 219–221, 242, 243, 243 n.150, 256

time frame of patent program: 129, 130, 223, 224

TiVo: 98 n.66

Top Down Budgeting: 16, 17, 133–135, 148, 149, 157–159, 161, 177, 178, 204, 206, 207, 228, 230, 232, 245, 246, 259

Toshiba: 99

Totaro & Associates: 80 n.50, 81 n.51, 83 n.53, 124 n.89, 226, 267, 271

Trend Micro: 98 n.66, 188

TRUE PATENT VALUE: Defining Quality in Patents and Patent Portfolios ("TPV"): 3, 13, 15, 23 n.9, 25 n.12, 26 n.13, 27 n.14, 28 n.15, 30 n.16, 31, 33 n.17, 33 n.19, 37 n.24, 39 n.26, 40 n.27, 41 n.29, 45 n.31, 48, 53, 67 n.41, 89 n.57, 90 n.58, 94 n.63, 97, 98 n.66, 110 n.76, 113 n.79, 124 n.86, 124 n.88, 125 n.90, 125 n.91, 224, 225, 226, 226 n.137, 241 n.143, 241 n.144, 241 n.145, 242 n.146, 242 n.147, 242 n.148, 243 n.149, 243 n.150, 268, 299

Trustifi: 188

Twain, Mark: 102 n.71, 271

two-part claim: See "Jepson claim".

types of patents by value contribution: 40 n.28, 245, 257, 258, 261, 263

U

United States Code, Title 35, section 101 (patentability): 84 n.54, 233, 233 n.141, 271

U.S. Patent Classification (USPC): 160 n.117, 178 n.122

U.S. Small Business Administration: 109 n.73, 266

Unified Patents: 103, 235

Uniloc: 98 n.66

United States Constitution (1787): 76 n.43, 272

University of Chicago Law School: 299

Unwired Planet: 103, 234

US 6,469: 11 n.2, 273

US 4,833,495: 59, 273

US 4,855,774: 59, 273

US 4,884,087: 59, 273

US 4,954,857: 59, 273

US 4,972,649: 59, 273

US 5,063,400: 59, 273

US 5,235,364: 59, 273

US 5,361,111: 59, 273

US 5,381,200: 59, 273

US 5,408,288: 59, 273

US 5,436,685: 59, 274

US 5,606,609: 53–56, 97, 188, 195, 196, 200, 219, 274

US 5,606,668: 48, 274

US 5,657,317: 96, 97, 274

US 5,682,379: 96, 274

US 5,835,726: 48, 274

US 6,359,872: 96, 274

US 6,374,311: 96, 274

US 6,389,010: 96, 97, 274

US 6,583,675: 96, 274

US 6,714,983: 96, 97, 275

US 6,847,686: 96, 275

US Des. 345,750: 59, 272

US Des. 356,101: 59, 272

US Des. 372,722: 59, 272

US RE 34,168: 59, 273

V

validity of claims: 21, 22, 24, 24 n.10, 25, 70, 210, 211, 225, 236, 237, 249, 262, 263

valuable patent: 82 n.52, 83, 85, 86, 94, 212–214, 262, 263

Venetian Statute of 1474: 76 n.43, 275

very valuable patent: 79, 82, 82 n.52, 85, 86, 212, 213, 262, 263

Vocus: 188

VSD ("validity", "scope", and "discoverability"): 21, 22, 31, 70, 82 n.52, 235, 238, 249, 252, 257, 262–264

W

Wagner, R. Polk: 24 n.11, 111, 112, 114, 119, 144, 144 n.112, 148, 270

Ward, Brad: 218 n.135, 275

Watchguard Technologies: 163, 165, 166

Websense: 163, 167, 168, 170–172, 174

Wikipedia: 19 n.5, 218 n.135, 275

WiLAN: 103, 234

Wild, Joff: 84 n.53

WIPO: 168, 173

www.truepatentvalue.com: 299

Y

Yahoo!: 161 n.119, 188

Z

Zix Corporation: 188

Zone Labs: 151 n.113

About the Author

Larry M. Goldstein is a U.S. patent attorney specializing in Information & Communication Technologies. He evaluates patent quality, manages patent portfolios, and is engaged actively in the drafting and prosecuting of patent applications. He is the author of **THE PATENT QUALITY SERIES**, which includes the three books *PATENT PORTFOLIOS: Quality, Creation, and Cost* (2015), *LITIGATION-PROOF PATENTS: Avoiding the Most Common Patent Mistakes* (2014), and *TRUE PATENT VALUE: Defining Quality in Patents and Patent Portfolios* (2013). He helped establish the patent pool for FRAND licensing of 3G Wideband CDMA technology, and he is a co-author of the book *TECHNOLOGY PATENT LICENSING: An International Reference on 21st Century Patent Licensing, Patent Pools and Patent Platforms* (2004). Mr. Goldstein holds a B.A. from Harvard College, an MBA from the Kellogg School of Management at Northwestern University, and a J.D. from the University of Chicago Law School. His web site is *www.truepatentvalue.com*.

Made in the USA
Las Vegas, NV
12 November 2024

11588914R20166